Shiva
The Lord of Yoga

Dr. David Frawley
(Pandit Vamadeva Shastri)

LOTUS PRESS
Box 325, Twin Lakes, WI 53181 USA
email: lotuspress@lotuspress.com
website: www.LotusPress.com

Front Cover and Line drawings by: Pieter Weltevrede
Shiva's Sacred Family line drawing by: Madhu Kirtana

For information address:

Lotus Press
Box 325, Twin Lakes, WI 53181 USA
email: lotuspress@ lotuspress.com
website: www.LotusPress.com

ISBN: 978-0-9406-7629-9
Library of Congress Catalog Card No. 2015940807

Table of Contents

Part V. Subtleties of Shaivism

Part VI. Glossary and Appendices

Illustrations

1. The Flow of Shiva's Grace

Foreword by Sri Lokesh Chandra

This work on Lord Shiva is a wonderful lotus that blooms from the calyx of the heart of Prof. Vamadeva (Dr. David Frawley). He opens before our minds the crystalline divine depths of trans-consciousness in a profound contemplation of Lord Shiva. Our crushing age of "un-man" is in dire need of spiritual waves in the sublime visualization of the Supreme Shiva, so that we drink the very sap of the divine, in Vamadeva's revealing spiritual illumination that appears directly to a person's spiritual light.

In the boundless profound depths of Yoga, Lord Shiva bathes our consciousness with the luminescence of being. In the simple and touching words of Vamadeva, we go beyond the confines of life to the eternal, the heartwork of the sacred. From our own inmost well-being, we return to a cosmos of Being that resonates in a rejuvenation of inherent radiance. Vamadeva is a wayfarer with his readers in the journey of enlightenment, so that "the flower's sacrifice ripens into the sweetness of the fruit" in the words of the poet Rabindranath Tagore. Lord Shiva is our eternal pilgrimage into the inner steppes of the mind and Vamadeva's presentation makes it into a joyful fullness. In the words of the *Aitareya-Brahmana*:

> *The feet of the wanderer are like a flower,*
> *Behold the striving of the Sun,*
> *Who is not wearied by wanderings.*

The *Linga Purana* states that Shiva is perceived in a fourfold manner: as the cause of existence, as existence itself, as the cause of liberation, and as release. As the cause of liberation and release, Shiva is the Lord of Yogins, holding within himself the power of life and the power of creativity. As Lord of Yoga, He transforms creative power into mental creativity and interiorized detachment that leads to release. In the *Kurma Purana*, Shiva says: "I the Yogi dance eternally." The ananda tandava, the "thunder bliss dance," is the dance of bliss in the hall of consciousness, the dance within the heart of man. His divine totality of creation, maintenance, dissolution, veiling-unveiling, and liberation is conveyed by the dynamic movement of his limbs. As he dances causing the waves of sentience to scintillate, he appears in the immaculate space of the heart (cid-akasha).

The five letters of the mantra Namah Shivaya are the levels of realization signifying the total commitment of the devotee to Shiva. They invoke one by one the five different aspects or facets of Lord Shiva: Sadyojata, Vamadeva, Aghora, Tatpurusha and Ishana. The *Panchabrahma Upanishad* states: "With the knowing of the five Brahmans, consisting of Sadyojata and others, as the preliminary step, one should know that all this phenomenal world is the Para Brahman, the Supreme Shiva, of the character of the fivefold Brahmans; nay we should know that whatever is seen or heard of, or falls within or lies beyond the range of his inner and outer senses, is Shiva of the character of the fivefold Brahmans alone."

"In the Brahmapura (the body that is the city of Brahman, the abode of the Brahma of the Micrososm), wherein is the abode of the form of a white lotus of the heart, known as the Dahara or small space...., in the middle of it is the ether known as the Dahara akasha (the small space that contains the entire universe). That ether is Shiva, the infinite existence, non-dual consciousness and unsurpassed bliss...., This Shiva is the witness established in the hearts of all beings.....and manifests himself to the seeker, in accord with the strength of vision and degree of spiritual development attained by the seeker. Hence this Shiva is known as the heart of all beings and the liberator from all the bonds of worldly existence."

Vamadeva presents the depths of Shiva as the Lord of Yoga in words of vision, as he himself is a devout Sadhaka. It is pleasure to travel along with him in a journey of devotion and purity, of creativity and beauty, so that we may discover the means of fulfilling our ultimate destiny. He provides a way to the transcendent in the yogic realization of Shiva to find the yonder shores of consciousness in the cosmic reality of Shiva.

Reading through the book, I was reminded that in every cycle of the universe an incarnation of Vyasa will write the inner aspect of the scriptures and Vamadeva (one of the five Brahmans), who has a direct experience the subtle realities, is such an incarnation of Vyasa. He show us the path where divinity truly dwells within us; there it must be worshipped ((*Taittiriya Upanishad 3.10*). Prof. Vamadeva leads us to the Puranic insight: "The supreme stage is your core, the Universe your shape. You are the unborn, Eternal (*Vishnu Purana 3.17.34*)."

Sri Lokesh Chandra
Delhi, India
February 2015

Note on Lokesh Chandra

Prof. Lokesh Chandra is the current head of the Indian Council of Cultural Relations (ICCR), a former head of the Indian Council of Historical Research (ICHR), Padma Bhushan, and a former member of the Rajya Sabha. He is regarded as the seniormost Buddhist scholar in India today and has produced over five hundred books.

Introduction
Sri Sivananda Murty

The following book is a profound work on Shiva as the Lord of Yoga and His form of the Linga. The author Sri Vamadeva Shastri or Dr. David Frawley needs no introduction. His world-respected books have explained in detail all about Vedic thought, Yoga, different forms of worship, mantra, and a host of related subjects that are both subtle and intricate.

Sri Vamadeva Shastri is no mere academic or intellectual researcher. He has taken the essence of Hindu Dharma and the higher teachings of Yoga seriously and adopted these as his way of life. He has proved himself to be a most competent commentator on many aspects of Yoga, Vedanta and Vedic knowledge. The present book on Lord Shiva that has flowed from his pen is an in-depth work of erudition and insight, reflecting many years of study and meditative experience.

Vamadeva has discussed the universality of Shaivism and Shiva Yoga. He establishes the inseparability of the yogic approach and the realization of Shiva and has dedicated a chapter to Raja Yoga. He has discussed the thirty-six tattvas of Shaivism, the twenty-five tattvas of Samkhya and a brief history of the Yoga of the Shaivites. It is obvious that there can be no single exhaustive compendium or treatise covering the nature and secrets of Shiva in the cosmos and beyond. However, Vamadeva has examined a broad range of these topics in a new and comprehensive manner. I believe that this work will be an important addition to the Shaivite literature for generations to come.

Rudra/Shiva in the Puranas

I would like to take this opportunity to outline the arrival of Shiva into the cosmos in which we live. A few words about Rudra Mahadeva, whose essence is Shiva Tattva, the transcendent truth:

Shiva as Hindu thought tells us is the final and third aspect of the Cosmic Reality. The manifest universe is complete only when the principles of creation and sustenance represented by Lords Brahma and Lord Vishnu are followed by the principle of the withdrawal and dissolution indicated by Lord Shiva.

According to the *Puranas*, which hold many yogic secrets, the primordial principle of Absolute Bliss, which is beyond all manifestation, appears in the universe as Shiva, known as Rudra Mahadeva. Shiva manifested later in the creation after the later cycle of Vivasvata Manvantara began, already long into the cosmic process. By the time that Rudra arrived all the higher worlds had come into being, waiting for the lower worlds to be filled with mortals.

It should be remembered that innumerable souls were waiting in the dark to be born into Prakriti or the material nature to experience the fruits of karma. The Earth and its surrounding Lokas were yet to fully evolve. After the arrival of Rudra even Brahma, the Devas, the Rishis, and the Prajapatis (lords of creation) could not recognize his essence and tried to downplay his importance. They had to learn bitter lessons for this. They had not yet recognized the need for withdrawal from the creation to take souls back to the Supreme and found Rudra's presence to go against the existing order of creation that they controlled.

Seven Manvantaras (cosmic ages) were reaching completion. Daksha descended to Earth and the creation of species on the Earth followed. The story of Daksha and Sati's birth as his daughter, who became Shiva's wife, only to only to have Shiva rejected by her father Daksha, is a well known subject in the Puranas. Daksha lacked the awareness to recognize Shiva's transcendent nature.

After giving up her body as Sati, Rudra's Shakti took birth anew as Uma/Parvati, the daughter of the Himalayan mountains, the personification of tapas and Yoga to draw in Shiva's influence for the benefit of the world. Rudra then became the goal of realization to release the soul from the bonds of rebirth. By virtue of being the principle of withdrawal from all creation, he became the giver of liberation.

Shaivite Literature

After the way to Moksha was established on the Earth through Rudra/Shiva, many great Rishis produced the *Vedas, Upanishads, Sutras, Agamas* and *Puranas*, among other sacred texts. The passage of time resulted in detailed teachings about Shiva and appropriate praise of Shiva in many forms and aspects.

Shaivism begins with Shiva as OM and as the essence of the Vedic deities as cosmic sound and light. The *Vedas* that manifest through OM and the entire Sanskrit alphabet are the sounds of Shiva. The essence of Shaivism can be found in the Rudram chant of the *Yajurveda*, reflecting prime Vedic mantras. In Vedic rituals the Rudram plays the main role, in which the word Shiva is first used for this supreme deity. Physical and material forms within our daily experience are highlighted in a symbolic manner. In later literature the concept of Shiva as the transcendent reality of Rudra is explained in profound philosophical terms.

The greatness and nature of Shiva is the subject matter of a vast literature with much analysis, synthesis and profound conclusions. For example, *Shiva Mahimna Stotra*, composed by the celestial being Pushpadanta, inspired Sir John Woodroofe to translate his poem as the Greatness of Shiva. Vamadeva (Dr. Frawley) continues drawing the reader into the study of Shiva as a living reality.

Shiva Linga

Shaivism is related to the linga. The linga form assumes great importance and the worship is dedicated to the linga rather than to the anthropomorphic form of Shiva. A miniature linga is worn by the dedicated Shaivite yogi. This is because Shiva is the giver of liberation who takes us beyond birth and death. To live in the presence of Shiva is to never die. The word linga is defined: "The moving universe is moving towards a single point of dissolution and that is the linga."[1]

The linga is a symbol of this cosmic point of dissolution that takes us beyond time and space. In the present book on Shiva Yoga, a detailed explanation is given to the various forms of the linga and the material out of which it is constituted.

Shiva Yoga

Shaivism is essentially Shiva Yoga, teaching the union of the soul as Jiva with the Supreme Shiva. Kashmir Shaivism and Shaiva Siddhanta as well as Shaivism in all parts of India north, south, east and west, extending to nearby countries are all only Shiva Yoga in various forms. These philosophies of Shiva Yoga constitute forms of dualism, dualism and non-dualism and non-dualism in different schools.

Shakti Yoga is also Shiva Yoga. After all, Shakti manifests as creation that is pervaded by Shiva. Everything in the universe from the smallest particle contains Shiva and Shakti working in unison together. Shakti is worshipped independently in many female forms, but these also reflect powers of Shiva. This integral Shiva-Shakti Yoga is esoterically explained by Vamadeva in his sections on Shiva and Shakti Yogas.

OM is Shiva; *OM Namah Shivaya* is the most important of all mantras. It can be added to Shakti or Devi mantras to give these more power.

Shiva is our destiny. Shiva is our destination. Shiva is our path. This is Shiva Yoga. Yoga is synonymous with Shiva. Shiva is the guru of all gurus, the supreme Yogi. We commonly speak of Shiva Yoga but not so much of Yoga relative to other deities. Ananda, the goal of Yoga as Samadhi, is also synonymous with Shiva, particularly as Shivananda. Shiva and Yoga are together at every point.

Shiva Yoga is *vairagya* or non-attachment, which is surrender, withdrawal and letting go. Shiva Yoga teaches us the "art of leaving," not only the art or rules of living. The body does not leave us unless we leave the body first by transcending body consciousness during life itself. True Yoga is about expanding out of body consciousness, not giving it more emphasis. Shiva is the guide of this process of going beyond body and mind.

Our current humanity is immersed in technology. In a few generations this fascination will get reduced and people will return to Yoga and meditation as their highest pursuit. Technology creates only a superficial attention, not any deep awareness. Our machines and equipment are but distractions from our eternal search for inner peace. We cannot be attracted to them for long. There is only lasting happiness and well-being through inner awareness, which is our Shiva nature, not through anything that comes to us from the outside or is made artificially.

This work of Vamadeva on Shiva Yoga is significant and distinct in many ways. It directs us to the inevitable awakening to our Shiva nature that is our true identity and the goal of all life. Shiva is accessible to anyone who sincerely and continually strives for his guidance and grace.

Sri Sivananda Murty
Peethadhipati, Sri Saiva Mahapeetham
Anandavanam, Bheemunipatnam, Vishakha District, Andra Pradesh, India
November 2014

Note on Sri Sivananda Murty

Sri Sivananda Murty, born 1928, is one of the most respected gurus in India today and head of the Shaiva Mahapeetham, an important south Indian Vedic Shaivite order. He is a great adept and teacher in Raja Yoga, Jnana Yoga, Vedic astrology, Homeopathy, and South Indian music. He follows the teachings of Ramana Maharshi and Trailanga Swami and is regarded as a Siddha Purusha.

He has been honored by the Shankaracharyas of Sringeri and Kanchipuram and by Tirupati Devasthana among many others. He is the author of many books and articles published mainly in Telegu. Vamadeva has been associated with him over the last twenty years.

Author's Preface

Any deep examination of the Yoga tradition leads one inevitably to an encounter with Lord Shiva – probably the dominant figure behind Yoga in all of its forms and aspects. Lord Shiva embodies the great traditions of Yoga, meditation, pranayama, mantra, asana, and Ayurvedic healing. If we were to provide these teachings a name and form in terms of a deity we would likely discover Lord Shiva as their essence.

In the figure of Lord Shiva we can discern that such yogic teachings are not simply ideas, practices, or disciplines, mere tools for us to use, but reflect the Divine reality of the universe that we can contact directly within our own consciousness. Yogic teachings themselves are outer formations of the inner deity who manifests through them. In higher Yoga practices, we are preparing for the Divine Being to manifest itself through us.

My intention in the present book is to help correct the distortions about Lord Shiva present in academic and popular accounts, which focus on the sensational side of Shiva and downplay his yogic implications. So far, few thinkers in the West have understood the profound wisdom and meditative insights behind such apparent figures of polytheism and nature worship as epitomized in Lord Shiva.

The present book teaches Shiva Yoga as an integral part of Vedic thought, not as a separate or contrary current as some scholars propose. It shows how Tantric and Vedic teachings reflect the same Rishi vision from different angles. In this regard, we speak of "Vedic Shaivism," though a few later Shaivite traditions in India have also forgotten their Vedic roots.

The book highlights the universal aspect of Shaivite philosophy; how it explains the higher awareness at work in the world of nature, as well the Absolute beyond manifestation. I have presented the cosmology of Shaivism in detail, including its subtle concepts of Nada, Bindu and Spanda.

I have addressed the complementarity of Shiva and Shakti as the cosmic masculine and feminine powers. I have indicated the main practices involved in the worship of Shiva, both inwardly and outwardly, from ritual to deep meditation. I have examined Shaivite Yoga practices and their inner teachings of Kundalini, Chakras and the Hamsa, which though often discussed are seldom understood in depth.

The book is intended more as a guidebook to practice. It is not meant to portray the ideas, methods, or history of Shaivism as only an intellectual concern. While we should acknowledge the universality of Shiva, we should also honor the specific teachings and traditions in humanity that have developed as a means of his expression. The book examines the views of various teachers from the Shaivite tradition who hold a living experience of Shiva, not merely the ideas of those who are looking from the outside the tradition and have never discovered Shiva in their own minds and hearts.

Above all, the book is an attempt to help us experience the reality of Shiva within ourselves, and reflects my own sadhana and meditation practices. It explores Shaivism for those that the presence of Shiva is a living and transformative reality.

The book is divided into six sections.

- The first orients us to the transcendent and universal meaning of Lord Shiva and how we must set aside all our preconceptions in order to approach him.

- The second explains Shaivite philosophy and cosmology, and its understanding of Reality on both individual and universal levels.

- The third focuses on Shiva and Shakti as the dual cosmic powers and their interrelationship, including the symbolism of their children Ganesha and Skanda.

- The fourth explains the practice of Shaivite Yoga relative to its prime views and practices, particularly as a form of Raja Yoga with a cosmic orientation.

- The fifth examines the connections of Shaivism with other Vedic disciplines like Ayurveda and Vedic astrology. It goes into Shaivite philosophy in detail and its relationship with other philosophical systems.

- The concluding sixth section and appendices contains a glossary, bibliography, resources, and footnotes.

The book reflects my studies and practice of Veda, Vedanta, Tantra, and Shaivism. It is based upon the work of Kavyakantha Ganapati Muni, the chief disciple of Ramana Maharshi, and his notable insights on *Vedas*, Vedanta, Shiva and Shakti. The book is not centered on the work of Kashmiri Shaivism but does afford it an important place. It includes my study of the Nath Yogis, particularly Gorakhnath, and the earlier Lakulish tradition of Pashupata Shaivism extending back to the *Mahabharata* and *Vedas*. It may differ from other accounts of Shaivism on the philosophical side, as several different approaches are possible.

I would like to personally thank Sri Lokesh Chandra for his kind and inspiring preface. Lokesh is one of the icons of Indian culture and thought over the last fifty years, who has influenced the country at a national level, and represented Indian culture and thought worldwide.

Most importantly, the book is based upon my interaction with the great modern Shaivite Gurus, notably Sivananda Murty, one of the greatest gurus in modern India today. The book is meant to encourage and inspire our own direct connection with Shiva, in whatever way is most authentic for us.

> I would like to dedicate this book to my Shiva gurus, notably Sri Sadguru Sivananda Murty.

> May that Supreme Shiva manifest within you and remove all limitations!

OM Namah Shivaya!
Vamadeva Shastri (David Frawley)
April 2015

2. Shiva as the great lord of meditation

Part I

Lord Shiva, the Deity Beyond Duality

Who they call the One Being in Vedanta, who abiding pervades Heaven and Earth, who as the Lord of all, there is no other, who is the imperishable Divine Word;

Who those desiring liberation as the inner reality search out by controlling the breath. May that pillar of awareness, who is easy to access by the steady Yoga of devotion, manifest for your highest well-being!

Hymn to Shiva

You are the sun, you are the moon, you are air, fire, water, and space, you are earth and you are the Self of all. And even this is a limitation for you, a transformation that you hold these worlds. We do not know any cosmic principle where you are not.

There are three *Vedas*, three states of waking, dream and deep sleep, three worlds, and three deities. The three letters of AUM describe you in all these three aspects. Your fourth state is indicated by subtle sound alone. You are all manifestation, as the giver of refuge, proclaiming your reality as the cosmic word OM.

Bhava, Sharva, Rudra, Pashupati, Ugra, Mahadeva, Bhima, and Ishana – these are designated as your eight names. Each one of these is described in the *Vedas*. To you of the most delightful nature, I humbly offer my surrender.

Reverence to the nearest and reverence to the farthest. Reverence to the smallest and to the largest. Reverence to the oldest and the youngest. Reverence to you as all and as the entire universe.

Greatness of Shiva of Pushpadanta, Shiva Mahimna Stotra 26-29

Everything is Rudra! May we offer our reverence to Rudra! The Purusha is Rudra; to that great being we offer our reverence! To the entire manifold and lustrous universe that has been, is and will be, everything is Rudra. To that Rudra may we offer our surrender!

Mahanarayana Upanishad 28.

We begin our journey into the transcendent reality of the Supreme Shiva by recognizing the immense mystery of life and consciousness that dwells within us and pervades us on every side. The following section endeavors to present the experiential reality of pure Existence behind the universe, as the foundation of our encounter with Shiva as the Supreme Being, Will and Power. Shiva is our ultimate origin and destiny and that of all creatures.

Approaching a Deity
Beyond Duality

Our lives are but a shadow, or a half light, as we struggle to find our way in a mysterious realm filled with powerful and intricate forces far beyond the boundaries of our limited creaturely minds. We have created over our short human history a few small island-like human societies in order to develop our personal and collective interests; yet in the process we have largely shut ourselves off from the greater universe beyond our control. Some of us have forgotten that we live in a vast universe of unknown forces and hidden dimensions, not simply in the current human society we are familiar with, which covers but a small portion on the surface of our planet.

Today we have further isolated ourselves from the cosmic mystery with a new sophisticated technology, and its glittering mass media that appears like a vast world of its own. Our technological prowess, which has emerged quickly over the past few centuries, increases the illusion that we are masters of our own destiny. We increasingly think that we can do or become whatever we wish – and that we do not need to honor or perhaps even recognize our duty to greater universe. Most of us now live in a media based reality of human news and have become removed from a direct experience of our own lives and natural environment. Instead of experiencing our own thoughts, emotions and sensations, we are caught in political, entertainment and social images following various scripts from the outside that muffle our own inner voice.

We ignore the world of nature and immerse ourselves in the little media boxes we carry around with us, now as small as a cell phone, which constantly distract our attention from the subtlety of life and its organic rhythms. We must remember that while the tools of technology have grown more numerous and sophisticated, they remain but a shadow of a greater reality beyond the merely human. Compared to the energy of a single star, like our Sun, all our technology resembles but a few brief flashes of lightning.

In spite of our technology and the alluring media realms that it can fashion, the greater world of nature and its immense forces continues to intrude upon us and challenge our view that we are masters of our world. This is evident in our era of climate change in which nature is beginning to fight back against our depredations on the environment. Nature does not conform to our expectations, reflecting powers of eternity that do not bow down to our transient capacities and concerns. Additionally, the effects of time, disease and the aging process eventually remove us from any false sense of lasting security in this fragile physical realm of man. A greater reality remains compared to which our human world is small and fleeting, if not inconsequential. And that realm is not without its own intelligence, feeling and laws – as well as its own wonder, beauty and grace!

We live in a vast multidimensional universe that we do not truly understand, and our ideas about it change radically with every new generation. Recent decades of science have caused us to extend our assessment of the age of the universe by billions of years, a length of time that a few centuries ago was scarcely imagined in the West. Science has similarly extended our assessment of the age of the human species by tens if not hundreds of thousands of years – periods that dwarf our existing records of human history.

Our technology seems to be moving faster than our minds' and perhaps even our bodies' ability to keep pace with it. However intimidating, this technology may be only harnessing a few outer powers of nature, not our higher capacities as a species. Clearly the world is not something entirely definable or predictable, much less static, whether in nature or in society. Something beyond our preconceptions remains ever ahead to challenge us to go farther.

If we look deeply within, we can easily discern that we do not truly know ourselves, nor have we searched out the depths of our own consciousness. We do not know who we are behind the veils of our shifting thoughts and outer roles in life. There is much hidden in our psyches that we have not yet uncovered nor yet suspect might exist, another universe of consciousness as it were. We hold to a limited sensory image of self that is the result of our outer interactions and do not know how to contact the core of our being that can never be seen and which no image can ever define.

There are potentials within each one of us that we have yet to actualize or even imagine to be possible. We prefer the habitual boundaries of our physical senses, expanded through our new technology but still only barely touching the teeming forces that pervade all of space. We do not know how to cultivate our inner senses, intuition, deeper feelings, and higher vision that alone can link us to the whole of life. We are happy with information, facts, and data at the surface and are losing the capacity for direct perception within. We seem more enamored of our own equipment and technology than of the greater universe that we can access through it. We are slow to move outside the field of our social conditioning that now is technologically intruding into our nervous systems and entering into our own bodies. Yet the aura of a greater inner universe continues to dawn around us.

The Greater Universe of Consciousness – The Face of Shiva

Modern science is beginning to recognize that the greater universe in which we live contains other forms of intelligence, perhaps very different than our own and more advanced. We are beginning to learn that our universe does not consist simply of matter, energy, or information but contains the reflection of a deeper consciousness and intelligence that pervades time and space as a whole. We are gradually moving beyond the concept of a mere anthropomorphic personal God made in the image of our human fears and desires, and beginning to recognize a cosmic awareness beyond all partiality and personality. We sense such a universal reality with wonder and doubt, trepidation and awe, but tend to keep our distance from it, feeling that it might make us feel insecure or unimportant. What is our place in a greater cosmos that seems infinitely more than what we are individually and also much more than what we are today as a species?

Approaching the experiential realities of this greater Conscious Universe is not an easy task. It takes us beyond our personal ego, contemporary society, and historical human culture. It requires a revolution deep within our psyches, a fundamental shift to a new level of insight beyond the intellect. Mere words cannot take us very far in this inner change of awareness, though spiritual teachings taken to heart can help set in motion its transformations.

First, we must recognize the primacy of the greater Conscious Universe over our social world and conditioned human mind. We must be willing to provide a special space within ourselves in order to dialogue with the greater universal being with honor and respect. For this to occur, we need to clear our psyches of wrong concepts, misperceptions, and beliefs, of which we have many varieties from many lifetimes, reinforced by our outer environment. We need to decondition our minds from the arrogance of human knowledge and render them into tools of a deeper inquiry beyond the field of our existing memories and expectations. If we hold to our usual opinionated reactions to mere words and let our habitual thought processes dominate, then the inner doors of perception are likely to remain tightly closed for us, whatever else we may do.

This greater field of consciousness behind the known universe has probably been better experienced by earlier human cultures, when humans lived more in contact with nature. The link to that cosmic experience has been preserved in spiritual and yogic teachings from throughout the world since prehistoric times. One of the most important encounters with the universal being is in the form of Lord Shiva and the yogic and mantric teachings associated with him throughout the history of India and nearby countries. Shaivite teachings remain a good point of entry for us to approach the higher reality beyond the visible world. Yet for this to occur we must look beyond the name or depiction of Shiva that we may hold to at a surface level and become open to the greater hidden reality.

Shiva indicates the supreme consciousness that exists deep inside us but outside our ordinary body-mind awareness, as the eternal silent witness ever present at the core of our being. To approach our Shiva nature requires a strong inner discipline, tremendous powers of concentration, and yet a pliable receptivity of mind and hearts – qualities that can only be developed with both sustained effort and grace. The realization of the Cosmic Shiva is a movement into an unbounded existence in which even our current universe is but one possible manifestation, one gem on an endless strand of gems.

The Non-Dual Reality of Shiva

Our world, both of nature and of humanity, consists of powerful dualistic forces and a dynamic play of opposites, either as complementary forces or as powers of conflict. We contain within ourselves the dualities of male and female, self and other, attraction and repulsion, birth and death that seem to pull at us from every side. Yet there is a mysterious point of harmony, balance, and integration between these opposites that is possible at a deep level, though it constantly seems to elude our personal efforts to reach it. The unity that we all seek appears extremely difficult to achieve and is something far more than any of the dualities that we encounter.

Shiva is ultimately a deity that represents the non-dualistic Absolute, beyond all the contraries and oppositions of this dualistic world of time, space, and karma. He represents the force of transcendent unity that is always more than the combination of opposites and holds simultaneously the power of both sides of all dualities. Shiva is a deity who transcends duality in his very nature, appearance and manifestation –which also requires that he embraces all dualities and resolves them back into himself. This makes Shiva difficult to understand for the dualistic mind that is caught in outer differences and distinctions, which dwells in its own opinions and conflicts as if it were the center of all.

Shiva reflects the supreme truth that dwells beyond both relative truth and relative falsehood. He is the Supreme Being that is beyond both relative being and non-being. He is the supreme Good that is beyond both relative good and evil. He embraces our world on both sides, above and below, and in the center and yet stands infinitely beyond it as well. He is One, yet he is all. He is everything and nothing, both within all things, outside of all things, and not limited by anything.

As such a non-dualistic deity, there is much regarding the portrayal of Shiva that seems contrary to our prevailing views of what is logical, right or appropriate. Shiva is portrayed as dispassionate yet he has the most powerful passions. He both destroys the ordinary God of love but then becomes the Supreme God of Love himself. He takes us beyond suffering, but to do this he can cause us excruciating pain. Shiva awakens in us a higher awareness, but for this to occur he must first take us beyond all our preconceptions, making us see the darkness of ignorance behind our lives. Shiva represents our higher Self that is the goal of all our aspirations, but to reach it we must allow our ego, its attachments and opinions to be dissolved, giving up our ordinary sense of self altogether.

The Challenge of our Encounter With Shiva

As such a non-dual deity, Shiva in his diverse names, forms, and actions is meant to be challenging for us to grasp. Lord Shiva is not meant to be easy to understand, nor can we present his reality in a simple manner that resolves all doubts for us as to what he actually represents. To contact the reality of Shiva we must first face all doubts and difficulties within ourselves and learn how to move beyond them with steadiness and grace. We must recognize the limitations of the mind and its particularized knowledge. The portrayal of Shiva is not meant to present us with only a good and pleasing appearance, any more than life is always kind to us. Our encounter with Shiva is meant to shake us up, to stir our inner transformative energies – to get us to question not only Shiva, but also to question ourselves and all that we may hold to be truth or reality.

Any real encounter with Lord Shiva is not likely to conform to our existing beliefs, hopes, or expectations. It may not leave us feeling more confident about who we are, or more certain that our lives are moving in the right direction. An encounter with Shiva may not initially make us feel happier or give us more prosperity or what we may regard as a better life. Shiva is not what we think

God is supposed to be, conforming to our opinions or hopes; Shiva is what the Supreme Divine truly is beyond the limitations of our minds, reason, and the fixed tenets of any particular faith or belief. Shiva is the supreme reality, not we ourselves, our ideas, opinions, books, or institutions. Shiva is the cosmic reality not our individual or collective imaginations and fantasies. There is no box we can place Shiva into, no formula or structure that the mind can arrive at that can hold Shiva.

To arrive at the state of supreme awareness that is Shiva, we must allow ourselves to be stripped bare of our personal conditioning down to a subconscious level, beyond the memories of the present birth and the perceptions of this present world. We must learn to see ourselves in all beings past, present, and future. We must be humbled back to the core of our being where no self-image prevails, and where there is no other that we have to conform to, please, or fear.

The human mind as it is today is not a conscious intelligence that we can rely upon to determine what is real. It is a conditioned response mechanism for biological survival and social development. But in the silence of the heart, where all is forgotten, one can know the truth. You are Shiva in your deepest Self and core being. *Shiva is the non-dual reality in which you personally are not there, yet in which you in your inmost essence of feeling and awareness are everything.*

So let us proceed in our encounter with a non-dualistic deity that has forms and aspects on all levels, but ultimately contains the whole of existence as a single unbounded Self. For this journey, we will employ a language that is philosophical and rational at one level, but symbolic and intuitive at another. In this process of unveiling Shiva, always remember that we are looking for the Supreme Truth beyond words, as a state of inner experience, not as a social identity or personal expression. Then you will find that Shiva is always with you as the very presence that envelops you on every side.

An Enigmatic Hindu Deity: How Shiva Is Viewed Today

The first thing for us to realize relative to Shiva and his unusual appearances is that he represents the transcendent reality that can only be portrayed in an indirect manner as it is inherently beyond words and thoughts. What we think about Shiva is not the reality of Shiva, particularly the modern mind's opinions that have little to do with that supreme truth beyond all concepts. So let us set aside or put in the background what we think we already know about Shiva and take a new look with our inner eye.

Many people have heard of Lord Shiva as one of the most important Gods of India since ancient times. Few are aware of his cosmic dimensions. Some know that Shiva is prominent in Yoga teachings and traditions, several of which are ascribed to him. Yet Shiva appears to be one of the strangest and most controversial of Hindu Gods, which overall seem quite bewildering to us in their diversity and in the details of their supernatural depictions.

The image of Shiva for the modern mind remains clouded by demeaning stereotypes rooted in older missionary and colonial thought, which found it difficult to appreciate spiritual teachings of non-western cultures, particularly those that had a boldly imagistic presentation. Yet even those of us who may not be affected by older prejudices may find the image of Shiva hard to understand. While Vishnu, the other primary Hindu deity, reflects a pleasant image of light, love, and devotion, such as we see in Lord Krishna, Shiva presents us with a depiction of raw power, paradox, and transcendence that challenges our conventional beliefs about reality, society, and religion.

Shiva has been identified with male energy and phallic worship, and is thought to personify sexuality more so than spirituality for the western mind. Yet while Shiva is a male deity and symbolizes higher masculine traits, that is only one of his many dimensions as the Lord of all powers. Freudian psychology has emphasized this sexual side of Shiva's symbolism and ignored Shiva's higher cosmic implications of which it is but one part. Our sexually obsessed culture tends to look down upon other cultures that include a sexual symbolism as part of a greater cosmic vision. To approach the reality of Shiva we must remember this important factor. The Freudian idea of the ego, superego and id constitute but a minuscule portion of the greater consciousness within us, which is the Supreme Shiva.

Shiva is associated with a cult of ecstasy, including at times the use of marijuana, and with sadhus and yogis who use this herb to worship him. This causes some to look upon Shiva as merely the deity of a drug cult. That Shiva's real ecstasy is Samadhi, the yogic bliss of Self-realization, is usually not mentioned in such discussions. Shiva's blissful symbolism, like the wine of mystic poetry, is that of a greater spiritual inebriation.

Shiva is often called a "God of destruction," after his ruling over the cosmic power of dissolution and transformation. He is sometimes thought to bring destruction in his wake and denigrated accordingly. That Shiva's dissolution is a movement into higher awareness is usually not considered. *There is in the end neither creation nor destruction but only the rising and falling of the realm of appearances from the Supreme Consciousness that is Shiva.*

Depicted as Pashupati, the "lord of the wild animals," or with a retinue of ghosts, carrying a trident and symbolized by a five pointed star, Shiva can have some resemblance to the "Devil" – a factor that missionaries have highlighted. Yet Shiva is also portrayed as a deity of the highest wisdom, delight, and compassion – as the friend of all creatures, however small or low – which includes wild animals, departed spirits, the sick, the poor, and the outcast. We seem content with looking at Shiva in a negative light, ignoring his universal symbolism, perhaps reflecting an inability to face the greater conscious universe itself, which is beyond our personal opinions.

The western mind tends to reduce Shiva to iconographic depictions and anthropomorphic appearances, which derive from a very different cultural milieu of ancient India. We seldom examine his formless nature, his mantric and light aspects that are universal in nature, though these are commonly taught in Shaivite literature as well. Shiva seems to us to be but one of a retinue of Gods or subtle beings of dubious divinity, not a name for God or the Supreme reality, surrounding himself with chaotic, if not destructive aspects of life, like the pagan deities of old. Many of these stereotypic opinions against pagan Gods are projected on to Shiva as well.

There are those who fear the energy of Shiva and reject it as something harsh, uncontrolled, animal, or sensuous. Many academics take a sensationalist approach to Shiva, reading human weaknesses and eroticism rather than cosmic transcendence into his mysterious nature. They misunderstand Shiva's cosmic power as something negative, a primitive adulation of the wild forces of nature, not an honoring of a supreme consciousness.

Shaivite Yogic Spirituality

Yet while Lord Shiva represents the universal reality, we cannot approach Shiva without regard for the actual teachings and traditions that he has developed in humanity. There remains a living tradition of Shaivism in the world today extending to numerous great Yogis, sadgurus, and spiritual masters and several different branches of Shaivism. Shaivism is part of the greater Vedic and Hindu tradition and reflects its power and knowledge.

We can contact Shiva today through his living teachings and representatives in a direct manner. These channels to Shiva do not simply represent an outer affiliation with Shiva but link us to the inner awareness of Shiva and keys to its ongoing manifestation in humanity. The many yogic paths that Shaivism has developed can be important to everyone. We can all join Shiva's vast family on Earth and contact its living representatives that have the greatest affinity with our own inner aspiration.

If we carefully examine the tradition of Shiva worship, we find something very different than the shadow of superstition usually cast upon Shiva. Shaivism contains among the world's most sophisticated spiritual, mystical, and yogic philosophies. It has preserved numerous texts of great depth, detail, and profundity on all aspects of life, consciousness, the universe, karma, rebirth and liberation of the soul. Shaivite teachings are not just theoretical but abound with practices relative to Yoga, mantra, prana, Kundalini, and the chakras that can take us to the highest Self-realization and God-realization.

Shiva relates to the unitary awareness beyond time and space, the supreme Brahman or Absolute, a universal consciousness such as modern physics is only beginning to suspect, might exist behind the known world. Shaivite philosophies include several systems of Yoga, Vedanta, Tantra, Kashmir Shaivism, and Shaiva Siddhanta that reflect a great sophistication in their theories, logic, method, and understanding of the means to gain true knowledge about eternal reality through inner perception and inquiry.

At the level of meditative insight, Shiva is a deity of endless time and boundless space, with his dance of fire symbolizing the process through which the entire universe is both created and dissolved at every moment. This transcendent side of Shiva inspired modern physicist Carl Sagan to associate Shiva with the highest knowledge of modern science. Shiva is a deity of the eons, not just an historical or cultural image.

Shiva is also an image of the highest refinement in human life extending to the highest Self-realization. Shiva is a great icon of art and culture in India, with extensive traditions of poetry, grammar, music, and dance associated with Shiva as their dominant influence. The influence of Shiva occurs in all the traditions and branches of Yoga in India from asanas to the highest samadhis. Shaivite thought covers medicine and healing (Ayurveda), astrology, and the occult sciences.

There are beautiful Shiva temples in all regions of India north and south, east and west, with extraordinary architecture and sculpture. These temples remain alive with many thousands of pilgrims visiting them regularly for festivals and holidays. Shiva has sacred sites throughout the Himalayas, extending into middle India and as far south as Tamil Nadu. Shiva is one of the great unifying images of Indian or *Bharatiya* culture. Yet we can find the influence of Shiva throughout Asia and extending into native traditions throughout the entire world.

Universality of Lord Shiva

Shiva is relevant to all of us, young and old, East and West, as a formulation of the highest truth and consciousness, the spiritual power behind nature, and the deeper Self-awareness beyond the known universe. We cannot understand our spiritual heritage and potential as a species unless we afford a prominent place for Lord Shiva and his teachings.

Yet we need not necessarily limit our views to the existing iconography of Shiva and his retinue of forces. That remains an important symbolism, but other depictions are possible, through the many aspects of nature. But we can appreciate the reality of pure consciousness behind the names, forms, and actions through which Shiva has been approached historically. It is not a question of merely embracing the name Shiva. Shiva has many names in India as in the famous *Thousand Names of Shiva* (Shiva Sahasranama). Other names like Rudra, Pashupati, or Bhairava have at certain times or in certain regions predominated. We can give Shiva a new name if we wish as his are eventually all names.

Our concern in this book is not with semantics or history but with what could be better called "experiential spirituality," which is what Yoga is really about. In such experiential spirituality, we are looking to the universal background behind the deity figure, not simply its outer implications in terms of time, place and culture. What is important is the actual experience of Shiva and the practical ways of gaining it, which have been well preserved in Hindu and Shaivite teachings. It is the "living" aspect of Shiva consciousness in humanity that is most important, which continues to evolve in its expression.

Approximately half of the more than one billion Hindus in the world are Shaivites, for whom Shiva represents the supreme Divine. Yet Hindus of every denomination honor Shiva at one level or another. Shiva is a prominent deity in the worship of Vishnu, Devi, Ganesha, Skanda, Hanuman and the other deity forms of Hinduism. Shaivism originally emerged from the older Vedic teachings and much of Vedic, Zoroastrian and pagan European traditions such as the Druids reflect Shiva aspects of fire worship and related teachings. Shiva as Rudra, the lord of the sound, is the origin of the Sanskrit alphabet that is the oldest and most perfectly devised of the Indo-European languages.

Shaivism has been popular historically in South India, particularly Tamil Nadu, where there are many famous Shiva temples. Shiva remains popular in North India, particularly the Himalayas, the great mountain lands of Shiva, with its many Shiva peaks, and Nepal, with its famous Pashupati Nath temple to Shiva in Kathmandu. Kashmir is a famous ancient Shiva land that influenced the cultures of Central Asia and China. Shiva is also connected to rivers with his most famous temple city being Benares or Varanasi on the Ganga.

Certain Buddhists traditions like the Tibetan honor Shiva as the great lord of the mountain with his trident as Mahakala. Mount Kailas in Tibet, the most sacred mountain for Hindus and Tibetans, and for Siddha Yogis, is the great mountain of Shiva. Shiva as a deity occurs in Tantric Buddhist texts.

Shaivism spread with Vedic and Indian culture in ancient times throughout south, east and central Asia, embraced by people of many different cultures and ethnicities. Central Asian Iranian people like the Scythians dominated territories from North India (Indo-Scythians) to the Ukraine (Scythia major) to the Danube River of Eastern Europe (Scythia minor) that reflected Shaivite influences. Shaivite and Buddhist kings were counted among the Indo-Scythian, Kushanas and Hunas that dominated these regions at that time.[2]

Shaivism spread south and east from India to Sri Lanka, Malaysia and Indonesia, where several important Shiva sites remain. Shiva worship once prevailed as far as Vietnam under the Champa kings until but a few centuries ago and had spread as far as the Philippines. Many old Shiva temples and lingas can be found in Vietnam today.

Today Shaivism is again expanding along with the global Yoga movement and the new Hindu diaspora to many countries of the world, particularly the English-speaking realm. This global relevance of Shiva is not new, but represents an important new expansion that is just in its initial phases. Wherever Yoga spreads, the power of Shiva cannot be far behind. Shiva remains a powerful image in the culture and thought of India that remains prominent today.[3]

Shiva personifies the inner strength born of our connection with all nature and all consciousness that can effectively deal with the challenges of our time and has a special appeal to the youth and for the future as well. There is great beauty, mystery, and depth to the figure of Shiva. It is the enigma of life itself, beyond the opinions and beliefs of the mind. So let us keep our minds and hearts open as we explore various sides of a Deity that encompasses all that is from the rocks on the ground to the unlimited Absolute.

Shiva, as the Great Unknown

We live in a magical and mysterious universe pervaded by an unseen intelligence and subtle energies, which extend far beyond the merely human and social concerns that dominate our daily lives. Modern science is still uncovering powers and dimensions of the universe, vast and small, that take us outside the boundaries of the known world as revealed by our senses into realms beyond ordinary time and space, physical reality, and personal identity. This sense of a great unknown and yet alive and magical universe is familiar to all mystics, yogis and poets – and with all who live with reverence for nature, which is the original state of the human mind and heart.

There is a profound sacred order to the cosmos, reflecting vast eonic forces working at a different level altogether than our ordinary historical, personal, and social agencies. This power of consciousness behind the universe is transformational and cataclysmic in nature; it does not conform to our expectations, needs or demands, or to the formulations and opinions of our human intellect. It has its own imperious logic and is not simply irrational in function. It possesses the precision of the universal being, not the limited focus of the human mind.

Our human knowledge works through a principle of familiarity. We impose our own mind created names, concepts, and forms upon the world and then think that we know what something is or what its true reality is likely to be. In this era of information technology we are particularly good at accumulating data, facts, and information about outer appearances that remain questionable. We are "data heavy" as it were, but weak in the field of life wisdom. We seldom experience reality directly for ourselves, where no thought enters and where no technology can intrude.

We easily confuse journalism, which is surveying opinions, with the pursuit of lasting truth. We forget that we must first investigate something deeply with a patient inner awareness, not merely with external cameras and recording devises, before we can have a sense of its true nature. To approach the reality of Shiva we need to put aside what we think we know about Shiva, or what we think we know about ourselves or the greater universe.

We dwell at the surface of the greater cosmos of consciousness and do not examine its endless depths. We are afraid of its unpredictable currents, in which our civilizational achievements can seem but a glimmer or a shadow. Yet besides our usual desires for the enjoyments of our familiar outer world, we possess a powerful inner urge to connect a greater unknown reality, even if we may not have a clear idea as to what that may be. This drive or impulse for transcendence is the basis of true religion and spirituality, among other deep searches for truth, though we may reduce these to mundane compulsions, scaled down into confines of the human world and our emotional needs.

This sacred cosmic mystery of the universe has been formulated in many ways in the different cultures of the world going back to the dawn of our species. It has been the prime concern of esoteric movements outside of ordinary society, including various orders of monks, renunciates and spiritual communities. If we look at India and its great Yoga tradition, we find that union with that mysterious unknown reality is the essence of India's cultural striving and the subject of a massive civilizational focus and endeavor.

The ancient *Upanishads* eloquently state even before the time of the Buddha:

> *Not what is known by the mind, but that through which the sages state the mind is known. That is Brahman. That is reality. Not what you honor here as an object.*

> *Kena Upanishad I.5.*

> *It is known to him for whom it is unknown and unknown to him for whom it is known.*

> *Kena Upanishad II.3.*

> *That from which speech and mind turn back without reaching; the wise who know that Self of bliss have no fear from anywhere.*

> *Taittiriya Upanishad II.9.*

Vedantic philosophy, the philosophy of the *Upanishads*, brilliantly echoes the search for what is beyond the known. It directs us beyond the mind and the mere creaturely to the cosmic reality. This requires a great leap of awareness, a revolution in the mind, and the awakening of a deeper sense of discrimination rooted in the eternal.

Yet as this cosmic reality is located everywhere and in everything, it cannot exist apart from our own being and must constitute our true nature. Our search for what is beyond the known is a search for our true timeless identity beyond the confines of our human personality. To reach that supreme truth, Vedanta unfolds a path of Self-realization that is relevant to everyone. *That supreme nameless and formless reality is described as the Supreme Shiva:*

> *His form does not exist to be seen. No one has seen him with the eyes. By the heart and the mind, those who know him dwelling in the heart become immortal. Some who are humble take refuge in him as the Unborn. Rudra (Shiva), what is your auspicious face, may that ever protect us!*

> *Shvetashvatara Upanishad V.20-21.*

Such Vedantic insights are rooted in an earlier Vedic vision. The ancient *Vedas* reflect this cosmic mystery in a special language of cryptic mantras of light and fire that cannot be translated and defy the outer mind in their formulation, as the following key Vedic verse indicates about our deeper Self:

> *He is the hamsa bird who dwells in light, the pervasive power in the atmosphere, the invoking priest at the earth altar, and the timeless guest in our home. He dwells in the human soul, he dwells in the supreme, he dwells in truth, and he dwells in space. He is born of the cosmic waters, born of the light, born of the great mountain, born of truth, he is the supreme truth.*

> *Rigveda IV.40.10, Mahanarayana Upanishad 12, Dahara Vidya*

Yet though this supreme truth takes us beyond all words and ideas, we must approach it through some type of expression in order to relate to it and bring it into our minds. Various spiritual teachings have arisen to help us approach this supreme truth, though it is ultimately beyond all concepts – and such teachings are merely provisional like a raft to take us across a river that must be discarded when we reach the other shore. We must learn to use the vehicle of the teachings without limiting the supreme reality to its terms and approaches.

Lord Shiva as the Great Unknown

It is as the great deity Lord Shiva that we most clearly confront the great cosmic mystery in yogic thought. Shiva is the embodiment of what is hidden, what is not what it appears to be, but reflects a vast and imperious power and motivation behind all that we see. What is the reality behind Lord Shiva, who is the great Lord of Yoga, and the supreme deity beyond all limitation?

Shiva is perhaps the most misunderstood of the Hindu pantheon, a paradoxical figure that suggests a reality beyond the bounds of convention or even reason. Shiva with his retinue of wild animals and ghosts, his trident, matted hair, the crescent Moon on his head that also bears the descent of the heavenly Ganga, and his behavior that acts in defiance of all ordinary norms stands apart from all other deities, appearing like the harbinger of a different order of reality.

The mysterious reality of the Cosmic Shiva is not merely a cultural or religious issue, some strange aspect of Hindu thought, but is relevant to the well-being of every individual. Shiva reflects the great mystery and cosmic power in which we all live, which overrides and transcends all our limited efforts as individual creatures.

To reach and unfold the power of the Cosmic Shiva is the key to our ultimate well-being and to the upliftment of the human race. Indeed, that Shiva consciousness is always working to enter more deeply into humanity, bringing us into alignment with the cosmos and spiritualizing all that we are. We can ignore this great unknown for a time, but we remain surrounded by it on every side. It holds the key to our future as well as to our obscure origins in the dark night of time. It embraces our lives at birth and death, waking and sleep. Our modern humanity trapped in the illusion of information technology needs to confront the cosmic Shiva once more, and is just beginning a new reckoning with this supreme mystery.

Shiva, we should note, is not simply the name of a Hindu deity. Shiva, which means "that which is auspicious," refers to the ultimately auspicious effect of our contact with the unknown, the nameless, the great mystery, what is beyond all limitation. In this regard, Shiva has no name and also an infinite number of names. Every name is a name of Shiva and yet he remains inexpressible and indescribable. Chanting the name of Shiva means going beyond all identities. It is the resonance of the cosmic silence. It is this inner reality of Shiva that we need to understand, not simply Shiva as a religious deity or a cultural form.

The Universal Trinity of Brahma, Vishnu and Shiva

Probably, the simplest and most common explanation of Shiva in the traditional literature is that there is a trinity of divine forces governing the process of time in the universe with Brahma as the Creator, Vishnu as the Sustainer, and Shiva as the Destroyer. These are the three faces of the eternal and the infinite, not three separate deities – three formulations and actions of the same Supreme Being or Brahman.

Yet this description causes the shadow of a destructive force to be cast upon Shiva – as if his cosmic role was to promote negativity and death. However, according to the view of Vedic philosophy, there is in truth no real creation or destruction of anything in the universe. The visible universe is but a manifestation of the timeless unmanifest, like the waves arising from the sea. We do not attribute the ocean with the action of creating and destroying waves. The wave arises from and returns to the sea, being nothing but water all along. When the wave goes back to the sea, it is a return, not annihilation. The wave falls back into the silence of the depths; a hostile and alien force does not destroy it. Shiva is the power of eternal return and transformation, not a mere force of destruction. He is not only the end but also the beginning and the essence both within and beyond the process of time.

Lord Brahma indicates the cosmic intelligence that initiates the world manifestation, setting forth the prime laws and principles that provide the structure for the universe. Lord Vishnu protects and sustains the manifestation, holding in equilibrium the powerful dualistic forces of which it is constituted. Lord Shiva completes and dissolves the manifestation, bringing all things to fruition. According to this view, Shiva is the great deity who dissolves all limitations, difficulties, sorrows and bondage, taking us back to the freedom of the unmanifest. Shiva is the state of mergence into which all things must return.

According to a deeper view, Shiva represents the transcendent beyond all manifestation, what is called *Para Brahman* or the Absolute in Vedantic thought. Vishnu indicates the cosmic lord or lord of the universe, the *Ishvara* of Vedantic thought. Brahma is the cosmic mind that works within the universe, the *Mahat Tattva* of Vedantic thought.

The Divine light in its higher essence beyond all form, person, and manifestation is known as Shiva. When the Divine light enters into human beings or individual souls it becomes Vishnu, the ideal soul or human being. When it becomes the basis of our intelligence and mind it becomes Brahma, the power of dharma. From our mortal world, we can only have an intimation of that supreme immortality of Shiva. Vishnu, on the other hand, takes a human form to guide, protect and save us. Brahma is ever present as knowledge, teaching and ritual.

We could say that Vishnu and Brahma are also aspects of Shiva. Or we could say that Brahma and Shiva are aspects of Vishnu, or Shiva and Vishnu are aspects of Brahma. No limited concepts can prevail here.

Shiva as the Supreme Reality

As the supreme reality, Shiva is looked upon in four main ways. We will discuss each of these in detail in separate chapters of the book.

1. Shiva is first the original clear light of reality that illumines all things, Prakasha.

2. Shiva is the immortal life force that is the basis of all energy in the universe, Prana.

3. Shiva is primal sound, OM or Pranava, the basis of all vibration and communication in the universe.

4. Shiva is the primal being or pure consciousness, Atman or Purusha, our own inner Self and the Self of all.

Shiva as the primal power of light is reflected in our search for Self-realization, our own inner light, and is not simply the worship of an external deity. This inner light is the real basis of life, the eternal energy of Prana that exists inherently beyond all birth and death. This Divine Prana in turn is ever resounding as the cosmic sound vibration Pranava, Divine Word that is both the manifest and unmanifest reality. This Divine light, life and word is our true being and Self-nature, the Purusha beyond the limitations of body and mind, which are but its instruments, our true Self-nature.

Shiva is the embodiment of mystery, but not merely the mystery of something unknown in the manifest realm. His is the mystery that transcends all that we have known, can know, or can ever hope to know with the mind. Shiva's true nature cannot be known to any outer instrumentality and does not dwell in the domain of word or thought.

We contact Shiva when we realize the limited nature of all that we can know or think, when our sense of self-identity fades away. This can make our encounter with Shiva into something awesome and at times frightening – facing the power of the great unknown that renders our lives but a grain of dust in the vast impersonal cosmic dance. Shiva is the being of cosmic consciousness far beyond the constraints of any creaturely mind and its compulsions. We are but facets of his greater reality, but also in our inner being are one with him. *We are Shiva.* That great cosmic mystery and supreme power is our true Self, in which we can find perfect peace and happiness – and need not fear at all, but should welcome with open minds and hearts.

Shiva as the Supreme Deity of Yoga

Those who practice Yoga may know something of Shiva but are seldom aware of his centrality to Yoga in all of its varied forms. Lord Shiva is probably the most important deity in the greater Yoga tradition. Shiva is often portrayed as the primordial Yoga guru, the original teacher behind the Yoga tradition.

The quest for Shiva – whatever name we may wish to use – reflects the essence of humanity's perennial search for immortality. Yoga as a sadhana or spiritual practice rests upon cultivating the Shiva consciousness of the highest awareness and bliss. This reality of Shiva is the power of silence, stillness, and non-doing, not the ordinary power of self-assertion and aggression. These are the secret powers of Yoga, which is Shiva's play.

This Shiva power of Yoga works through inaction, peace and balance, in which one is centered in one's own being and grasps the entire universe as a manifestation of one's own thoughts. The power of Shiva is no mere outer force that displays itself for personal gain or recognition, nor the outer effort to control that makes a show of itself in order to gain adulation. Shiva is the spiritual force that turns things around, draws things within, and takes them back to their source, in which a deep unity remains beyond all expression. Shiva symbolizes the balancing and calming effect of all Yoga practices. Shiva is the still point of Yoga that is the highest and most transformative state of balance.

Shiva is the supreme guide to meditation and calming the mind, the supreme guru of the quest for enlightenment, teaching us to observe, contemplate and not react, providing us with a cosmic view of all the events in our lives and the emotions in our minds, so that these can never overwhelm us. Yet Shiva is not the deity of a mere intellectual meditation approach, any limited rational philosophy, or personal self-analysis. Shiva is the deity of merging the mind back into its source in the infinite, giving up the personal mind for the universal consciousness, like the wave returning to the sea. Shiva takes us beyond the preconceptions of the mind, with its conflicts and dualities, to the formless consciousness that pervades all space and is not bound to any memory patterns, fears or desires.

Shiva is *Yogeshvara* or the "Lord of Yoga." He is the ideal or archetypal yogi, ascetic, monk, swami and sadhu. Worshipping Shiva as the Lord of Yoga within ourselves we can master all aspects of Yoga and meditation through his grace alone. The worship of Shiva pervades the Yoga tradition from the most ancient to modern times. The Nath Yogis, from whom much of Tantric Yoga, Hatha Yoga and Siddha Yoga arise, were followers of Lord Shiva who is *Adi Nath* or the original guru.[4] Shankara, the great guru of non-dualist or Advaita Vedanta, who also taught Raja Yoga and Bhakti Yoga, was regarded as an incarnation of Lord Shiva. Shiva is the great guru and all true gurus can be regarded as his channels or conduits. Shiva as *Mahadeva* or the great deity behind all deity formations is the ultimate guide of all.

Return to Shiva

A return to the original clear light of reality, which is the Supreme Shiva, is the essence not only of yogic spirituality, but also of all true science, art, philosophy and psychology – of all true culture. The search for our inner Shiva nature does not limit us to a description of Shiva, but opens us to the greater powers of the conscious universe and its unlimited number of worlds, souls and creatures.

To achieve this higher state of awareness that is the Supreme Shiva, we can practice Shiva Yoga or the "Yoga of Shiva," of which there are many varieties in the diverse Shaivite traditions. There are special rituals, mantras, pranayamas, mudras and yoga practices relative to Shiva in his many appearances and approaches, from outer forms of deity worship to formless inner meditation practices.

Yet we can also approach Shiva in a personal manner today along with or apart from the formalities of older Yoga traditions. To contact that state of Shiva or profound peace is a simple matter of allowing ourselves to deeply contemplate nature, and to move into our own inner nature beyond the mind, giving up our psychological identity to a universal sense of Self. To contact Shiva we must be willing to let go of everything, we must be willing to surrender the mind's need to know for a willingness to be and to be all. This is not at all easy, though it is something that we can gradually approach by cultivating the life of Shiva, which is the life of meditation as our highest pursuit. Meditation is the highest culture, though it does not need to express itself. It is the culture of a deeper awareness beyond the outer productions of body and mind.

As the Shiva force manifest within us, it creates a certain palpable pressure inside our minds and nervous systems for us to purify, to change, and to transcend all that we have thought we are. We must allow the currents of this Shiva energy to move within us and strive to follow their impetus and motivation. They can facilitate a deeper healing that dissolves all our life problems and not merely suppresses them. This requires that we do not resist the higher Shiva force, but rather welcome it as the call of our true nature. Such a surrender to Shiva is like an inner death but also an inner rebirth, the resurrection of our higher Self-awareness that was latent in the darkness of the subconscious mind.

One may ask: *Does it matter what one calls that supreme reality or how one conceives it, even if one does not know the word Shiva or understand the yogic symbolism of Shiva?* Such a reality beyond description is not limited to a name, but connecting with the power of Shiva through traditional yogic ways of knowledge can be a great aid in understanding that supreme unknown.

That higher Shiva consciousness has approached humanity throughout history, and has established certain paths of access to itself, not merely in outward books and institutions but in the human mind and heart. These ways of higher knowledge do require individual adaptation and change in form according to outer changes in time and culture. Yet they maintain a certain continuity and consistency, a reality in the collective mind that can make our inner journey quicker and more efficacious, if we learn to follow their currents. Yoga helps us return to that great mystery of Shiva by the paths of previous great Yogis and sages whose blessings can guide us along the way, step by step. Shiva is not just the great unknown but also the highest knowledge for which teachings and gurus will ever remain accessible for those who are receptive to them.

Shiva, the Hidden Deity of Nature

Shiva is a deity of nature, much more so than of any human formulation. Even Shiva's human depiction is replete with the symbolism of nature as mountains, rivers, plants, animals and sky. His depiction is non-historical, reflecting the vast cycles of nature and the enduring powers of eternity. Shiva indicates a universal reality far beyond any books about him, academic depictions, or institutions, much less any anthropomorphic form in which he may be portrayed.

Understanding Shiva requires examining the whole of nature, including recognizing a deeper divine nature that exists behind the apparent inanimate forms of the outer world. The world of nature is the manifestation of deeper unseen, mysterious forces, and of the primal power of existence beyond all forms. As a manifestation of a greater consciousness, nature is an expression, not a reality in-itself, and has a message to teach us. The world of nature is a doorway to a deeper consciousness, which is Shiva. Nature is creative intelligence in expression. This creative intelligence does not shape nature from the outside but develops it from within, with the outer world that we see but the waves of a deeper ocean.

The world of nature portrays a universal language of energy and form, directing us to an unseen power and presence beyond all apparent limitation. Each creature, plant, rock formation, planet or star has a teaching, is telling us something to us about the universe as a whole. This inner reality of nature is better translated through poetry, image, and symbol than through facts and information, which keep us constrained to the surface of the world. Nature is the supreme scripture and ultimate revelation for both the mind and the heart, beyond any human words or formulas. We must learn to decode the forms of nature, which is to discover their transcendent Shiva essence.

Shiva as a deity of nature is best expressed through nature, from the rocks on Earth to the cosmic space beyond. Like nature, everything we see depicted about Shiva is symbolic and indicative of something greater. His sacred animals are forms of energy. His weapons and ornaments are cosmic powers. We can experience the Supreme Shiva easily in nature, if we look to what nature is reflecting at a deeper level, though we may lose Shiva if we look at him according to human depictions alone, particularly accordingly to the views of those who have never experienced his awesome presence.

Nature and Spirit

Nature arises from a deeper spirit, presence, peace, and power, of which the outer forces of the natural world, with their constant changes, are but shifting movements and expressions. There is an expanse to nature that brings a sense of vastness into the human mind when we open up to primacy of the natural world. Nature suggests to us a Divine presence as her hidden counterpart, lord, or in-dwelling consciousness.

We have all experienced a sense of wonder or magic in the sky, clouds, ocean, mountains and forests, which draws us into the contemplation of Spirit, God, or a Supreme Reality. This is true not only of the religiously minded but extends to all people, young and old, educated or uneducated. We live in a wonderful and beautiful universe whose greater reality and deeper meaning remains far beyond anything that the mind can name or conceive as ultimate. There is something immense about the universe and its overflowing currents, where all our measurements, however intricate, fall short.

We can feel and intuit the existence of a vast spirit behind nature in the great outdoors, even if we may not agree upon its name or depiction. So-called primitive people are strongly aware of this sacred spirit in nature, as nature is their primary environment, more so than we modern humans who are caught in our high tech and urban environments. In the wilderness, we sense a cosmic reality beyond our ordinary lives in human society. We can see with our inner eye another horizon beyond the sky. The great God, deity, or spirit of nature is often conceived as a sky God, holding the Earth in his embrace and opening to infinity. Yet he also dwells within the Earth and her growths and landforms, as the soul of the Earth. These are all facets of Shiva.

Shiva as the Great Deity of Nature

Shiva in Hindu thought is portrayed as the God of the wild. He is the deity of the mountains, forests, jungles, and deserts – regions largely uninhabited by human beings, where not only wild animals but also subtle beings, like nature spirits and Devas, roam freely and express the Cosmic Spirit in ways unknown to we ordinary human beings. While Shiva has a human appearance, particularly as the yogi in the mountains and forests, he also has animal, plant and rock forms. As embracing the wild, Shiva relates to our deeper spiritual and cosmic impulses that require we break away from mere human convention, and express our true nature that is more at home in the wilderness than in the artificialities of human society.

Shiva's sacred sites are located in nature, defined by the beauty and the power of the land, waters and sky. Shiva's most important temples are the hills and mountains. We can find these sacred sites of Shiva in every ecosystem. He has sacred stones, plants, rivers, stars and fires. Yet even Shiva's manmade temples are designed to reflect the structure of the cosmos, not simply human concerns and have their importance as well.

Shiva is not a deity of time or of historical revelation defined by special human mediators or messengers. He represents the eternal power in nature that pervades all life. We need not do something special or travel far to discover the presence of Shiva. We only need look more deeply into the energy fields behind the visible forms of the world, and become aware of the sacred space within our own minds and hearts.

Shiva is first of all the great deity of the mountains, the very personification of the indomitable mountain spirit. He represents the same qualities of grandeur, height, stability, and power that we feel in the mountains, and the same expansion of vision as we discover looking out from a mountaintop and surveying the surrounding world. Shiva is the sacred world mountain and has many sacred mountains of his own. These Shiva peaks include the Himalayas, the highest mountains in the world, particularly in the Indian state of Uttar Khand, which include the origins of the Ganga, Shiva's sacred river. Most important is Mount Kailas in Tibet in the Transhimalayan range beyond that has the appearance of a gigantic crystal, from which many great rivers of Asia arise nearby. Shiva is the entire universe that is shaped like a mountain of consciousness. Shiva is the mountain lord, which is the lord of all existence.

Along with sacred mountain are sacred mountain waters, rivers, lakes and waterfalls. These mountain waters are the Shakti or Goddess powers connected to Shiva as the Supreme Deity. The mountain draws in the rain clouds whose rain brings about the origin of the rivers. Shiva as the mountain lord aids the descent of the Heavenly Ganga or river of Heaven that falls on his head as the summit of the mountain. Only the head of Shiva, or the higher consciousness, has the power to bring the cosmic waters of consciousness, the lightning streams of higher awareness down to the Earth and to our human realm. Pouring water on the head of Shiva, whether as a statue or the linga, reflects his connection with the cosmic Goddess streams and allows these to flow upon us.

Shiva's dance is the infinite dance of life. All of nature is present within us and forms the inner worlds and islands of the psyche. Shiva represents the mountain of the spirit, which is the mountain of the spine, and the chakra centers that we ascend as we rise in consciousness to meet Lord Shiva at the top of the head, the summit of our inner mountain. Shiva represents the wild spaces and the vastnesses in our own minds and hearts that few of us have the daring or the aspiration to approach, as they require that we leave the familiar world behind.

Throughout history, yogis, mystics and poets have gone out into retreat and silence in nature, generally into the mountains, in order to find God or the cosmic reality. They have put their books aside and left their institutions for a direct encounter with the reality beyond the human. The deity of the wild that they find in their journey of self-discovery is the essence of Shiva and the Great Spirit in Nature, whatever name they might decide to eventually use in order to describe it. It is a deity of energy, fire, light, and sheer transcendence over all things merely human, not a deity of words, ideas or dogmas. Shiva appears in the raw spiritual experience of the unknown beyond all theologies, philosophies, and religious organizations. It requires a sacrifice of self and mind to the unknown power in order to access the reality of the Supreme Shiva.

Shiva as a Pagan Deity

Shiva as nature deity can be traced back to ancient and prehistoric humanity and the very dawn of our species. As a God of nature and the wild, Lord Shiva has a special affinity with pagan and nature Gods of all traditions throughout the world, including ancient Greco-Roman Gods like Pan and Dionysius.[5] The ancient Celtic image of Cernunos, the horned God and lord of animals, has a special resemblance to Shiva that seems to be more than a coincidence, with his horns, his sitting pose and retinue of wild animals around him. Such Shiva like images reflect a deity both within nature and beyond it.[6] These images are no less sophisticated in their portrayal of the cosmic reality than abstract philosophies, indicating the power of raw experience over the rational articulation of the mind that usually comes in at a secondary level.

Looking back to early humanity, we could say that Shiva is the deity of the shaman, and as such reflects the oldest formulations of the sacred in humanity. Shiva is the lord of the dance, of ecstasy, of the drum, of dream and trance that the shaman works with. To Shiva belongs the sacred fire and the sacred plant, the Agni and Soma of the ancient Vedic lore in India. In fact, the *Vedas* are nothing but the mantric expression of Shiva, with the four main Vedic deities of Agni, Soma, Surya, and Indra or Fire, Sun, Moon and Lightning as the four aspects of his light. Shiva resembles the supreme deity of light in Shamanic traditions.[7]

All over the world there are great ancient traditions of the worship of megaliths, standing stones, and sacred mounds, extending to pyramids and obelisks. These suggest to us the ascending energy of Shiva and intimate an early era in which a type of Shiva worship prevailed throughout the planet. Along with sacred stones and mountains are dragons, serpents, and magical electrical and lighting forces. These reflect the power of Shiva as the lord of the serpents, lightning, dissolution and transformation.

As the lord of immortality, Shiva resembles deities that take us beyond death and the boundaries of our world defined by time and mortality. Shiva has affinities with Egyptian Osiris as our inner guide in the after death state with both being symbolized by a corpse – the state of Shiva consciousness beyond the physical body and senses and dead to the outer world. Yet we do not find Shiva depicted in the role of the sacrificed or mutilated deity. He is a militant deity who defeats and destroys the powers of darkness and remains whole and complete.

The Indian mind – and the pagan mind in general – reveres the deity as both residing in nature and as transcending nature. It experiences God within all of nature but as not limited to the outer forms of nature. It does not see God in a human role creating the world as something outside of himself that he must rule over. It regards the deity as manifesting through nature as its own self-expression, with the human being as a special manifestation of the deity striving to awaken within its own creation. This primal religion of nature can accept both pantheism (nature as God) and monism (the unity of all) in a single embrace. It does not limit divinity to the existing state of nature, but does not place God against nature or outside of nature either. The supreme divinity is impersonal, with nature as a manifestation of natural law going back to the Spirit, not nature as a hostile force against the spirit.

If we look to the deity as it manifests through nature, it is a deity that can be quite different than our human conceptions. Nature does not present us with a deity that is kind or predictable to us, or anthropomorphic in form. Nature does not present us with a deity that suits our prejudices, confirms our identity, or promotes one religious community against another. Nature shows us a deity that is awesome, unlimited, and beyond the control of our will and desires, either individually or collectively. The deity behind nature is not merely an historical God but the inner power of biology, geology, and ultimately all the energies of the cosmos.

The deity in nature that we find in the wild includes the destructive forces of nature through the Sun, fire, lightning, storms, and earthquakes. It is a power that we can only bow down to in reverence and humbly seek its guidance. Even Jehovah in the Bible is portrayed as a God of thunder, lightning, and the Divine Word, factors in common with Shiva, not a mere human deity for our personal salvation. We must remember it is not our place to scale down the Divine into our familiar world, but to break open the shell of our world in order to discover something that we might call Divine or transcendent.

Shiva is also the deity of the wild side of human beings and relates to what is unconventional, forbidden, or unknown. Shiva is a force of revolution and trans-formation, which ever seeks to break up the status quo in order to lift us to a new and higher level of existence. There can be a certain restlessness or discontent about Shiva energy that ever pushes us to go farther and not to simply stop short or stagnate at any level or with any final achievement. There is something daring and fearless about Shiva energy, which is not content with any mere established order or any predictable result. Shiva always tries to break the boundaries and go beyond them. Yet Shiva is not just a blind rebel against convention, which is a mere emotional reaction, but represents the power that ever strives to grow until the highest goal is reached – a goal in which we move beyond all time and space and become Shiva himself.

Shiva is not a deity of human excesses, much less human weaknesses, habits, or addictions. He is the deity that helps us transcend our conditioning, not simply act opposite to it, which is only to be controlled by it indirectly. Shiva breaks down all limiting concepts, ideas, identities, habits, and routines of the mind. He does not throw us back into the unconscious but takes us beyond it to a universal awareness. Shiva as a deity who does what is forbidden indicates a power that takes us beyond the outer view of reality and its preconceptions.

Shiva does not emphasize our lower unrefined animal nature as it is, or blind emotions. Shiva represents the energy of our spirit, emotions, prana, but as turned into tools for higher awareness, as connected to the Cosmic Spirit. Shiva shows us how to transcend our animalistic weaknesses, not by suppressing them but by releasing the deeper energy or spirit hidden behind them. It is the human perversion of animal energies, as in the destructive forces of lust and greed, that is the problem, not these energies in their own nature.

Shiva awakens the powers of the wilderness and cosmic space within our own minds and hearts. He unfolds a space, time, and energy within ourselves that is greater than anything we can experience on the outside. Shiva's mantra is the call of the wild, the voice of the wilderness that helps us understand all creatures great and small. He allows us to leave the human world and its conflicting opinions behind and return to the entire universe as our own greater home. He takes us on an inner journey to the highest summits of awareness and bliss. His is a challenging force that is ever testing us, expanding us to go beyond what we thought were our limits.

Shiva impels us to transcendence as the power of our own inner will and deepest motivation. The peace of Shiva is a state of perpetual transcendence, in which no attachment to the past, form, or fixed identity is possible. In this regard, Shiva is the great psychologist and lord of the mind who removes the traumas and excesses of our human nature, affording us a cosmic mind that holds all the powers of nature as our own inmost Self. Shiva heals and revitalizes our natural spirit and original awareness.

Shiva and Shakti: Male and Female Powers

Shiva is also a formulation of the cosmic masculine force, which is not simply male sexuality but the cosmic ascending and expanding energy that has many forms and manifestations. This cosmic masculine energy pervades all of nature as its assertive and motivating power. It is only symbolically masculine by reflecting masculine qualities. In the human being, Shiva takes the power of the male but shapes it as a spiritual energy rather than simply crude aggression.

Shiva in his iconography is associated with many symbols of the cosmic masculine force that we find worshipped throughout the ancient world and in native traditions. These include mountains, fire, Sun, the sky, pyramids, standing stones, obelisks, and trees. Shiva does not merely indicate some peculiar Hindu God of little relevance outside of India; he reflects a universal symbolism and cosmic reality. Shiva is the cosmic pillar that is the pillar of Dharma that upholds the entire universe by a pervasive power of truth, peace, equanimity and compassion.

As the cosmic masculine force, Shiva is not a mere glorification of male sexuality, he is also the great ascetic and yogi, reflecting the highest self-discipline and inner equipoise. He indicates the power that pervades the universe and allows us to ascend in consciousness to our highest potential of Self-realization.

Shiva forms a duality as the cosmic masculine force, along with his complimentary Shakti or cosmic feminine principle. Shiva does not represent a masculine force as opposed to the feminine force but as working complementarily beside it. Shiva and Shakti together show the complete unfoldment and yet complementarity of both male and female principles, each supporting the other in a dynamic manner. Shiva's Shakti has the independence of the Shiva nature behind her.

Shaivite and Shakti traditions and teachings are woven together in a beautiful and powerful manner. They hold that the masculine force and the feminine force should each be afforded a place of respect and allowed their full development – and that this development works best when both the powers are honored together. Shiva without Shakti is a deity without power. Shakti without Shiva is a power without deity.

Shiva and Shakti are the Divine Father and Divine Mother in all their names and forms. They are Spirit and Nature. The worship of Shiva and Shakti as the dual cosmic powers represents the natural religion of humanity and the entire universe, which revolves around honoring these two forces in all their manifestations in both the animate and inanimate realms. We find this honoring of the dual mystery in all native and traditional cultures, and in the ancient world overall. Shiva is the standing stone, pyramid or obelisk, while Shakti is reflected in the ring stone, the altar or the cave such as we already find worshipped in the earliest humanity long before what we call history began.

Shiva's Yoga of Nature

This current ecological age requires a new encounter with Shiva as the great Lord of nature. Nature is not just an outer organic bio-system, but also the manifestation of a supreme power of consciousness. Nature is not just a process of material evolution but a manifestation of consciousness, with that Spirit seeking ever greater expression as it takes on more refined life forms in the plant, animal, and human kingdoms. Beyond nature is a spirit that can never be conquered, which has endless energy, and cannot be resisted once it manifests. This power of nature we can also call Shiva.

Today we are trampling down nature in many ways, polluting and damaging the sacred Earth and her family of creatures, great and small. One can feel the wrath of Shiva slowly developing, not as a mere emotional reaction but as a protective force of nature. Yet Shiva is a power of eternity. He cannot be pushed quickly into action, much less intimidated, but once his forces begin to move, there is nothing that can stop them. Shiva is an appropriate deity for this ecological age. Contacting his energy can help us find a way beyond our technological excesses to the eternal beneficence of nature.

We can no longer look at humanity apart from nature, or God apart from nature. And we can no longer look at nature apart from consciousness or apart from ourselves. Our true Self and eternal being is our inner nature of which the outer world of nature is a changing expression in the realm of time. This Shiva or Spirit Self is calling us once again. This call of the wild is the call of the Divine Word, which is not simply human concepts, but Divine feelings powers, and principalities.

We need to return to the world of Shiva as the Great Spirit, which is our true origin and home, and our place of renewal, renaissance and transformation. We need to enter into the universe of Shiva, which is a conscious universe of power, bliss, peace, and transformation.

Yoga, properly practiced, develops the secret powers of nature within us to help us manifest the Great Spirit working behind nature. Yoga is nature's natural practice of spiritual growth through cultivating stillness and inner power, the grace of Shiva. Shiva's Yoga is first of all a Yoga of nature, but nature as imbued with consciousness and grace, not nature as a blind or mechanical force.

Shiva holds all the powers of nature and the force of higher evolution hidden within. Shiva Yoga requires uniting our inner being with the greater universe, not simply working out our personal or human potentials. It includes our connection with other worlds, other solar systems, other intelligent forms of life, and other planes of existence – including recognizing the consciousness that pervades all space.

Shiva Yoga requires utterly abandoning and surrendering our personal desires to the indomitable universal force, and letting it take us where it will. Shiva Yoga requires leaving the human world behind in our consciousness and embracing the vast. Devotion to Shiva is not devotion to a form or image but devotion to the power from which all form arises, which is to the seer of all. Loving Shiva is not about loving a personal deity that resembles us but opening to the power of universal love that is not afraid of death or sorrow. Shiva Yoga is the Yoga of nature to hold the entire universe within the core of our hearts, with our heart located everywhere. We will now explore that Shiva Yoga in some of its many facets.

3. Dakshinamurti, the Lord of Wisdom

Part II

Shiva's Cosmic Reality

Meditation on Rudra-Shiva

Let us meditate upon the Self as Shiva in the form of Rudra: Who has the appearance of a transparent crystal, who has three eyes and five faces; Who carries the Ganga River on his head, who has ten arms and is adorned with all ornaments.

Who has a blue neck and who carries the crescent Moon on his head, who wears a serpent as his sacred thread; Who is dressed in the skin of a tiger, who is the most adorable and grants freedom from fear.

Who carries a water pot and a mala (rosary), with a spear in his hand, who is effulgent, who has matted hair and a hair tuft at the top of his head.

Who is mounted on the back of a bull, who carries the Goddess Uma as his left side, who is moist with nectar, peaceful, and is invested with all heavenly enjoyments

Who is conjoined with the deities of all the directions of space, who is honored by Devas and Asuras alike, who is enduring, eternal, pure, steady, unchanging, and immutable; Who is the supreme Ruler, the all pervasive Lord Rudra, who holds all forms.

Laghu Nyasa of the Rudram

There is only one Rudra, with no second to him that exists. He rules these worlds with his ruling power.

He has all faces, heads and necks, who dwells in the hearts of all beings. As the adorable lord Bhagavan, he pervades all, he moves through all as the auspicious Lord Shiva.

Shvetashvatara Upanishad III.2.12

The following section presents the higher reality of Shiva through a cosmological view linking him with the cosmic principles of light, energy, time, space, sound, and awareness behind and beyond all manifestation, with Shiva embracing all as Being-Consciousness-Bliss. It is a journey to the highest reality beyond the known world.

We can enter into the vast universe of Shiva from any point in time or space, as Shiva (peace and bliss) is the nature of the cosmos and the essence of life. This "Shaivite Cosmology" forms the basis of Shiva's Cosmic Yoga taught in the fourth section of the book.

Shiva as the Supreme Brahman

The Power of the Absolute

Behind the visible universe of time and space that is always changing, exists an unmanifest timeless reality that never changes even for an instant. This supreme reality existed before the Big Bang that brought our particular universe into being, and will continue long after our universe comes to an end many billions of years in the distant future. It holds the potential for innumerable universes like our own, as but reflections of its transcendent nature beyond all limitations.

This supreme reality is ever perfect and pure, untouched by any possible disturbance, agitation, or sorrow. Nothing that happens in any world or in the life of any creature can affect it. Our physical world is but a transient realm of shifting shapes in the shadow of this deeper immutable truth, located far from its inner light. Yet this transcendent reality is not unknown to us. It is the deepest core of our own Self and inner being that is the eternal witness to all the worlds. To connect to it is the highest aspiration of all our searches for truth and divinity.

Various philosophical systems East and West have posited a metaphysical or ontological Absolute behind the known world of time, space and causation. This Absolute principle has been identified with God or regarded as a reality beyond God. In Yoga and Vedanta, this supreme principle is called *Brahman* or the "Supreme Brahman," referring to the ultimate Godhead that both contains and transcends everything that can be conceived or experienced. Yoga and Vedanta teach us how to realize this Absolute within ourselves, not merely how to think about it at a mental level.

Lord Shiva is not just a deity form or aspect of universal energy, in his highest formulation Shiva represents this Absolute or Supreme Brahman into which everything is dissolved and on which everything is founded. In this ultimate sense, Shiva is not merely God or the Lord of the Universe. He is the unbounded presence of the Absolute in which God, the soul, and the world merge into pure unity beyond all division.

Brahman means, "that which is ever full," and refers to an endless expansion in a state of fullness, not from a state of deficiency or want – a blissfully serene state of overflowing perfection. Shiva is the deity of this cosmic fullness both within and beyond the worlds, which arise from his unlimited Shakti or endless creative power. Shiva embraces all possible worlds, yet contains more than can ever be expressed in any world or creature. He holds the power behind the worlds and a higher energy that can never come into form.

The Enigmatic Symbol of the Impersonal

How, one might ask, can that nameless and formless supreme Being be symbolized or personified at all, much less in the strange iconography of Lord Shiva or other bizarre Hindu Gods and Goddesses? Yet if we look deeply, we can discern that as the great mystery, Brahman requires such an indirect revelation as analogy, symbol, and metaphor.

Shiva represents the impersonal formless reality of Brahman more so than he does any personal deity. That is why Shiva's personality is paradoxical, contrary, mysterious, and transcendent. Shiva's unusual personality, his nature forms and supernatural powers, is an intimation of the impersonal. It is a symbol to draw us from the personal to the impersonal levels of our own awareness. Even our own creaturely existence in body and mind rests upon a higher impersonal consciousness that has never been born and will never die, and which reflects the reality within us of the Absolute Shiva.

The Supreme Brahman is still, quiescent, and serene – a state of perfect peace and equanimity. It has nowhere to go and nothing to accomplish, as it has no connection with the realm of cause and effect. It is beyond evolution, growth, decay, birth, or death. It has no instruments of body or mind, subtle or gross, individual or cosmic. In that reality of the Supreme Shiva there is no world, no soul, and no God. There is only one plenary Self-existence through which all else is possible but has no necessity to occur. This is the state of "Shiva Nirvana," mergence into the Shiva as the only reality.

Yet that Supreme Being is not only transcendent and absolute, it is also the ground of all becoming, form, and action. It is the true nature and real substance of all things behind their outer transient appearances. It is located not only beyond the highest heaven but beneath the very Earth on which we tread. It is not only the Supreme Divine; it is also our own deepest Self-awareness, which is the presence of Shiva within us. It is not only beyond time and space; it is ever present in the core of our own hearts, closer to us than our own thoughts, dwelling in all of its unbounded fullness at every limited point in space and time.

Shiva as Sat-chit-Ananda: Being-Consciousness-Bliss

I. Pure Being: Sat

Shiva as a Sanskrit term implies auspiciousness, peace, quiescence, and stillness, which are the qualities of Pure Being, *Sat*, the highest principle of yogic insight, the Supreme Brahman. Shiva indicates that impersonal beneficence, which is the source of blessings for all, which judges none, favors none, but shines like the Sun with equanimity upon all.

Shiva represents pure Being or *Sat*, which is the principle of unchanging truth or *Satya*. *To seek Shiva is to seek truth. To seek truth is to seek Shiva.* That supreme truth is not an idea or conclusion but the Absolute existence beyond all relativity and contradiction. That Supreme state of Being is an immutable, formless, impersonal awareness. It is beyond time and space, person, location, form or name, action or result. It is supreme Truth that is the support and basis of all limited or relative truths.

The world of becoming, time, and change is only possible because of the support of the eternal ground of Being on which it depends. There is only One Being in all becomings, however various these may appear to be. All diverse becomings are but becomings of One Supreme Being that is beyond time, space and action. All manifestation is a form of the unmanifest that is ever transcendent and pure.

Shiva is not simply Being at a philosophical level, which is only a construct of the mind, but Being as our own true nature, our own inmost Self that is one with all existence. There is only one Self-existing Being behind all innumerable bodies and minds. The reality of all becoming is the serene and enduring being of Shiva. We are all developing in various ways in order to contact and merge into our greater Being that embraces all that we can possibly be and yet does not need to become anything at all. Becoming arises from Being, is sustained by being, and returns to being in the end. That being is not an abstract principle but the supreme Divine nature of Shiva.

The Permanent and the Impermanent

There is a common statement in spiritual thought that "everything is impermanent." There is indeed nothing at all in the outer world that is permanent, even for a second. Shaivite philosophy teaches us that everything in the manifest world of name and form is constantly changing every moment. There is no creature great or small, and no world up to the highest heaven that remains without change or movement, and nothing that does not eventually come to an end. Yet this does not mean that there is nothing that is permanent.

Shiva is permanent. The essence of Reality is permanent. Truth is eternal. Pure Being is above and beyond all change, which is only phenomenal. Behind everything that appears to be transient is a permanent reality, which is ultimately the core of our own being, our true Self.

Pure consciousness is beyond all variability and has no discontinuity. That permanent reality is the basis of all the changes in the impermanent relativity, which arises from it like waves from the sea. Without a single enduring ocean, the play of shifting waves could not be possible. Impermanent forms are but the waves of a greater permanent consciousness; otherwise we would not be able to note their changing nature, which is only possible because of the reflection of the changeless Self within us.

The essence of the soul is eternal and never dies. No one is ever really born or dies. The soul simply changes its outer garb while its inner essence remains continuous.[8] We all seek the permanent and wish to endure forever. No one wants to die. The permanence that we naturally seek reflects the highest truth of our own enduring Shiva Self. Once we discover that inner steadiness of eternal peace and awareness, we will find permanence, tranquility, and repose in everything, including throughout all the inevitable vicissitudes of life. Only the outer world changes; the inner core of our being like the axis of a wheel does not change, though everything changes around it.

Nothing has any reality of its own except as a manifestation or appearance of Shiva's enduring reality. We need not fear change or impermanence because the ground of our being is unshakeable, untaintable, and beyond all limitation. Shiva represents the eternal and timeless ground of being. All outer phenomena of body and mind are transient and fleeing, but the inner essence of being does not undergo even the slightest fluctuation within itself. The Being of Shiva is the state of pure Self-awareness, consciousness without any object, bliss without any desire.

All the objects and energies of body and mind are but temporary formations of forces, elements, and qualities that are merely appearances of the light of consciousness. If we take the apparent object to be real in-itself, we fall into ignorance. If we recognize the light both in the object and in ourselves, we grow in awareness. The light of consciousness or presence of Shiva is eternal, like a mirror that is devoid of movement. The objects of name and form that appear in this mirror of consciousness have no separate reality. Yet as appearing in that eternal mirror, all objects themselves are also eternal and unborn.

The Transformative Power of Being

Though Being is static in itself, it is also the ultimate source, origin, and support of all creative powers. Being constitutes the central point of stillness upon which all movement in the universe depends for strength, coherence, and continuity. This is the still point of Shiva at the heart of the world, around which the entire universe revolves. Shiva is a state of perpetual transformation that itself does not change.

The highest power of transformation is that of Being itself, not anything that can be done or attempted. If we simply rest quietly in the stillness of our own nature, all that is magical will unfold of its own accord without any special efforts of our own. This transformation power of Being or *Sat Shakti* is the supreme Shakti of Shiva. It is identified with Kali, the Goddess of Eternity, the Shakti or power inherent in the Absolute.

Being is a state of transformation, which never changes – a transformation forever into and unto itself. This means that if we can rest in our inmost being all the secret powers of the universe will be revealed to us spontaneously at every moment. Resting in our Shiva nature gives us all powers, not to our human ego but to our deepest soul.

This Shiva principle of transformation means to rest in the core of one's being, and let everything move around you – to be the center or the spoke of the revolving wheel of Samsara, the phenomenal world, which is to go beyond Samsara and to be Nirvana yourself. Being is the point that is everywhere and yet embraces the most distant horizon from a space beyond.

Sadvidya – The Knowledge of Being

The ground of Being that is the Supreme Shiva is ever present within us as the ground of our own experience. It is pure Self-awareness without an object, incident, event, or possibility. This state of pure Being is the foundational light on which the mind and senses operate and from which our inner prana arises as its electrical force.

The simplest way to contact the presence of Shiva is to dwell in the presence of Being, which is to recognize the background presence in which we live, perceive, and hold our awareness. Behind the names and forms there is one Being in all things that can be called Shiva.

Being is the one thing through which being known everything in essence is known. This knowledge of being is not a matter of information, but of identity, of contacting the power of identity in the mind, which is our ability to become one with all. Being is common to all beings, in all their diversity, as the substance out of which they are fashioned, like ornaments made of gold. That One Being is the same and changeless in all becomings and constitutes their inner reality. Knowledge of being is the all-knowledge of Shiva, which is the all knowledge of the state of peace that dwells behind all things that move.

This teaching of the "knowledge of Being" or *Sadvidya* occurs in the *Chandogya Upanishad* in ancient times[9] and in the *Saddarshana* of Bhagavan Ramana Maharshi in modern times.[10] If we give our primary attention and awareness to Being – which is the presence, space, and light behind all that we see – withdrawing our minds from outer distinctions of name and form, we can enter into the Supreme Reality through all that we perceive. All that we do will be rooted in Self-realization, which is abiding in the presence of all.

Whatever we do in life, we should constantly remember our ever present inner Being, which is the Being of all and remains outside of all changes, disturbances, and appearances – the most simple essence yet the supreme and highest Truth. If we know the essence of Being, we know all. If we miss the essence of Being, our knowledge is but ignorance and illusion. To dwell in immutable Being is to dwell in Shiva and to dwell in bliss.

II. Consciousness - Chit

Being is inherently Self-aware and conscious of itself. Being is intrinsically Self-being. A being that is not aware of itself has no true existence or independent reality. It is a mere unconscious formation that must rely upon a higher intelligence.

True consciousness is inherently a consciousness of being, which is the primal state of pure awareness prior to the arising of any subject or object, the clear light of existence. To be conscious of something outside ourselves, but not be aware of our own inner being is a state of distraction, not true knowledge. It is an ignorance that causes us to lose our inherent peace and happiness. To be aware of our own being is the root of all knowledge. If we abide in that, knowledge of all being must descend upon us.

A being that depends upon something outside of itself is not an Absolute or Supreme Being, but a relative being caught in a process of becoming. Such is the secondary reality of the creatures and objects of the world, including we humans. Only a self-aware existence is a true and independent reality. An unaware existence must be dependent and produced. Yet true self-awareness is not a bodily identity but being one with existence itself.

The Self-awareness of Being can be defined as consciousness in the true sense of the word as unmodified pure awareness without any object apart from itself. Such Absolute consciousness (chit) is not mind, which is a creaturely or embodied consciousness bound in the process of time and action. Embodied consciousness or mind is but a reflection of pure consciousness into an organism limited in time and space. Pure consciousness is the light beyond the mind. Yet it is only through the light of consciousness that the mind can function and perceive.

Even cosmic mind, the intelligence behind all nature, is but a vast reflection or manifestation of pure consciousness that transcends all thought and action.

The essence of meditation is to cultivate pure consciousness, Self-awareness or detached observation. It is to dwell in wakeful discernment, to silence or negate the mind. Then we can merge into the awareness that is beyond the mind, using the mind only as an instrument but no longer taken in by its fears and desires.

Shiva represents this supreme consciousness (Chit) and Shakti is its power to visualize, create, and express (Chit-Shakti). All manifestations of Shiva and Shakti as universal forces derive from the supreme Shiva consciousness and are dependent upon it. The Shiva principle becomes the mind in creatures and the Shakti principle becomes the prana or vital energy. Self-awareness is the root of all knowing and the basis of all life.

III. Bliss or Ananda

Self-being and Self-awareness is inherently a state of bliss, joy, peace, and contentment. An unhappy existence or miserable state of mind cannot last and no creature is willing to endure it for long. An unhappy consciousness is a contradiction in terms. Unhappiness implies ignorance, lack of consciousness, darkness, and contraction. Awareness naturally brings calm, peace, detachment, and delight, releasing us from all ignorance and sorrow. Bliss is the very power of existence and the attitude of pure awareness rooted in internal peace and contentment.

Shiva reflects this supreme bliss or Ananda in his symbolism and in his action. Shiva is a deity of the ecstasy born of pure consciousness, not merely human ecstasies induced by drugs, sensations, or entertainment. He represents the Self-aware Ananda or bliss, which is beyond all thought and description. Existence is inherently ecstasy. Existence as the duration of Being implies a state of elevation, detachment, and exaltation. The Self-aware Absolute is the most exalted of all things, the Supreme Deity, Parashiva.

Ananda is the fullness of feeling inherent in Self-aware existence, the inner being that feels all and gives feeling to all. Ananda is not simply feeling good at an emotional level. It is not an emotional high that must be eventually followed by an emotional low. Ananda is the state of fullness that is Self-aware existence, which has the ability to translate all experience – which is essentially Self-experience – into beauty, growth, delight and transformation, even what may be ordinarily felt as pain, sorrow, disease and death.

Bliss and Emptiness

The problem for us in our ordinary state of consciousness is that we find happiness mainly in action and sensory enjoyment. When we are doing nothing, or when nothing is happening, we feel bored and easily get depressed. We regard the state of being or mere existence as a type of emptiness, if not sorrow, a state of lack rather than one of fullness. We do not equate existence with essence, or the ultimate concentration of joy, but with a state without essence or value. We do not equate being with the summit of the cosmic mountain but with its unrefined base.

The state of emptiness that we feel when we are not active is not the state of being or pure existence. It is the emptiness of the mind that is the reflection of our ignorance of the true nature of reality. As we are always looking outward for happiness, that process creates an inertia or emptiness within that covers over our real internal bliss. Our inner world is empty and lacking because we have not cultivated it. If we provide the same attention to the inner world that we do to the outer world, we will discover an even greater and more lasting fulfillment within.

We similarly find our main happiness in relationship, not when we are alone. We associate being around other people, being in a crowd or, better yet, having a large number of people following us with happiness and success. This also reflects our lack of connection with our inner being and core awareness that is not a separate self but is the Self of all beings. The inner state of aloneness can hold the entire universe.

Unless we first face and break through our inner emptiness and ignorance, we cannot find lasting peace and joy. This requires that we turn our energies within, stop pursuing happiness on the outside, and cultivate inner contentment. It is a daunting struggle at any period in human history, as our natural tendencies born of karma are to look without through the senses. Yet it is even more daunting today in our media age that keeps us externally engaged, stimulated or distracted almost perpetually, with its vast new array of sensory, predominantly audio-visual enjoyments.

We must remember that higher states of joy and peace are associated with conditions of inspiration and contemplation, when our breath literally stops and we are drawn into a profound silence. One of our greatest sources of peace and renewal is the state of deep sleep, when all action of body and mind is drawn to a minimum. The happiness of sensory enjoyments, on the other hand, eventually wears us out. Desire makes us active and we confuse that restless movement born of desire with life. True happiness and bliss calms us down and makes us content wherever we are. So even in our own experience, we can find a natural coexistence of stillness and happiness.

Ultimately emptiness, space and being is bliss, and a bliss that is unlimited, unqualified and immutable. Realizing this requires that we empty ourselves of all thought, desire, expectation and memory. What makes us miss the bliss of being is our misperception of who we are and what the universe is in essence, which is an unfoldment of the fullness of being.

Being is the perpetual ever self-renewing bliss of Shiva. Outer action is the play of Samsara or sorrow, which is to be caught between alternating pleasure and pain. To transcend sorrow we must go beyond all outer seeking to the inner wholeness and completeness of our Self-nature. Shiva as the great lord of Yoga is the image of perfect bliss and peace that we should emulate in order to go beyond every sort of pain.

Ananda and Transcendence

Ananda exists in all things as their essence, even in tragedy and death. Ananda begins with peace and is the delight born of unshakable peace that is not disturbed by anything. Suffering occurs in life so that we go beyond outer pleasure that is transitory to Divine bliss that is eternal. Suffering is Ananda inverted and the bliss in it can be redeemed by awareness and love.

The bliss of Shiva not only transcends death; it turns death into immortal joy. What makes death painful is the fear of non-existence. If we look within our deeper awareness and recognize our eternal existence, then death is no more than a change of clothes for the soul. Shiva is honored as *Mrityunjaya* or "the one who gives us victory over death." Shiva or Rudra is honored not just in the good and the beautiful, but also in what is painful and difficult. It is easy to find joy in what is beautiful, comfortable, happy and secure; but can we find bliss even in opposition, enmity, disaster or calamity? Shiva provides us the inner peace to allow that to occur.

Shiva represents that Self-aware ecstasy that cannot be overcome by external difficulty or suffering. Just as a truly happy person cannot be rendered sorrowful by a pinprick, so too Shiva cannot lose his poise, cool or composure by any external difficulties. Shiva can swallow all the poisons of life and turn them into nectar. He does this by accepting them fully in the ground of existence, which transforms painful becoming into blissful being.

Shiva as Fullness or Purna

Shiva represents the state of fullness, wholeness, and completeness, *Purna*. He is not deficient in any way; even in space, emptiness or in the void he is completely full and Self-sufficient. The wholeness of Shiva is present in each thing and in every individual soul. Fullness of being is everywhere and pervades all space. This fullness of Shiva, like streams into the sea, can take in all limitations, taint and sorrow without losing anything. To accept this universal fullness and wholeness is to touch the presence and power of Shiva.

The wholeness of Shiva dwells within each person and in every object. Everything is an appearance or mask of the eternal Shiva, in which there is no gain or loss, no coming or going, no beginning or end. Only when we discern the light and presence of Shiva in each thing will we know the truth of the object, and understand it as a manifestation of our own inner being. Each one of us is the permanent, full, whole, and complete reality that permeates every aspect of our being. We can move from whatever we observe directly into the Supreme Shiva as the presence of awareness that holds everything.

The Uniqueness of Shiva

In each thing in the universe there is something unique, whether a person, a species, a force in nature, or an event in time. That unique factor is its *linga*, meaning its "characteristic mark" or Shiva nature. Shiva is that which gives power and preeminence to each thing. Shiva is not apart from anything. Shiva is what makes each thing what it is. Shiva is that which is. Shiva is the essence of being in all beings.

Shiva is that which is unique in all things. To perceive the unique is to perceive Shiva. To honor uniqueness is to honor Shiva. That which is unique in each thing is its true nature, which in turn is a reflection of nature as a whole. The uniqueness in each thing is one with the uniqueness in all things. This is the Shiva aspect of Shiva.

The uniqueness of Shiva and his creative force or Shakti, can be found in each thing. Each thing has a unique nature that in turn has its unique power or capacity, its special Shakti. Human beings have the unique nature as intelligent beings, with the unique power or capacity to find the truth. Each individual human being reflects intelligence and its power in a different way. So far we are still at a very preliminary level of manifesting that deeper intelligence overall, but much more will unfold during the further course of human evolution.

Everything is a manifestation of Shiva. What we see through our senses are but crystallizations of the light of Shiva. What we discover in the formless reality beyond the universe is the transcendent nature of Shiva. All things constitute Shiva's dance within his own being, which is also his dance with his own Shakti. To access Shiva consciousness is not to become lost in some unusual cult but discover the essence of all, which is ultimately bliss.

Shiva as the Supreme Self – Paramatman

Who are we in our true reality and essence? What is our enduring nature apart from our shifting outer appearances in body and mind? Who were we before this particular birth, and what will we be after we leave this world?

What is our true Self and identity beyond our outer self-image and social identity? Is there anything within us that is enduring or eternal beyond the continual flux of thought, emotion, and action that constitute our ordinary state of existence? ----These are some of the fundamental questions that we should all seek to answer in order to make our lives truly meaningful.

We all possess an innate sense of Self, a sense of being a person, a conscious subject with its own dignity, not just a mere inert object for others to manipulate. We have a sense of our own independence and self-existence as an individual. We want to be happy, free, and aware of what is occurring on in our lives, not dictated to or lorded over by others.

Politically speaking, we want to be free to determine our own destiny and not be under the control of others, to have our own vote and representation. Economic wise, we do not wish to be in debt to anyone or owe anyone anything. Similarly, we have a spiritual sense of freedom, a desire to no longer be bound by the limitations of the external world, the opinions of other people, or even to the dogmas of one faith or another.

We all feel something unique, priceless, and invaluable about ourselves – something far more than our outer possessions, titles, or bodily identities. We feel a sense of wholeness, integrity, or continuity about who we are that is more than all our outer life expressions and achievements. We possess an awareness in the present moment that is more than the sum total of our memories in the past, and is capable of approaching life in ever new and creative ways.

We want to know the truth for ourselves and do not like being told how to think or how things are supposed to be. We want to experience life for ourselves and not simply take what others say or describe as real or final. Yet we seldom take the time to turn our awareness within in order to discover what our inner sense of being, value, and continuity might truly be.

We are usually content with an illusory outer freedom to achieve and acquire in the external world, which is to be a slave of desire and attachment. We seldom question what true freedom really is, which requires freedom from desire and from time, not simply the ability to get what we want. We all want to be free to be ourselves and to express who we really are. Yet the self we choose to be is not usually our true or divine Self, but some physical, sensory, mental, or ego driven outer self that is ignorant as to the nature of the impulses that drive it and which are seldom its own.

We can with some effort and concentration contact the presence of universal forces, Gods and Goddesses, or Divine energies within ourselves, at least as a possibility or as a metaphor. Even those of us who may not believe in any higher reality still aspire to do something great and enduring in life, and can find a sense of wonder contemplating the greater universe in which we live. No one wants to be limited, little, or small or feel content with being insignificant. No one wants to be dependent, controlled, or told what to do as if we had no real power or intelligence of our own, even children.

We do not want to be treated like an object, image, ornament, or possession, even by those close to us. All beings want independence, Self-power, and mastery extending ultimately to the whole of life. We want to expand the boundaries of our sphere of influence to include our friends and family, community, nation and humanity, extending to all nature and existence. Our sense of Self is greater than our personal identity or bodily form, more malleable, and capable of much more than what we already have become.

Such intuitions of a potential greater reality within ourselves reflect a deeper Self-awareness behind our ordinary personality. This sense of pure and unbounded Self-being is called the *Atman* in Vedantic thought, specifically the *Paramatman* or Supreme Self, once we understand its core as the Self of all beings. Our sense of Self that is currently limited to the body can be expanded to include the entire universe. This inner state of Self awareness can be accessed in silence, balance, and stillness through the practice of Self-inquiry and meditation.

This sense of Self is the root of the mind and all the five senses, which are but extensions of its sense of being. Only if we have a sense of our self first can we then perceive other things through our senses. Self-being is our most powerful and enduring core experience, the ground of our soul. But we usually project our Self-identity outwardly into the formations of the external world in which we lose ourselves. We must develop that intuition of Self inwardly as unity with all. Then all our problems will dissolve without further effort.

Shiva symbolizes that inner Self which is ever free and has the power to transcend all outer forms and expressions, time and karma. Shiva symbolizes the Atman within us, our inner center and core identity as pure consciousness. *We are Shiva, and our Shiva Self is the universal Self.*

Shiva and Purusha

The term *Purusha* is used in Vedic thought to indicate the higher Self or Person beyond the mind. The goal of Yoga is dwelling in the Self-nature of the Purusha beyond the limitations of the gunas or qualities of nature.[11] Purusha is usually interpreted as "Puri-sha": he who dwells (sha) in the city (pura) of the body, or the indwelling spirit.[12] This term for dwelling (sha) relates to Shiva as the one who dwells in, fills, and permeates all things. Shiva is the Spirit that informs, pervades, sustains, and upholds all objects and actions in the universe. To dwell in our own inner being and in the presence of Being is to dwell and abide in Shiva, in immutable peace and contentment.

Purusha means person or subject and refers to our original sense of Self, wholeness, and unity. We are not simply a conglomerate of bodily parts, but have a sense of Self that can use the body like an instrument, and which imparts wholeness, integrity, and harmony to all our outer actions. When we look back on who we are we find a continuity of awareness and memory, not simply an identifiable physical appearance. We are aware of ourselves as individuals, as subjects, not as mere bodies, objects, instruments or images. Even if our body is somehow impaired, injured or deficient, we do not wish to be regarded as anything less than a whole person.

Purusha is the principle of independence and mastery over all external influences, knowing that we are sufficient in our own nature, regardless of the uncertain changes that might occur around us. None of us wants to be under the power of the external world, to be a slave, a servant or a dependent. We all have a sense of being full and complete in our own nature independently of any external influences. This reflects our inner nature in which we are masters of the entire universe.

Yet Purusha does not stand for the ordinary human person or bodily ego. The Purusha is the consciousness inherent in light, the indwelling spirit of the entire universe, of which the human being is one manifestation. True subjectivity is not a matter of bodily identity but of Self-being that transcends all objectivity. To discover the Cosmic Person we must give up our little personhood and circumscribed sense of self. We must take the sense of Self beyond our creaturely body and mind to embrace all of nature.

There is a sacred, priceless, and immeasurable dimension within ourselves, which is the most intimate aspect of our being. This is our Purusha nature. We would not trade our life or being for anything. This sense of personhood is present in all human beings and animals, even in plants. One can intuit it in all the formations and forces of nature. *Personhood is a universal presence and quality, not simply the expression of creaturely existence.*

In addition, the term Purusha refers to certain positive masculine qualities such as strength, independence, fearlessness, and steadiness. Like Shiva, Purusha indicates the higher cosmic masculine power, not simply the biological male identity. Shiva is symbolized by a bull that also indicates the Purusha, spirit, or cosmic masculine force. This is not merely the bull as a symbol of virility, but the bull of dharma or cosmic law. The bull represents the spirit or the Purusha, the enduring principle of awareness that holds all things together and gives significance to all. Shiva is the original person or *Adi Purusha*, the Cosmic Person or Supreme Self whose body is the entire universe and who rules over all, not as something external but as his own expression.

Your Shiva Self: Yourself as Shiva

Jiva is the yogic term for the individual Self (Jivatman) or individual reincarnating soul, of which the ego is a manifestation in the current life. Shiva is the name for the Supreme Self (Paramatman) beyond the cycle of death and rebirth. The term Jiva implies movement, energy, and life, while Shiva indicates calm, presence, and awareness. Our evolution in consciousness is a movement from Jiva to Shiva, from outer identity to inner being. This is the ascent from the individual subject or person to the universal subject or person, from the "I am the body" idea to the "I am all" realization.

In your true nature you are Shiva as the universal being. All nature is your embodiment and but a small part of your greater being. You are no mere limited body or mind. You are not simply human or limited to any other type of creature. You are in all beings and all beings are within you. You are the Self, spirit, energy, and motivation in all creatures and in the entire universe.

To truly know Shiva is to know oneself, which is to know who we are in our own nature apart from all external influences and outer conditioning factors. To truly know oneself is to know Shiva, because at our core we are the universal Being in manifestation. To know yourself is to know yourself as Shiva, and to cease to be a Jiva or limited soul.

Your true Self is your Shiva Self not your Jiva Self, your universal Self, not your personal Self. This fact is very difficult for us to understand in our current era dominated by psychology, which focuses on the human, personal, and memory based self, giving importance to analyzing it and unraveling its past. Letting go of that human memory based self, which is a fiction of time, we can find a greater equilibrium and harmony in our eternal Shiva Self.

We feel more significant in life as we expand our sense of self out of our individual body to our greater family and community. Better than this is to expand our sense of Self to include the entire universe as our own family, which is to return to the state of Shiva. When you enter into this inner composure that is the state of Shiva, you will know the entire universe as yourself. All of boundless space will be your body and all time the unending movement of your life.

If we inquire deeply as to our true identity, we realize that we cannot be limited to our outer nature as body or mind, which are but instruments of our outer expression. We are the being who exists behind these instruments and are more than their functions that are constantly changing. Our inner nature cannot be quantified or objectified but is of the nature of pure consciousness.

You as pure consciousness do not have eyes and ears, for example. It is your body that has eyes and ears. You are the consciousness and energy through which the body and its organs function, like the electricity that runs them. However, you are not limited to your outer instruments any more than electricity is limited to the equipment that it runs. The inner electrical force within you is a power of consciousness, not simply a material force. It can and will leave the body, and can inhabit any number of bodies, gross or subtle, or dwell in its own nature without a body. That inner spiritual power is your Shiva nature. In your Shiva nature you are beyond birth and death, name and form.

Similarly, your true nature cannot be defined by thoughts, emotions or memories. These are but changing functions of the mind. Your inner nature remains continuous regardless of the changing moods and actions of the mind. You have the power to stop the mind, if you learn how to meditate and dwell in thought free awareness.

Learning about Shiva implies learning about one's deeper Self, not simply exploring a foreign or ancient deity form and its cultural implications. It requires searching deeper than our outer physical or psychological self to the very core of identity within ourselves – to the principle of pure identity in which we can become all that we see. It is a process of meditative inquiry in which we uncover the various veils of Maya or illusion about who we are and find the Divine purpose behind our birth. When we remove all the veils of false identity about ourselves, Shiva alone remains.

This Shiva Self is our inner being, our inmost Self behind our changing outer self. Shiva is the mind behind the mind, the eye behind the eye, the speech behind speech, the prana behind prana, the true Self behind the ego. Whatever faculty or expression we have is only possible because of the power of Shiva or Shiva's Shakti behind it. The Shiva Self is the pure I, the self-vibration of pure being that is not yet differentiated into subject and object. The Jiva or ego is the impure I, the self that is identified with body and mind and caught up in its reflection in the external world. Jiva is the shadow of Shiva in the outer world but connected to its core light within the heart.

Shiva's Yoga of Meditation

True meditation is a practice of Self-inquiry, called *Atma-Vichara* in Sanskrit, a search within for the true Self, the Atman or Purusha at the core of our being. Self-inquiry consists of following out the prime question "Who am I?" back to the source of our being in pure consciousness. Shiva as the power to calm the mind to mirror the inner Self is the great lord of meditation.

Classical Yoga is primarily a Yoga of Meditation and Self-inquiry – the search for the Purusha. The Yoga of Shiva is a Yoga of universal Self-knowledge. The knowledge of Shiva is Self-knowledge and Self-realization. This is not only to recognize Shiva as the consciousness within oneself; one must learn to recognize the presence of Shiva in all beings. All beings are but masks or appearances of Shiva who is the true Self of all. If we remove the mask of body and mind behind all creatures, we will discover Shiva as the indwelling Self. Shiva hides himself in the form of different living beings, and then discovers himself once more through all. Learn to honor and recognize the presence of Shiva in all creatures and everywhere, and everyone will treat you like Lord Shiva!

Shiva is the central point of the universal and Supreme Self within us, our inmost core existence. To approach the reality of Shiva within ourselves, we must first surrender the little or outer self, the ego that constitutes our ordinary self-identity. We must let go of our outer distractions and disturbances and embrace our inner witness Self that does not allow anything external to break its composure. This Shiva consciousness is not far from us. Shiva is the detached, calm and silent aspect of our own deeper awareness. We can most easily access Shiva as the "witness consciousness" or *Sakshi Bhava* within us. The eye of Shiva is ever awake within us teaching us the truth of all.

Shiva is not something alien to us but constitutes the very essence of our being. We need not fear his presence or his power, but he does require that we dissolve our ego in order to enter into his reality. This is an inner cleansing and purification, letting go of our limited identities as being this or that person to find that we are the Supreme Person in all. It is the dissolution of the ego into the true Self. To discover Shiva is to return home to our deepest heart. This means remembering who we are in eternity and no longer being taken in by the mask of this particular life. Life is but the play of Shiva, veiling and revealing himself in ever wondrous forms of joy.

I am Shiva

The highest teaching of Shiva Dharma is the direct and immediate realization of your Shiva Self as the Self of all.[13] Try to develop and continually cultivate a connection with that inner core of your being. Never forget that you are Shiva and all other powers must dance around you.

- Remember *Shivoham*, "I am Shiva," and all will be Shiva or blissful for you!

The famous *Mahavakyas* or "great sayings" of Vedanta and the *Upanishads* have their implications in terms of Shiva that you can also meditate upon, contemplate and affirm:

- *Aham Brahmasmi,* "I am Brahman" or "I am God" is the same as *Shivoham* or *Aham Shiva*, "I am Shiva."

- *Sarvam Khalvidam Brahma*, or "Everything is Brahman" is the same as Everything is Shiva.

There is a famous Hymn to Shiva called *Nirvanashatkam* or "Six Verses in Praise of Nirvana" by the great guru Shankara, which epitomizes this higher Self-knowledge.

1. *I am not the mind, intelligence, ego or conditioned awareness. I have no ears, nor tongue, nor nose, nor eyes. I am not space, air, fire, water, or earth. My nature is the bliss of consciousness (Chidananda), I am Shiva, I am Shiva (Shivoham)!*

2. *I am not Prana or the group of Pranas, nor the seven tissues of the body, nor the five sheaths (koshas). I do not have any mouth, hands or feet, nor organs of reproduction or elimination. My nature is the bliss of consciousness (Chidananda), I am Shiva, I am Shiva (Shivoham)!*

3. *I am beyond attraction and repulsion, greed and delusion. I have no infatuation or envy. I have no Dharma, no goals, no desires, nor even any seeking of liberation. My nature is the bliss of consciousness (Chidananda), I am Shiva, I am Shiva (Shivoham)!*

4. *I have no virtue or vice, nor happiness nor sorrow. I have no mantra, no pilgrimage, no scripture, and no form of worship. I am not the enjoyer, the enjoyment, or the object enjoyed. My nature is the bliss of consciousness (Chidananda), I am Shiva, I am Shiva (Shivoham)!*

5. *I have no death, no doubt, and no distinctions of family. I have neither father, nor mother, nor birth. My nature is the bliss of consciousness (Chidananda), I am Shiva, I am Shiva (Shivoham)!*

6. *I am beyond all thoughts and beyond all form, existing everywhere and transcending all sensory knowledge, with no limitation, no liberation and immeasurable. My nature is the bliss of consciousness (Chidananda), I am Shiva, I am Shiva (Shivoham)!*

Shiva as Pure Light – Prakasha

Our lives are defined and determined by light in myriad forms. We live in the great mystery of light. Yet as light illumines all, we feel no darkness in this mystery. The play of light is a mystery of radiance, wonder, beauty, and grace with which we are at peace and feel a deeper knowledge and wisdom.

Reality is of the nature of pure light and everything that we see is composed of light. Modern physics teaches us that matter is a condensation of light, and energy is the power of light. Light makes everything obvious, but its true nature is not revealed. There are many forms of light within us from body to mind and spirit.

There is one thing that all deep thinkers can probably agree upon and which all religions portray – that the highest reality is pure light. We can all recognize and honor a Supreme Light or light of truth, but what is the nature of that highest light? Light is an outer energetic phenomenon that reveals the world around us. The light of truth, however, is an inner light of awareness that is not visible. It is the light of the seer, not the light of the seen. It is a power of enlightenment that can dispel our inner darkness. This recognition of an inner light changes how we view the universe that is based upon light.

Shiva's nature is defined as pure light, *Prakasha Matra*, the pure power of illumination, the self-revealing essence of all. This light of Shiva is not simply light in the outer world, or the light of the mind. It is not the light of God as some distant being or luminary in a Heaven beyond. The light of Shiva is the light of Being that has no name or form and yet makes all names and forms possible. Shiva is the light of being, consciousness, and bliss that connects these three aspects of the Absolute together. He is the light of self-being, the self-illumining, supreme light that is self-aware and blissful in its own existence.

The light of Shiva is the inner light behind all outer light forms in the universe. It is the basis of all inner illumination as perception, meaning and understanding. This supreme light of Shiva, endures even in darkness, sorrow, sleep, and death. It is the inner essence of light that is the basis of all existence and the ground of all experience. This pure light precedes time and space and is the origin of all intelligence and wisdom.

The term Shiva – which refers to silence, endurance and abidance – suggests an all-pervading indwelling light. Shiva is the pure light behind and beyond the universe, the original and immutable radiance that consists of pure illumination without any boundaries. The light of Shiva is the light of pure existence, the foundation and support of all. The light of Shiva is the background glow behind the visible universe, the Sun behind the Sun. The light of Shiva is clear and invisible, yet illumines and gives meaning to all, including dispelling the darkness of the mind and heart.

The light of Shiva is the light of being that underlies all forms of energy and becoming. Existence itself is the original light through which all things appear and can be contrasted. The light of being has no form or color, but makes all form and color possible. It is the state of pure revelation like space in which all things exist and are revealed. It is the light of presence that is the supreme presence of light.

The light of Shiva is the basis not only of all forms of light but also of sound, reflecting the connection between lightning and thunder in the world of nature. The light of Shiva is the origin of the Divine Word that is the word of Shiva. Shiva represents the original light of the Vedic teachings from which all Vedic mantras arise. From that light of truth all great teachings and philosophies arise. The light of Shiva is the source of all meaning and comprehension.

This light of Shiva dwells within us as the light of our own self-awareness, which is our deepest light. In this regard the famous Vedic prayer: "lead me from non-being to being, from darkness to light, and from death to immortality,"[14] is a prayer to lead us back to the presence of Shiva within us.

The Light of the Seer or the State of Seeing

We are the light of Shiva and Shiva sees through our own eyes. This light of Shiva is the light of the seer within us, not merely the light that is seen externally. The light of the seer is the self-illuminating state of seeing, which is the nature of the Purusha as pure illumination. It is not light contained in an object, instrument, faculty, or organ of the body and mind. The light of the seer can perceive all forms of light that are like sparks arising from its power.

It is through the light of Shiva that we see. Shiva is both the light of seeing and the light out of which the objects seen are composed. It is self-effulgent and is its own subject and object. The light of Shiva is the unity of light of the seer, the light of the process of seeing, and the light of the object seen.

- Whether it is the seer, the power of seeing, or the object seen, all are manifestations of the same light, and can only be connected according to the unity power of light.

- Meditate upon this supreme light of Shiva that connects the knower, the knowing and the object known, and you will never fall into sorrow.

This clear light of Shiva is said to be transparent like a crystal, the *sphatika* or crystal linga of Shiva. When one worships that crystal pillar of light, it is a recognition of the supreme light of reality, the state of complete illumination and perfect peace.

Shiva is portrayed with his third eye open, indicating his ruling over the power of perception and awareness. The third eye is the inner eye of unity that perceives oneness, reality and eternity. Opening the eye of Shiva is the key to understanding the light of Shiva and the Supreme Light of truth.

The Four Forms of the Light of Shiva

Shiva has four light forms as Sun, Moon, Fire and Lightning. These symbolize different aspects of light on different levels of the universe, individual and collective, inner and outer. They are not simply scientific aspects of light but metaphors of the power of light. They reflect different manifestations and energy of the original clear light.

The Sun here is not the light of a single star but the light behind all the stars and the overall power of illumination. The Moon is not just the reflected light of the Sun, but also the reflecting power of all forms of light. Fire is not just the physical fire but the color, heat and transformation inherent in all light. Lightning is not just electrical energy in the atmosphere but all electrical and propulsive forces in the universe, up to the power of consciousness.

1) Surya – Shiva as the Sun or All-illuminating Supreme Light

> The light of Shiva as the supreme light of reality is radiant like the Sun. It is self-effulgent, self-illuminating, the source of all light, and the light of lights. The Sun shines through the light of Shiva, radiating light, love, life, and intelligence on all. The inner Sun of the spiritual heart is the abode of Shiva. This is the light of the Self and the light of Prana.

2) Soma – Shiva as the Moon or the Attractive Light of Bliss

The light of Shiva is sometimes said to be white like the Moon. It is cool, peaceful, serene, untainted and undisturbed, a source of endless beauty and delight that nourishes the soul. The light of Shiva is said to be as brilliant like a million Suns but simultaneously as delightful as a million Moons. This is the calm light of the peaceful mind.

3) Agni - Shiva as the Universal Fire or Hidden Light

The light of Shiva is the source of all warmth. It is the universal Fire or Agni, also called Rudra. There is a power of heat, fire or combustion, hidden in all creatures, objects, and energies in the universe. This is the immanence of Shiva in all. The fire of Shiva is working within each creature in order to ripen it to its highest potential.

4) Vidyut - Shiva as the Electrical Force

The light of Shiva is the source of all power and energy that arises from it like lightning. Lightning is the basis of all light and each form of light has its own lightning or energy projection. The electrical force of Shiva is behind all energies, powers, and forces in the universe from subatomic to supragalactic levels. This lightning aspect of Shiva is the basis of Shakti.

Sometimes the light of Shiva is only said to be twofold as Agni and Soma or Fire and Moon, the red and the white bindus or energy powers. Fire and Moon stand for the two main aspects of light in its active and receptive roles, light as the power of illumination and light as the space created by it.

Agni represents the fierce or wrathful forms of Shiva that are protective in nature and remove negativity from body and mind. Soma represents the soft and compassionate forms of Shiva that are inspiring and dispense grace, affirming that which is positive. The fire of Shiva is the great purifying power that burns away whatever is not enduring. The moonlight of Shiva is the great rejuvenating power that vitalizes our higher essence of bliss.

Shiva is worshipped through special Fire rituals and offerings, starting with the *yajnas* and *havans* of Vedic culture. In these fire rituals, Soma or the mystic plant juice is the highest offering, and symbolizes all the offerings as a whole. As Agni and Soma are the two main aspects of Vedic worship, Shiva is a deity of the Vedic process, which is unifying Agni and Soma on all levels from fire and water to consciousness and bliss.

From the union of Agni and Soma (Fire and Moon) arises the Sun, the golden light that blends the red and the white energies together. The Sun is the great Vedic symbol of Atman or Purusha, the Supreme Self that is Shiva. Shiva is sometimes connected to the rising Sun as the dawn of spiritual knowledge. The Sun as the pure light is the illuminating power of Being. Agni and Soma are speech and mind from which the Sun as prana arises.

Sometimes the original light of Shiva is related to lightning because lightning is the original light or spark that starts or sets in motion the other three light forms as Sun, Moon and Fire. Lightning in particular is the force that descends from Heaven and enkindles the Fire on the Earth. Lightning is the basis of Shakti or energy, which is the electrical power of Shiva. Lightning is the power of perception and discrimination. It is the weapon of the Gods that removes darkness.

Sun, Moon and Fire each have their respective lightning energies or electrical forms as the solar lightning, lunar lightning, and the electric Fire. Sun, Moon and Fire relate to the three eyes of Shiva with the Sun as the right eye, the Moon as the left eye, and Fire as the central Third Eye. These three also relate to the three main channels of the subtle body with the Sun as the right or Pingala Nadi, the Moon as the left or Ida Nadi, and fire as the central channel or Sushumna Nadi.

The original clear light of Shiva creates the four energy centers within us as it diversifies, which govern over the seven chakras. The four lights of Shiva are the four lights of Yoga. In Tantric Yoga these four energies centers are often more important than the seven chakras which are defined according to them. All four are rooted in the supreme light of Shiva.

1. Head, Thousand Petal Louts – Moon and mind
2. Third eye – Lightning and perception
3. Heart – Sun, prana and Self
4. Root – Fire, speech

In this system, the seven chakras are divided into three groups of three, with the Navel (Manipura) and Throat (Visshuddha) chakras having roles in two of the three groups. The Third Eye has an independent value as Lightning but can be part of the lunar triad as well.

Three Fire Chakras

- The root, *Muladhara*, root or earth chakra forms the receptacle for the Fire, the Earth altar on which it burns.

- The second, *Svadhisthtana*, sex or water chakra is the site of the flame itself but also indicates its fuel, the oil through which it burns.

- The third, *Manipura*, fire or navel chakra, represents the radiance or ascending flame of the fire.

Three Solar Chakras

- The third *Manipura*, fire or navel chakra also represents the descending light from the Anahata or heart chakra of the Sun and the heat of the Sun.

- The fourth, *Anahata*, air or heart chakra is the Sun itself, and connects to the inner spiritual heart beyond the chakras, the seat of the Self or Atman.

- The fifth, *Visshuddha*, ether or throat chakra, represents the ascending light of the Sun.

Three Lunar Chakras

- The fifth, *Visshuddha*, ether or throat chakra represents the reflection of the Moon. It is connected to the tongue and the power of speech.

- The sixth, *Ajna* chakra or third eye represents the lightning coming from the Moon or clouds.

- The seventh or crown chakra, *Sahasrara Padma*, the thousand-petal lotus of the head, indicates the sphere of the Moon. The head and mind hold the cool energy of awareness like the Moon.

Movement of the Kundalini

The movement of energy up and down the spine in Yoga is that of the ascending fire of Shiva or Kundalini rising from below, the Agni-Rudra of the *Vedas*. The descending grace or moonlight of Shiva is the nectar or Soma falling from the lotus of the head above.

These two forces of Shiva and Shakti cross over in the heart as the region of the Sun. They also meet above in the Third Eye as the place of lightning. The light of Shiva ever flows within us and is the basis of all other processes within us and in the universe.

Shiva and the Night

Shiva is often a deity of the nighttime, particularly the dark of the Moon but also the dark night of innumerable stars. This connection with the night reflects Shiva's mystery and transcendence of the ordinary visible known world. His connection with the dark of the Moon shows the mind (Moon) as merging into a higher reality, the beyond the mind state. Yet Shiva is not a deity of the darkness of ignorance, but of the darkness of the unknown that is the secret light and the highest knowledge.

The night indicates Shiva's relationship with dissolution, peace, and silence – the conditions in which our world is put to rest. The night of Shiva is the inner light beyond both outer light and darkness. It is the universal light lit by innumerable stars and suns.

Shiva is also a deity of wakefulness, the God who never sleeps, even during the night, whose eyes never blink, and whose perception never falters. He is the light that persists even through darkness, the wakefulness that is ever present behind all things. This is another aspect of Fire that can be enkindled at night to remove the darkness.

Staying up all night chanting and meditating is a special practice for worshiping Shiva, particularly on Shiva Ratri, the great night of Shiva. Shiva never sleeps, even in the state of deep sleep. Shiva is always aware, with his third eye open, whether the world exists or not. Shiva is the light that endures even through darkness. He is the inextinguishable fire. The light of Shiva illuminates all states of consciousness and all objects of perception without any diminution.

Prakasha and Vimarsha

The light of awareness has the capacity of reflecting upon itself and knowing its own self-reality. This self-knowing power of the inner light (Prakasha) is called *Vimarsha*, which means the power of reflection and deliberation. The supreme light is self-effulgent. The supreme knowledge is self-knowing. It is from this reflective capacity of the light of consciousness that the universe comes into being. The universe exists as part of Shiva's own self-knowledge and reflection upon his own reality. Once we understand through Vimarsha that universe is a reflection of Shiva, we can directly enter into the light of Shiva.

Vimarsha or the power of reflection relates to the Vidyut or electrical force among the four forms of light. Yet each power of light or Prakasha has its own power of reflection or Vimarsha. The lunar force has the reflective power of meditation. The solar force has the reflective power of prana and self-awareness. The fiery force has the reflective power of speech and investigation. The lightning energy holds all powers to uncover, reveal, and perceive.

This power of reflection or Vimarsha is the basis of Shakti, which begins as Shiva's ability to know himself, and extends to the ability to create all things and yet remain beyond them. Light is self-illumining. In illumining himself, Shiva creates the entire universe as his Self-revelation. Shakti is Shiva's reflection upon himself through which he knows himself as he is through the entire universe that arises in the space of his own consciousness. Shiva is the light through which Shakti moves as lightning. By developing the lightning force of inquiry or reflection on our inner Self, we can move from the mind to the beyond the mind state and know the highest truth.

Shiva as Mantra and Primal Sound

Shiva is always worshipped with chanting, music and sacred sound in all of its profound manifestations. The sound of Shiva, which is the resonance of peace and grace, flows through all beings and the entire universe, as the basis of their very heart and vitality.

Along with primal light, Shiva is also *primal sound*, called *Pranava* in Sanskrit, which refers to the original vibration behind the universe, known and unknown. Pranava indicates more than sound in the ordinary sense. Pranava is the self-arising sound vibration behind all forms and energies in the universe. Pranava sets in motion all forces and actions in the universe consisting of sound, light, energy, prana, mind, and consciousness.

Pranava is the Divine Word or Word of God, which is the sound of Shiva. This Divine Word is not a mere verbal utterance, but the energy of intelligence behind the universe, which is light and sound in unison. Shiva indicates the transcendent unity of sound and light along with their related faculties of seeing and hearing (*drishti* and *shruti*, or vision and revelation). Pranava is the sound of light, which is also the light of sound. While Pranava indicates the primal sound vibrations in all of its forms, it is most connected to OM, the most important of the seed mantras, which directly puts us in touch with its power.

In the human body, this primal sound vibration indicates the open mouth that produces all sounds. It reflects the original cosmic expansion out of singularity into infinity. Shiva is identified with Omkara and is frequently lauded as its personification.

> *All yogis ever meditate upon OM united with the bindu (point focus) as the means of fulfilling all desires and granting liberation. Reverence to OM!*[15]

The great name mantra for Shiva – *OM Namah Shivaya* or *Reverence to Shiva* – is an extension of OM and is a prayer for the peace, blessings and grace of the Divine Word. Shiva is the energy of OM as expansion, ascension, and the power to go beyond all limitation, linking us to Being, Consciousness, Bliss, and Love absolute.

Pranava as primal sound is not simply sound as a sensory quality accessible to our physical ears, nor any sound that is produced by external action or friction.

Pranava relates to unstruck sound that is self-produced and not the result of any external contacts, as is the case with ordinary sounds.[16] Pranava encompasses all energy and vibration in the universe that itself consists of vibration.

The primal sound OM is inherent in both space and light and is the basis of time.

- Space carries and is sustained by a subtle sound vibration that creates and sustains its etheric field. Space is the field of unmanifest sound.
- Light produces sound, particularly through lightning and fire, which is its energetic action. Sound is the basis of energy and prana.
- Sound as vibratory movement creates time as the first of all movements, and holds all time within itself, which is the unfoldment of its potentials.

Pranava as primal sound is the basis of all sounds both verbal and non-verbal, including speech and music. It is the basis of all words and languages, starting with the sounds of the alphabet that are its prime manifestation. The letters of the Sanskrit alphabet arise from Shiva's drum that he plays during his dance of fire. All words are names of Shiva or his own Self-expression.

Pranava is the basis of all music as the original musical note and its cosmic rhythm. All music, extending to the music of the spheres, is the music of Shiva. That inner music is the source of all dance as vibratory frequency or sound in action. Each creature has its own sound vibration or portion of the Divine Word, its distinctive place in the dance of Shiva. It has its own dance or vibratory movement, which is based upon the current of its prana.

Pranava is the basis of the inner sound current called *Nada*, which flows through the spine and the sushumna, and which connects us to the cosmic sound current. Those who develop a one-pointed mind hear these inner sounds when they close their ears and listen within. The spine is often compared to a reed or bamboo flute, through which Divine music is made by the Divine breath or Prana. Each soul is a manifestation of primal sound, a play of music as well as an articulation of the Word. The musical word is the chant, which is mantra, through which all wisdom arises.

Awakening the Divine Word and sound current and allowing it to flow through the spine is the basis of higher Yoga practices, and forms our natural inner chanting or prayer. Our inner soul body is the manifestation of our portion of the Divine Word at the core of our being. It is a body of light and sound, word and music, energy and consciousness, Shiva and Shakti.

Shabda Brahman

All aspects of sound from gross sound to transcendent vibration are called *Shabda* in Sanskrit. The manifest universe is said to be *Shabda Brahman*, which is Brahman or the Godhead with qualities that are all based upon sound. *All differentiation in the universe originally occurs only owing to sound.* This is not mere differentiation created by words but that created by vibration in all aspects.

The Supreme Brahman is the unmanifest state of Shabda, with sound in its latent and transcendent state, the Godhead without qualities. That soundless state is the ultimate point of harmony within and beyond all sound and meaning. All sound exists to draw the mind into a deeper state of silence. Silence holds the supreme meaning of unity beyond all relative meanings of articulated sounds. Silence is the one thing that means all things and holds all potential differentiated meanings within itself. All meanings of words and ideas exist to draw the mind into a state of transcendence where no thought stirs.

An important method of Yoga practice is to merge the mind into the Divine sound current or Shabda Brahman, which then naturally takes us to the silent and unmanifest Brahman, in which all vibration is turned within and outer sound ceases. This is to merge into the OM current in which the entire universe is dissolved, which then takes us beyond all manifestation. It is to enter into the subtle body of sound and its chakra system and then dissolve these back into pure light and unbounded awareness.

Svara

Shiva as primal sound relates to the concept of *Svara*, which means "sound vibration" and "accent." Svara also refers to the vowels, which form the root of the alphabet, as consonants without a vowel cannot be pronounced. Svara refers to the mantra OM as the ultimate expression of all vowels. Svara indicates melody and harmony, which suggests unity and self-abidance. Svara is the essence of bliss and self-identity behind all sounds either as words or music. As accent, svara refers to the meaning, intent, or focus behind the sound of the world.

There is a famous statement in the *Upanishads*:

> *He who is lauded as svara (sound) in the Vedas, and is established in Vedanta, Who is beyond the forces of nature, we laud him as Maheshvara (Shiva) or the Supreme Lord.*[17]

Svara means the essence (rasa) of oneself (sva). It resolves all sound and music into the inner vibration of the pure I am, the single note of "I am all," as the song of bliss. Such music is the basis of the ancient *Samaveda* or Veda of Song, harmony, oneness that is considered to be the highest of the *Vedas*. The *Samaveda* is closely related to Shiva as the Divine musician and chanter. The Vedic name for Shiva is *Rudra*, or "he who makes sound," which is also Agni or Fire, the deity of speech. The sound he makes is Soma or the watery nectar, which refers to music and to bliss.

Svara relates to the essence, energy, vibration or meaning behind all sounds. It is the prime melody that is the harmony and unity of all. Creating harmony in our Yoga practice refers to unifying all our thoughts in the mantra. As such, Svara is OM and Pranava, primal sound and the Divine Word.

There is a special relationship between the terms Svara as tonality, *Sara* as meaning the inmost core, and *Rasa* referring to the essence. *Svaravati,* what holds the power of sound, relates to *Sarasvati,* the Goddess of wisdom, who holds both Sara and Rasa, the inner essence. Svara is the vibration of unity and harmony, which is the basis of all music and indicates the unitary vibration of the same Self and light in all beings. It is not the outer meaning but the inner meaning that is the bliss of consciousness.

Shiva as Nataraj, the Lord of the Dance

One of the most common forms of Shiva is *Nataraj* or the "Lord of the Dance." In this depiction, Shiva is portrayed performing the powerful spiraling *Tandava* dance or "dance of thunder," with a ring of fire around him. This is the dance of universal transformation.

Shiva is the great lord of the cosmic dance that constitutes all existence. This is not just an artistic image but reflects the dance of waves and particles, creatures and worlds, in this universe of circular and spiraling unfolding and evolving powers. The universal movement is the dance of Shiva, as the dance of peace, harmony, energy, and transformation. To surrender to that dynamic dance is to enter into the highest equipoise of stillness.

To Shiva are attributed 108 primary dance poses and accompanying gestures (mudras) that define the essence of all expression. Gestures are motions that reflect sound and music, manifesting it into form, enhancing their meaning and power. The ultimate gesture or "mudra of Shiva" is to remain silently aware at the core of our being in the face of the entire movement of life, in resonance with the Divine Word.

Shiva's Mantras

Shiva is the essence of all mantras, which can be called the "sounds of Shiva." He has own special mantras as well. Shiva is the lord of cosmic sound or the cosmic music, particularly the great mantra OM from which all the *Vedas* and all mantras are said to derive, and the entire universe generated. The thunderous music of Lord Shiva is the origin and end of all.

The Sanskrit alphabet is said to arise from the beating of Shiva's drum, whose resonance pervades all space and establishes its background rhythms, showing that all words and meanings are inherent in space and not simply produced by human beings.

Shiva most specifically represents the vowels among the letters. Vowels are open sounds that can be resonated endlessly, whereas consonants are projections in a moment of time.

- The prime vowel sound-A (the a sound as in "*a* book," the most basic opening of the throat) is sacred to Shiva as representing pure light and the Supreme Shiva beyond all manifestation, into which everything is ultimately negated, the Supreme Brahman.

- Shiva relates also to the *anusvara* M-sound (the M-sound at the end of mantras like OM , consisting of a nasalization of the vowel followed by a closing of the lips). This sound represents dissolution, as a drawing all sounds back to the vibration at the soft palate of the mouth that vibrates the entire head.

- Shiva is the vowel-O, which unites the infinite A-sound, with the vibratory force of the U-sound (U-sound as in "p*u*t").

Shiva's primary mantra is *OM Namah Shivaya*, the most widely used Shiva mantra. It is more powerful if received by special initiation, but can be used by anyone who feels an inner connection to Shiva. *OM Namah Shivaya* takes the form of the Goddess or Shiva's consort.

- *OM* is said to be the face of Shakti or the Goddess.
- The syllables *na* and *ma* are her two feet.
- The syllable *shi* is her heart.
- The syllables *va* and *ya* are her right and left arms.

Apart from OM, the main bija for Shiva is Hum (pronounced "Hoom"). Sometimes it is extended as Haum.

- *Hum* represents the cosmic fire or Agni, as well as the power to burn up or explode. It is the weapon mantra, the fire from Shiva's third eye. It is Shiva's Rudra form and relates to his Tandava dance or dance of dissolution.
- *Haum* (Ha plus Aum) represents the Cosmic Prana ever expanding in the region of the head and the thousand petal lotus. It connects both the Agni and Vayu or Fire and Air/Prana aspects of Shiva energy as the cosmic Spirit.

Shiva has an important threefold set of bija mantras as *Haum Jum Sah.*

- *Ju☐m* (pronounced "Joom") indicates light and velocity, quick illumination or vitalization, including power of healing.
- *Saḥ* (*a* as in th*e* followed by a soft h-sound) represents Shiva's being, power and stability. It is the nature of the Purusha.

Haum Ju☐m Saḥ reflects the speed and power of Shiva's energy moving into us and taking us beyond our ordinary mind and life with the energy of the standpoint of this Cosmic Prana. This mantra takes us beyond all difficulty, death, suffering and sorrow.[18]

- A very powerful Shiva mantra *is: OM Haum Ju☐m Saḥ Nama Śiva☐ya!* It is probably the strongest form of the Namah Shiva mantra, as it is empowered with special bija mantras. You can chant this whenever you aspire to greater awareness, Prana, healing power, protection and peace.

Another important bija for Shiva, particularly in Kashmir Shaivism is *Sauḥ*:

- *Sauḥ* combines the stabilizing s-sound with the expansive au-sound and the Visarga-h, for holding and directing the energy of Shiva and Shakti. It also reflects the power of the Moon and the Soma or nectar of immortality and is said to be the immortal bija. It is commonly used in the

Shakta Upaya or the energetic practices of Shaivite Yoga. It relates to inhalation and the drawing in of the Shakti energy, particularly into the heart. Sauḥ is also regarded as a bija of the spiritual heart, particularly in the ability to withdraw our awareness into it.

Perhaps most notable for dealing with all of life's difficulties and dangers is Shiva's aspect as *Tryambakam*, the "Three-Eyed One" or *Mrityunjaya*, the one who takes us beyond death, as the Rishi Vasishta lauds in the *Rigveda*.

> *We worship the three-eyed one, who is fragrant and increases nourishment. As a gourd from its stalk, may he release us from death but not from immortality.*[19]

This is a mantra of fragrance, nourishment and natural growth and development. It also occurs in the famous but much longer Vedic *Rudram* chant to Shiva in the *Yajurveda*, in which one learns to honor the Divine power not only in beauty, bliss and happiness, but also in sorrow, difficulty and death. Shiva helps us to embrace both sides of dualities so that we can move beyond duality to the essence of oneness. Once we reach him, there is no more death and sorrow, which are revealed as but the shadow of a deeper unending light. *The Vedic Rudram contains most of the names of Shiva that predominate in later Shaivism and is the best extended set of Shiva mantras.*

Sibilants and aspirated sounds (h and s-sounds) relate to Shiva as Prana, the power of the breath. Prana and Pranava go together as Prana creates sound and vibration creates the breath and vital energy in general. Pranava is not only primordial sound but also primal Prana. *Hamsa* and *So'ham* Prana Mantras also relate to Lord Shiva, but we will examine these later in the book under the topic of the Hamsa.

There are many hymns, poems or *stotras* to Lord Shiva in classical Sanskrit that are commonly chanted by his worshippers. Many of these hymns are by the great Vedantic guru Shankara.[20] There are many kirtans, bhajans or shorter devotional chants and songs to Lord Shiva that are becoming popular today throughout the worldwide Yoga movement.[21]

All sounds are ultimately the sounds of Shiva if we take them back to their origin in the heart. If we let the natural chant of Shiva arise within us it will take us to the highest truth and grant us the most profound wisdom. We should learn to dwell in the sounds of Shiva, which are the sounds of all nature, and the sounds of peace.

Shiva and the Universal Prana

Life is not just a biological phenomena; the entire universe is alive in every particle and every point of space. Our transient individual lives are but small portions of an eternal cosmic life. Nothing really dies, only forms change. That universal life is our true life and the entire universe is our greater body and organism, ever evolving into the Supreme.

Shiva is Prana as the supreme life-force, the original power of feeling, knowing and action at a universal level before and behind any creaturely expressions. Shiva is the Supreme Life behind all limited forms of life. Shiva is the Lord of eternal life, and to enter into Shiva is to live forever within our deeper Shiva nature.

Shiva is not merely prana in the biological sense of the breath and vital force, but in the inner sense of the Spirit and cosmic breath, the "breath of God" or "breath of Brahman," from which the entire universe arises. This Supreme Prana is ultimately the power of Eternal Being. We all live through this greater prana or life-power of Shiva, without which we could not even take a single breath or have a single heartbeat.

Shiva is the cosmic life that flows through nature, which upholds the biosphere on Earth, and energizes the atmosphere with wonderful displays of storms and seasons. Shiva is the cosmic life energy that flows through space linking the worlds together, which is present in the most distant stars and galaxies, imparting consciousness and movement to the entire universe. This cosmic life force of Shiva holds the potentials of the different bodies, senses, and minds of creatures, through which it seeks to become aware of itself in the outer world.

The great Prana (Maha Prana) of Shiva is the *Kriya Shakti* or prime power of action in the universe, which is a play of consciousness. Even inanimate forces of nature are manifestations of Prana at a lower level, containing the seeds of life and awareness latent within themselves. From this great Prana arises all powers of energy, electricity, magnetism, attraction and repulsion.

This great Prana of Shiva is the basis of will-power or *samkalpa shakti*, through which all our drives and motivations arise, from simple biological urges to the will to realize the highest truth and Divinity. This Divine breath of Shiva is the origin of impulse, energy and aspiration on all levels. Whatever we do or attempt is an expression of the life of Shiva, the cosmic life of which our individual life is but a phase or an aspect.

The cosmic power of action or Kriya Shakti is inherently a force of intelligence, reflecting the working out of a higher will. It manifests through the law of karma and dispenses the fruits of actions for all souls in the universe. Yet the same Shakti can take us beyond karma by connecting us to the power of spiritual knowledge. It becomes the Yoga Shakti and power of meditation that leads us beyond time and karma. The great Prana that sets everything in motion also eventually propels us to transcendence.

This great Prana of Shiva enlivens not just the physical but also the subtle body. The subtle body, with its chakras or energy centers, is our body of prana that connects us to the higher Prana of Shiva by which it is activated.

Shiva's connection with Prana begins with his Rudra form in the *Rigveda*. Rudra is an atmospheric deity, whose sons, the Maruts or Rudras, are deities of the storm, thunder, and lightning. Shiva grants immortality that is his own nature as the Supreme deity of life.

The Prana of Shiva

The Prana of Shiva is the current of Self-awareness, ever reflecting the Divine I am and its unfoldment. It is the arising of the Self-energy in all creatures through which all other forces are set in motion. This Divine I is the pure I that exists beyond all outer identifications and limitations. It knows itself equally everywhere and as contained in all things.

This pure Prana of the pure I before it is identified with body or mind is the Prana of Shiva. The ultimate source of Prana within us is our own being and sense of Self. Our sense of Self, however we hold to it, is the basis of our motivation and action on all levels. Aligning to the pure I of the inner Self connects us with the supreme power of Prana that can work magic and bring about instantaneous healing and transformation. We must learn to return to the origins of life at the core of our own awareness. When the Prana of Shiva is flowing within us we can move beyond birth and death, joy and sorrow, and can feel all beings within our own hearts.

This supreme Prana is called the *Prana Purusha* or "Self that is made of Prana" in Upanishadic thought. It is not simply the Self of the vital sheath (pranamaya kosha) that mediates between body and mind, but the Prana that exists behind all the sheaths and bodies of the soul. This inner Prana or inner spirit is the source of bliss or Ananda, the Ananda Prana. It is the breath of Being, the energy of the Self ever flowing into itself. It is life beyond birth and death, and dwells everywhere without the need of any embodiment. To know that supreme Prana is to know our true Self or Purusha beyond all darkness. To know our true Self grants us the Prana or vitality of the entire universe.

Shiva as the great Yogi represents the Prana in its state of release from birth and death, life liberated from all sorrow – a state of perpetual peace, serenity and well-being in which the Self breathes the universe within itself, without any friction, stain or duality. The goal of our lives is to move from the creaturely Prana of the Jiva or individual soul to the supreme Prana of the universal being or Shiva. This is to move from the bodily breath of inhalation and exhalation to the cosmic breath of the coming and going of all the universes, the *Atma Shakti* or power of Self-being in all. While the breath of the Jiva creates additional karma for us, the breath of Shiva returns us to peace and freedom from all desires, moving us beyond all time.

Prana, Sound and Pranava

The Universal Prana through its outbreath creates sound at a cosmic level or Pranava, just as speech arises from the exhalation of the human being. Similarly, Pranava or the universal sound vibration carries the energy of the universal Prana. Prana is one with Pranava or primordial sound. The Universal Prana and the Divine Word are one. The sound of the breath is the basis of all other sounds. The sound of the breath energizes all other sounds in the body, extending through the respiratory, circulatory and nervous systems, and allows the vocal organs to function.

Shiva as Maha Prana creates Pranava or primal sound as his breath or exhalation. The *Vedas* are the manifestation of the breath of Shiva. The *Vedas* are the breath of Shiva as Primordial sound. Shiva's breath moves through OM, which is the seed mantra of the cosmic prana. Shiva's Prana is a mantric force that calms the mind and brings in a deeper intelligence.

Prana and Time

This universal breath creates the movement of time according to its rhythms of expansion and contraction. Time is not an abstract continuum but a rhythmic flow like the breath. Time is the Prana that is moving through the cosmic space like a series of waves sustaining the universal life. The entire cosmos is breathing according to long cosmic time cycles or Maha Yugas, which mark the lifespans of the worlds and their presiding deities.

The unmanifest Brahman beyond the cosmos also has its own breath or vibratory potential, but this is held within itself and has no outer expression. The manifest universe is the life of God and manifests from the Divine Prana as it externalizes. Yet that Divine life never dies with the coming and going of the worlds.

Through controlling Prana and the breath, removing our consciousness from identity with the body and mind, we can go beyond time. We can move from the ordinary time bound breath to the eternal breathless Prana within us, which occurs when we turn our awareness within at the timeless center of our being.

Prana and Electrical and Magnetic Energy

This supreme Prana like the power of lightning energizes all forms of light in the universe from a physical level of fire to the light of the mind and ultimately to the Self-effulgent light of consciousness. Each form of light has a lightning that sets it in motion. Similarly, each form of light creates its own energy or lightning, its power of action. Every form of movement in the universe generates energy or electrical force, like the flowing of water that generates electricity on Earth. Prana moves like lightning and the higher Prana gives us a lightning like perception and direct realization of the Supreme truth.

Prana has the electrical force to create and transform but also the magnetic force to draw all things back into itself. Shiva holds that cosmic magnetism and draws all creatures back into himself. Shiva is the central vortex of cosmic energy, the Self-awareness that reabsorbs everything. In the same process, Shiva creates the electrical energy of Self-realization, providing us the inner power to activate the subtle faculties. Even the force of gravity holds a portion of the energy of Shiva, who holds all the worlds together.

Prana and Space

The universal breath like air pervades all of space, which holds and carries its power, taking us to the supreme space of consciousness. Prana or air is the power of movement inherent in space and space is Prana in a state of rest. The cosmic Prana creates space as its energy field, which in turn gives it power. Space is the body of Shiva, and the cosmic breath is his movement. Shiva is a deity of the air, space, and atmosphere, with the thunder as his voice and the lightning as his eye.

To create Prana we need first to create space. This pranic space is not any ordinary space defined according to distance; it is the inner space of Shiva that is the space of peace within ourselves. To draw in prana from nature works best we are when in a natural location open to space, the mountains, sky, stars, or clouds. Shiva is this natural breath of space, which is the movement of the cosmic life. When we create space in the mind in meditation, we similarly create a new prana in the mind that is sacred and immortal.

Shiva and Prana Yoga: Unitary Prana

Yoga works to take us from the outer dualistic prana bound to the cycle of birth and death to the inner unitary prana that is immortal. This is the movement from the darkness of ignorance to the light of knowledge. The outer dualistic prana is reflected in the dualism of inhalation and exhalation in the breath and the duality of energy between the solar and lunar currents of the right and left sides of the body and brain. These dualistic currents are biological in nature and have psychological counterparts as well.

Through the practice of pranayama, Yoga works to balance and calm the dualistic movement of the breath, increasing our power of retention, and eventually taking us to the breathless state. In the breathless state, prana or vital energy flows directly through the spine and does not depend upon the movement of the breath through inhalation and exhalation.

Through Yoga we gradually learn to withdraw our prana or life-energy within, silencing our outer sense and motor organs, mind and emotions, until we reach the unitary state of prana that sustains the concentrated or one-pointed mind and holds our deeper self-awareness. This state of the unitary Prana is the state of Shiva. The unitary Prana is the Prana of Shiva, which is the deathless prana, the immortal prana that pervades and transcends the manifest universe through the supreme space of consciousness.

Shiva is the unitary prana behind the dualistic movements of the breath as inhalation and exhalation or the dualistic movements of the mind through attraction and repulsion. To reach the higher Prana of Shiva we must first balance the ordinary dualities of prana, energy and emotion within ourselves.

This unitary prana flows in a state of balance and peace. If we can merge into that prana we can go beyond the breath, which is to go beyond life and death. The unitary Prana of Shiva is the prana of prana, the breath behind the breath. The unitary breath of Shiva pervades all space and light. It is the basis of the universal life.

Prana as a term in Vedic thought often refers to the spine, specifically to the flow of the energy of consciousness through the spine, not merely to the breath. The prana upholds the spine, energizing the subtle body and its chakra centers. Once we calm, balance and unify our prana, all these inner energy centers, powers and potentials must manifest for us. All prana, extending to the breath and senses organs, is a manifestation of the immortal Prana of Shiva, broken into waves of vital energies and impulses, like waves upon the sea. If we turn our individual prana within, we can contact and merge into the universal prana of Shiva.

The Breathless State and the Inner Breath

The Yogis seek to reach the state of *Kevala Kumbhaka* or a continuous state of retention of the breath in which our individual prana is merged into the Divine or inner consciousness. Then a unitary prana of higher awareness remains steady behind the outer movements of the breath and life-force.

The Shiva Yogi can go beyond the need to breathe altogether, remaining in a trancelike state of Samadhi. An inner pranic current runs through the spine and there is no longer a limitation to ordinary breathing through the lungs. An inner flow, bliss or Soma flows from awareness itself. When the duality of the breathing process is suspended, the mind is put to rest and the universal consciousness manifests through us. We can merge into the inner breath and live in our body of Prana or subtle energy.

Sahaja Prana or the "Self-born Prana" is a further development from Kevala Kumbhaka and is the natural Prana of the state of Shiva. In the Sahaja Prana state the outer breath may continue, but the consciousness remains in a calm and detached manner rooted in the inner unitary Prana, no longer identified with the physical body and its process. The inner breath or unitary prana flows behind the breath in a state of unitary awareness and observation. This allows us to conduct all of our ordinary bodily and mental functions without losing our connection with the unitary prana or universal life of Shiva.

In Raja Yoga, there is another approach to Kevala Kumbhaka or the breathless state. This does not depend upon outer breathing exercises but only on the use of the mind. In this process, called the "breath of the witness" (Sakshi Prana), one observes the breath with constant attention, recognizing ones true Self beyond the fluctuations of the breath. This also takes us to the Sahaja Prana.

Ordinarily we breathe unconsciously and automatically. When we perform breathing exercises like pranayama we begin to breathe consciously. This changes the nature of the breath and turns it gradually into a force of awareness. When we are aware of the breath, we become able to go beyond the karmic patterns and emotional disturbances rooted therein.

When we observe the breath with full attention, we are holding our awareness in the inner breath, the breath of the witness. We no longer identify ourselves with the breath but hold to a unitary state of awareness beyond the fluctuations of the breath. This breath of the witness is the prana of the state of seeing and gives energy to our deeper perceptions. If we follow this practice of observing the breath, our breath will naturally deepen, slow down and connect us to a deeper source of prana within our own awareness. Observation of the breath can lead us into the breathless state, where the outer breath falls away and our prana is rooted in our inner consciousness.

Actually we are always in the breathless state. It is only the body that breathes. Our inner consciousness is inherently beyond the outer fluctuations of the breath. Dwelling in the breathless state of consciousness as our true being – whether the body breathes or not – is the highest form of pranayama. When we no longer identify with the body then we are in the natural breathless state, and cannot be affected by what the body does. This is dwelling in the deathless Prana of Shiva.

Sounds of the Breath as Sounds of Shiva

The breath reflects certain natural sounds that connect to certain letters of the alphabet. Most important of pranic sounds are the s-sounds and h-sounds that have a hissing or air type quality, such as the yogic Prana mantra *So 'ham*. Inhalation as a drawing in of energy reflects the mantra *So*, while exhalation and the release of energy marks the mantra *Ham*. So indicates receptive or lunar energy, while Ham reflects projective or solar energy. So'ham is also a Shiva mantra.

The Yogi works to balance the So'ham current within. This can be done in two primary ways. The first is to expand these natural energies with So as inhalation and Ham as exhalation. The second is to reverse these energies with Ham as inhalation and Sa as exhalation. The So'ham approach reflects a nurturing lunar energy. The Hamsa approach reflects a purifying solar energy. Both have their places in Yoga practice. Shiva is not only So'ham but also Hamsa.

Once inhalation and exhalation are balanced, they become withdrawn into an inner peace. Then these same sounds "Hamsa So'ham" continue to reverberate within the spine and the sushumna as the natural sounds of the Self, So'ham "He am I," and Ham Sa," I am He," referring to the Supreme Self. These sounds can also develop into *Shivo'ham*, "I am Shiva." This is the inner flow of the non-dualistic breath, which is the breath of Shiva.

Shiva Prana Yoga Practices

There are many Prana Yoga traditions connected to Lord Shiva. They are reflected in several Yoga practices.

• Nadi Shodhana

Alternate nostril breathing is the main practice for balancing the pranic energies within us. It can be used to balance the right and left or solar and lunar nadis, as well as the Agni and Soma energies in the body overall or in the different chakras. Use the mantra *Ham* for breathing through the right nostril and Sa or So for breathing through the left (*So* for inhalation and *Sa* for exhalation).

• Hamsa So'ham Pranayama

As Shiva is prana, the natural sound of the breath is the Name of Shiva. Follow the natural sounds of the breath as *Hamsa* or *Soham*, "He am I" or "I am He" (referring to our Shiva nature). Or simply *Shivoham* or I am Shiva. *Hamsa* is more solar and *So'ham* more lunar in its energy. The same mantras can be used to hold the Prana in the Sushumna. Internally chant *Hamsa Soham* while meditating in silence and holding the awareness in the spine.

• Yoga Nidra – the Sleep of Shiva This consists of withdrawing into our inner core prana and consciousness or the state of Shiva that holds all knowledge and all power. It is the ultimate practice of Pratyahara.

• The Breath of the Witness – Sakshi Prana Consciously observing the breath, one moves into the state of the seer, which is the immortal witness beyond the breath. One enters into the unitary power of consciousness that is beyond birth and death, breath and no breath. Learn to recognize your inner awareness as the breath behind the breath.

Shiva and Vital Energy – The Value of Being Shiva

Shiva is not just associated with the Supreme Prana but with all aspects of Prana, life, and vitality. Shiva is full of life and vital energy because he is rooted in the Supreme Existence that never dies nor suffers any diminution or defeat.

Shiva relates to the positive attributes of Prana and vital energy that extend to emotional and psychological levels. One way to worship Shiva is to cultivate these vital powers of Shiva within ourselves. These help us overcome the ego, and its capacity to get easily disturbed. The ego is a knot in Prana, a pranic weakness that needs to be surrendered or released.

Shiva represents daring, the ability to challenge the unknown. He searches out difficulties and is willing to make a way forward for others to follow. He is ever seeking to transcend and go beyond. He is daring in the higher sense of ever willing to go forward, evolve, and follow a higher path. As such, he represents evolutionary energy and innovation.

Shiva represents fearlessness. He is not afraid of anything, even death. He is not careless and does not expose himself to unnecessary risk, but he cannot be held back or intimidated by any threats. Shiva grants fearlessness to his devotees. Wild animals become gentle around him, and ghosts and spirits become calm and peaceful.

Shiva is independent and rests self-assured in his own nature. He is not dependent upon anyone or anything. He does not take anything from anyone, nor does he look down upon anyone. He does not cultivate dependencies, either for himself or for others. He is willing to stand alone against the entire world for a cause that he believes is right. Shiva is self-reliant and does not look for anyone to save or redeem him. He cultivates this self-reliance in his devotees and does not turn them into his dependents.

Shiva is the principle of self-confidence of the highest order, which is the confidence of being the Self and master of the universe, not simply that of being a strong or powerful person. Shiva does not need to accumulate property or power. He has the highest power of the Self of all, owning everything and nothing.

Shiva is cool in the colloquial sense of the term. He is not disturbed or thrown off balance by anything. He never loses his composure nor becomes hot headed regardless of circumstances. Through the inherent coolness of his mind he can handle the highest heat and lightning force of awareness and not be burned by it. Yet when necessary he can control or dissolve anything and project the hottest fire without burning himself.

Shiva is ever patient with the steadfastness of eternity. He is never in a hurry nor requires quick results. He bides his time as all time belongs to him. He knows how to wait and can act with great force when the appropriate and most efficacious moment for action arises. Yet he does not wait for others, he waits for his own right time of action. The value of Shiva is in enduring results, not in short term gains or displays.

Shiva is beyond all illusion. He has no desires or imaginations. He is not taken in by any schemes, advertising or propaganda. He cannot be lured by any fantasies or promises. He has no expectations, no opinions or preconceptions that can cloud his perception or judgment. He is ever clear and sees things as they are.

Shiva is not obsessed with himself. He knows how to observe others with detachment, extending to the entire universe. Shiva has no self-image. His Self-image is the entire universe. He sees himself in all beings and all beings in himself, as the *Upanishads* state.[22] The mind of Shiva is inherently contemplative, and has a space for all beings to be free and to be what they are, which is Shiva, ever happy and auspicious. Shiva is willing to be one with all at the level of the highest truth but does not seek to conform to anything externally. He goes his own way, not as an ego assertion, but as a return to the One Self of all. We can benefit by cultivating such attitudes of Shiva within our own lives.

Shiva, Time, Space and Beyond

We live in a universe defined by time and space at an outer level as the field of our experience, our action and our lives. Yet what we experience as chronological time or locational space through the senses are but surface views of a greater existence that we do not truly know. Time and space contain many dimensions, hold many creatures, worlds, eras and world-ages, interwoven into a tapestry that is immeasurable, without limit and full of consciousness.

Time is the breath, life or prana of the Universal Being that we call Shiva. Space is the mind or field of manifest awareness of Shiva. Just as we as individuals have our individual pranas and minds, to Lord Shiva belongs the universal prana and mind. Yet as the inner being or Self, Shiva transcends prana, mind, time and space altogether.

Shiva as Pure Being or the Supreme Brahman is the ultimate resort of all, the unchanging foundation. Behind all the cosmic principles, tattvas, elements, and gunas – however we may formulate them – remains the presence and power of Shiva. Shiva as the peace of Pure Being is the ultimate Tattva or truth principle behind all existence. Time, space, causation, and karma are but outer manifestations of Shiva and his diverse Shaktis. All worlds and creatures are his forms.

At the highest level, Shiva transcends all forms of number or determination. Shiva is sizeless, as the veritable *Upanishads* say, "smaller even than the atom and greater than the entire universe."[23] Shiva is timeless and holds eternity and all of time in the singularity of a mere instant. Shiva embraces us on every side, above and below, within and without, to the right and the left, from the smallest to the largest, in the moving and the static. He is the past, the present and the future and what is beyond all time. Shiva is full and perfect in every limited thing and yet more than the greatest that we can conceive.

The Reality of Space

The field of space in which we exist and act is a field of light and consciousness. We perceive objects that appear in the space around us, but seldom observe space itself. Though space is much greater than the objects that appear within it, we often ignore it altogether. We endow objects with various characteristics but regard space as devoid of qualities, as having little significance of its own apart from the objects that occur within it. We see life and intelligence as residing in embodied creatures, but do not attribute consciousness or life to space itself.

Yet space is important for both our bodies and minds. We have various spaces within our bodies, which hold prana and allow for energies to move. Our bodies are built around various hollow canals and spaces such as the gastro-intestinal tract. Space allows us to breathe, which is to take in the atmosphere around us. The channels in the body allow substances to come in and out of the body and link it with the world around us. There are spaces between the joints of the body in which prana can be held, which help us move.

Our sensory openings in the head are largely orifices, subtle spaces that provide room for impressions to enter the nervous system and brain. Each of our five senses helps us open out to the space around us, most notably the ears and the eyes. Our prana requires space in which to move.

The mind is formless like space in its appearance and action. The mind functions best when we have space in which to think and to observe. Our mind space is the key factor in our intelligence and in our psychology. There are spaces or gaps between our thoughts, through which we can contact the background space of the mind. There are gaps in our consciousness between the states of waking, dream, and deep sleep. Such junctures in space are points of transformation that can link to higher states of awareness. The dream world has its own space related to the space of imagination in the mind.

There are many forms of space in the external world, with caves and cavities in the Earth, currents in the space of the atmosphere, and various types of space between planets, stars and galaxies extending to the unlimited space beyond all manifestation. Space, whether external or internal, is not empty but holds various forces, waves and particles, some in a state of latency, others in invisible currents like the wind. We may not recognize these forces, as we do not regard space as important or real in itself.

Space is the prime reality of our world and our lives. Space embraces us on every side. Yet we seldom embrace space. We do welcome space at times and do not want to be cramped, limited, or put into a corner. Artists like to create a certain artistic space in which their creations can be produced and viewed. We like to have our space in life to expand, but a space in which to do or accumulate things, a defined space or territory, not an empty space. We seldom afford space any value of its own or recognize the sacred presence that permeates space. Yet space is one of the best ways that we can understand our true nature and Divinity as a whole. In the recognition of the power of space we can gain access to the Supreme Shiva.

Shiva as the Lord of Space

The presence of Shiva encompasses all space, and the highest space of consciousness is the presence of Shiva. Space is the body or field of energy for the manifestation of Shiva. This includes physical space, the space of prana, the space of mind, the cosmic space, and the unlimited immutable space of Brahman. The space of Shiva comprehends all things in the universe as a single place that can never be lost or forgotten. All beings and all events remain forever in the space of Shiva that is our universal home. Each one of us holds a different location or abode in the eternal space of Shiva.

Shiva is the great lord of space and grants space, freedom, and the full scope of movement to all. He abides everywhere behind everything and as the space between things. To perceive this unitary space is to know the presence of Shiva. The presence of Shiva is the supreme space of being, consciousness, and bliss, which underlies all forms of space. The face of Shiva can be found in everything and looks at us from everywhere as the beauty of space.

As space, Shiva is the highest heaven at the summit of the worlds. The highest world is the world of Shiva, from which he surveys all the worlds. Shiva is also the Supreme Space beyond all manifestation, even the highest heaven, from which he looks down upon all creation. Cosmic space is twofold as the pure space of consciousness beyond all manifestation, and as the space of the mind that holds all karmic patterns and seeds of creation and is the basis of manifestation from the higher to the lower worlds. Shiva envelops both types of space.

Shiva as space reflects a practical Yoga teaching. To realize Shiva, which is peace and presence, one need only create or make room for space, not merely physical space but the space of being and awareness. Such space is not a wall of separation but a link of consciousness. Wherever we go, we should create space, acknowledge space as sacred, and afford each creature its own space. This is to create the space of Shiva everywhere. We should observe and honor space, and not let our minds become limited by outer forms that are but colors or flowers arising from space.

To find Shiva we must create a space for Shiva to manifest. Whenever space is created, the power of Shiva naturally arises. Whenever a sacred space is created, Shiva must arise within it as the sacred presence of Being. Whenever a healing space is created, the healing power of Shiva as the universal Prana will become activated. Yoga is about developing higher forms of space inside ourselves, through which the cosmic forces can manifest.

The chakras from the root chakra to the lotus of the head are not simply locations in the body but centers in which we can experience subtler levels of space. Each chakra opens up another realm of space, another Loka or realm of vision. Make sure that your Yoga space, both inwardly and outwardly, is filled with the space of Shiva that can hold all things. To develop Yoga or the state of unity there must be a space that unites, which brings together not by removing differences but by affording them a common space to exist without friction.

Shiva as the Great Lord of Time

We experience time as past, present, and future primarily as our own birth, growth, decay and death. Time has its rhythms, seasons, and dance throughout all existence. We live in the movement of time that constitutes our lives, defined as our lifetime. Time is the great deity or cosmic power that we must all face and be humbled by in the end.

Yet if we look deeply, we see that time like space is a coordinate of the mind. If we slow down and concentrate our minds, we can slow time down, just as when we expand our perception of space we can make our world larger. The mind recognizes and measures time relative to the movement of objects in the external world or the development of energies in our own bodies. But if we turn our minds within, we find time will fade away as we silence our thoughts. Time and space exist relative to the seer who witnesses them. If our witnessing consciousness becomes complete, then we can witness all of time and space within ourselves.

In our deeper consciousness we witness time and space from a point of pure presence. All time can be defined as presence. The reality of the past is that it once was present. The reality of the future is that it will eventually become present. And the present moment occurs in an enduring presence. That timeless presence, which is the background of all time, is the eternal presence of Shiva. It is Shiva's time which is all time and beyond time.

Shiva represents eternal time, pure continuity, and endless duration. He is the immutable and changeless, the unperturbed silent witness of all. Shiva is present at every birth and at every death, giving blessings to all. He is ever equal and kind to everyone, great and small. Shiva ever abides as *Sadashiva*, always auspicious.

Shiva as eternal time is the energy that dances on the stage of Shiva that is infinite space. Time is the movement of space, the waves formed on the ocean of space, which is the dance of Shiva. The dance of time is Shiva's fiery dance of dissolution, his Tandava or dance of thunder, which also has its power to create, preserve and transform, as well as to ripen and mature.

Space and Time

Time and space are not different but constitute the active and passive, the expressive and receptive, the electrical and magnetic aspects of the same reality. Time consists of currents in space and space forms the background and latent energy of time. Space in motion is time and time at rest is space. In this regard, space is eternal and time is unbounded.

Space consists of sound or vibration, which is the seed of time. From that time-space vibration all mantras abide as the root ideas of the Cosmic Mind. Sound upholds space and imparts meaning to all existence. Sound creates time as the basic movement of the breath. From the unmanifest sound of space arises the manifest sounds of air, which is the movement of space. Out of the sounds of air all other sounds are created. The mind has its own special space that holds all words, sound and meaning.

The movement of space is the dance of the cosmic air or *Vayu*, from which the breath or Prana of Shiva arises. The breath of Shiva creates time, which is transformational movement in space. The mind is our inner space in which our own life-energy moves. Yet air and prana as the movement of space are also time. They create their own times and the lifetimes of both all creatures and all worlds.

Prana, Pranava, Akasha and Kala or primordial life energy, sound, space and time are ultimately one and intimately related as powers of consciousness. Each is a manifestation of the other. Each is contained within the other. And through mastering one, the others can be mastered. Time is a manifestation of space and carries the energy of Prana or the universal life. Time is the Divine Word or Pranava that directs the destinies and karmas of all creatures and all worlds. The energies of time, sound, and Prana are but the vibrations of space and one with it.

The power of time (Kala Shakti) is the Goddess Kali, who is the power of action (Kriya Shakti) in the universe bringing about the full unfoldment of the cosmic dance of Shiva. This original power of action does not simply promote any type of activity but energizes the evolution of consciousness. Kali is also the Prana

Shakti as the power of eternal life that overcomes all death and limitation. Kali is Shiva's own Shakti or the power of Shiva in his own nature, his ability to be himself. Kali is ultimately the timeless presence of the supreme space of Being into which everything is dissolved.

Shiva and Death

Our ordinary life that exists in the shadow of death is not a true life or real existence but a form of death and limitation, a condition in which our inner Self and soul remains in bondage. The life of Shiva that exists beyond death is the true life of the spirit, in which we go beyond the shackles of the body to a state of freedom that pervades all existence. We awaken from the dream of limited life to the reality of unlimited life and boundless intelligence.

Shiva is the great lord of eternity who takes us beyond death. He is the very death of death. For Shiva there is no death and no breath but only a continual Self-awareness of I am as a single existence. The key to going beyond death is to die while alive, which is to turn our prana, senses and mind within and merge them in our deathless Shiva Self.

Shiva is *Yama*, the God of death that controls all things. Yama is also the principle of Self-control that is the first of the eight limbs of Yoga. Yoga begins with a recognition of death and the arising of our inner search for immortality. Without death we would not be impelled to grow or strive or try to make the best possible usage of our time. Shiva is time that brings each creature to the completion of its life cycle. Time is the realm of our experience in which not only our body but also our soul grows, matures, and evolves. Time takes us beyond time as we grow in the spirit, if we accept the presence behind time that is the eternal Shiva.

Death is the great guru or teacher in the *Upanishads*[24] and many ancient texts. Only when we face the inevitability of our death are we willing to look into who we are and the meaning of our lives. Death is the power of cosmic negation, the great law of impermanence, which nullifies any separate value in the transient world and all that it contains. Death is the doorway to eternity, causing us to look beyond the fluctuations of time to a greater reality. To die while yet alive, withdrawing the mind, prana and senses into the spiritual heart is the way to become Shiva and live in Shiva forever.

Shiva, Causation and Karma

As ruling the power of time, Shiva governs the power of causation bringing about creation, preservation and dissolution, the birth, maturation, and death of all creatures and all worlds. This is the form of Shiva as *Maheshvara* or the cosmic lord, and his wife Durga as *Maheshvari*. As the cosmic ruler, Shiva looks over all phases of our lives and aids us in all transformations. He does this by conferring on us the inner peace that is the point of transformation at every juncture in time.

The causative power of time reflects the karmas of souls, creating the bodies and the worlds necessary for their experience. As Shiva dwells beyond karma, we can transcend our karma through the worship of Shiva.

Like other Vedic systems, Shaivism teaches us that the effect has no other reality other than that of the cause. A clay pot has no reality apart from the clay out of which it is fashioned. The pot is a form or appearance made from clay as its substance. A wave of the sea has no reality apart from the sea. So too, everything born of Shiva by way of name and form is ultimately Shiva in its nature and essence. When we move back from the created aspect of our nature to the power of creation and then to the uncreated essence, we merge back into the Supreme Shiva.

Shiva as Inner Time and Inner Space

Shaivism notes that time and space are but waves and rhythms of the eternal and infinite ocean of consciousness. Relativity must rest upon a greater reality and cannot exist of its own accord. Shiva is the sole reality behind the relative world. Behind our relative appearance of body and mind is our inner reality as Shiva, who holds all time and space in the singularity of his being.

Shiva dwells in inner time and inner space, which is sacred time and sacred space, time and space defined by Shiva or the state of peace. Sacred time is eternal or unending. Sacred space in infinite and indivisible. Inner time is the time created by Prana or the unitary breath. Inner space is the space contacted between thoughts by the meditative mind. We can only find the supreme truth if we create the space and time for it within ourselves, and a space and time that is sacred and aware. When space and time become sacred, space and time are dissolved into pure being and pure presence. All limitations and definitions fade away.

We must learn how to live in the time and space of Shiva, which alone can take us beyond time and space to a non-localized, non-chronological reality of pure experience. This is to embrace the sacred as our true existence and recognize our outer lives, their locations and events, as but episodes of the greater cosmic drama of transcendence.

We create the sacred time and space of Shiva by letting go, surrendering, and opening up to the inner presence that dwells behind all visible things. This takes us beyond all limitations of time, space and karma to the essence of all. We all struggle very hard in our lives, often for things that are not really good for us. Most of that struggle is unnecessary and only breeds sorrow. We can at any moment enter into the consciousness of Shiva and all will be bliss. Let us embrace all time and all space in the Supreme Shiva, and then even the changes and displacements of life will only give us greater wisdom and peace.

4. Shiva and the Descent of the Ganga

Part III

Shiva and Shakti:
The Dual Cosmic Powers

Reverence to the two Shivas, who are new and youthful, whose forms are intertwined with each other; the daughter of the mountain and he who rides the bull, reverence again and again to Shankara and Parvati!

Reverence to the two Shivas, who are the lords of the universe, the rulers of the universe and the two forms of transcendence.

Reverence to the two Shivas, who are the supreme healing powers, who are adorned by the five syllable mantra of *Namah Shivaya*.

Reverence to the two Shivas, who protect all creatures, whose hearts are bound to protect the three worlds, who are worshipped by all the deities. Reverence again and again to Shiva and Parvati!

Umamaheshvara Stotra

In this section we will examine Shiva and Shakti, the dual Cosmic Powers, their interrelationship, their Yoga, and how to approach them. Shiva and Shakti form the complementary powers of existence that underlie the greater universe of consciousness and bliss. We can find them behind our every thought, breath and word, as well as in every rhythm in time and nuance in space.

Shiva and Shakti:
The Cataclysmic Universe

We live in a dynamic universe shaped by powerful forces that are unpredictable, uncontrollable, and ultimately unknowable to the mind. In both our individual and collective lives sudden periodic changes occur of a cataclysmic nature that usher in new levels of manifestation, altering the equation of energies in a fundamental and enduring manner.

Though there are periods in nature and in human history during which little change appears to be happening externally, powerful currents are always working behind the scenes that will eventually – and often when least expected – emerge with great force and without regard for our personal or social well-being, sometimes wreaking havoc until a new equilibrium can be formed again. New paradigms and new eras are brought into being through the sudden dissolution of the old. Such quantum leaps in the movement of time are part of the nature of time itself.

On Earth we can observe many transformative forces through earthquakes, volcanoes, hurricanes, floods, and forest fires, which are usually occurring at some location on the planet at any given moment in time. The greater universe has numerous transformative events through black holes, quasars, collisions between galaxies, and collapse of stars, just to mention a few. The origin of the universe is attributed to the Big Bang – which is perhaps the ultimate such transformative event – with its own unknown antecedents that were dissolved to allow it to happen.

Modern science is aware of these transformative events and is developing a "cataclysmic" view of physics, life, and evolution, where sudden changes leave their mark upon long time cycles and are often the dominant forces in natural evolution. Human history is shaped by Ice Ages with quick and devastating onsets and endings, which includes major floods. Such a great world flood that raised ocean levels over three hundred feet marked the end of the last Ice Age some ten thousand years ago, from which our current cultures and civilizations gradually emerged, leaving what existed before difficult to determine and lost to our memory.

Transformative forces of nature are responsible for maintaining the cosmic order, which consists of powerful electrical currents that rest upon the proper state of balance. Should that state of balance be disrupted, these same forces when calm can cause radical reorientation and destruction. At key junctures in time, transformational forces naturally bring about major changes within the cosmic order, removing one status quo in favor of a new level of development that may be very different from what preceded it. This apparent disruption of the cosmic order is an inherent part of the cosmic order. Our own psyche is shaped not so much by the regular events of life as by unexpected and powerful changes, whether traumas, chance encounters, or sudden inspirations. A play of lightning forces circles our lives on all sides.

We can easily observe the cosmic rhythms that weave a continual play of transformation. The movement of day and night causes light and temperature patterns to vary in a significant manner within twenty-four hours. The movement of the seasons brings about dramatic changes of heat and cold often in a period of days. There is the process of our own birth, growth, maturation, decay, and death, which affects all embodied creatures.

All natural time cycles are marked by short phases of transformation, return, or revolution at various juncture points, in which the energy that has appeared to be in a steady state quickly and dramatically changes. Such juncture points, or *sandhis* in Sanskrit, include sunrise and sunset, new and full moons, solstices, eclipses, and longer astronomical time cycles. Most notable for the continuity of our own awareness are the daily junctures between waking and sleeping. Our own consciousness does not remain steady even for a single day, but must merge back into a latent state of unknowing in order to renew itself to continue.

Transformation may be upward or downward. The disease process, whether for body or mind, results from disrupting a positive state of balance, in which background conflicting forces come out in the form of toxins and disturbances. Diseases often manifest during the change of seasons, particularly from warm to colder weather. If we do not prepare for such changes of seasons, our health is likely to decline with their advent.

Such junctures as the points between inhalation and exhalation, or between one thought and another, hold a tremendous power for higher Yoga practices and can be used to direct our awareness upwards, if we concentrate our awareness there. We can learn to use the transformational points in our lives to help our energy ascend in a radical manner. Using points of natural transformation in a positive and conscious manner is perhaps the essence of Yoga.

We as human beings are but guests in a vast world that follows its own imperious laws, from minuscule time periods to eonic cycles. Nature does not function for our personal benefit, though it does contain many resources that can be beneficial to us if we learn how to use them in the right manner, with respect for their power and their periodicity. We must learn how to ride these waves of transformation rather than be swept away by them.

We must learn to understand the laws of nature, which are the "laws of Shakti," the irresistible universal Divine force and its indomitable will. We cannot expect laws that govern long natural time cycles through geological or astronomical forces to change in order to suit our transient needs in the short period of our human history. Our current twenty-first century is facing a stern reckoning with the powerful Shakti of the Earth that is bound to humble us, if not dramatically require that we reduce our numbers, before this century ends. We are servants of the cosmic order, and should not try to be its dictators.

We as human beings can carve out little islands of security for ourselves in which we can remain comfortable for many years, if not most of our lives. But there remains the changeable nature of life in terms of our decay and death at a physiological level, depressions and wars in society, and natural disasters that eventually wear down if not wash away our little islands altogether. If we learn to honor these great forces of time, and hold to the eternal essence of our own being, we can move through all such unpredictable changes, however potentially traumatic, with awareness, beauty and grace.

The Power of Shiva

This cataclysmic power behind the universe is the power of Shiva in manifestation. Shiva's power or "Shiva's Shakti" works to promote transformation, not merely dissolution or destruction. This usually requires upsetting the existing order or status quo and removing its inertia. If that existing order becomes rigid, it may have to be broken down altogether. If that order is adaptable, the Shiva power will be more a force of flowering and new growth.

Sometimes even the higher force works through conflict by placing opposing forces in close proximity in order to force them to work out their differences or perish. Such a clash or conflict of opposites occurs on many levels, though opposing forces can also form attractions and become complimentary as in reproductive processes.

We must recognize the supreme power of Shiva in order to find harmony with the greater universe of consciousness. One may designate that Shiva force by another name, but we cannot ignore or avoid the universal force of transformation, except at our own risk and peril. We are not in control of ourselves, our physiology, our society, nature, or the time cycles in which we live. The world and our own individual nature follow cosmic laws and cycles of transformation that we must adapt to, and understand as the working of our own deeper nature. We must be ready for transformation at every moment of life, being willing to let go of the past, cast away our identity, and embrace the currents of the great unknown and cosmic mystery. Each day should be such a transformative event or we are failing to truly live.

Meditation on Shakti

The following is a stage by stage meditation on Shakti in the universe that can help us understand our relationship and our ultimate identity with it.

- We are all confronted with a vast, marvelous and almost magical world appearance, particularly through the diverse forms of the world of nature. That appearance is full of change, dynamism, mystery, and hidden depth. We must recognize and honor this great creative display and its myriad unfoldments.

- Behind this vast world appearance is a secret power of unlimited proportions of which the realm of appearances, however extensive, is but a surface intimation. We must learn to intuit the presence and motivating power of this secret force behind what we see.

- There is a supreme power or Shakti of transformation (Parinama Shakti) behind the visible universe and its forces that is beyond all control, definition, or prediction. It is the higher will hidden behind the workings of nature. We must first honor this force, respect its wisdom, and recognize it as sacred. We should strive to align ourselves with its impetus and motivation, though we may not understand the design of how it operates.

- This supreme power of transformation that exists in nature also exists within us behind the dynamic and impulsive movements of our thoughts, impressions, and vital energies. We should recognize this universal power as the real driving energy behind our lives and learn where it is directing us at the deepest level, which may be different than where we personally wish to go.

- We as individual souls are a manifestation of the supreme power of transformation behind the entire universe, a play or dance of the highest Shakti. This universal power forms the synapses of our brains, the rapid movements of our sensory impressions, and our ability to communicate with thousands of words. It connects us with past and future lives, subtle currents and secret destinies.

- This same universal power of transformation dwells within our deepest core being as the Kundalini Shakti that can take us to higher levels of awareness, if we learn to awaken it within us.

- That supreme power of transformation or Maha Shakti in the greater universe is also our own inner Self-power and immortal pranic energy within our hearts.

- We are one with that supreme power or Shakti that is our true Self, for which our bodies and minds are but waves of perpetual change.

- All that the Supreme Power does throughout the universe is but a manifestation of our own deeper Self, its intelligence and guidance. We should align our outer life and action according to its inner direction.

- If we can consciously embrace this supreme power of transformation, the inner Divine force, it will guide us to our highest potential, the state of Self-realization and unity consciousness. We must learn to surrender to that ever dynamic Shakti in order to reach the quiescent state of Shiva that no change can disturb.

Shiva's Point of Power

Behind both the vastness of the apparent universe and the secret powers within it, is yet a greater presence and power of peace. From that supreme peace all powers emerge and hold their vitality. This place of peace is the stillness at the core of our being.

The entire dynamic universe rests upon a still point of pure energy and awareness, which never changes, and is never limited to the field of time and space. There abides within us that same point of changelessness and transcendence, which is the "still point of Shiva," like the eye of a hurricane at the core of our being. When the mind is still, Shiva is present as changeless, unbounded awareness, Self, and bliss, held in an all-pervading vibrating singularity.

This same still point endures behind the universe and pervades it at every level, supporting all transformation like the axis of a moving wheel. That changeless power of change is the unchanging nature of Shiva. Once we learn to hold to that still point we can maintain our peace and composure whatever disruption may be happening externally, from whatever source nature, deity or man.

Meditation upon the Still Point of Shiva

- Recognize the vast world appearance and its innumerable changes as an unlimited display of light.

- Recognize the deeper hidden force that both energizes all appearances and transcends them, the great Shakti, like a perpetual dance of lightning.

- Recognize the stillness of Shiva and the Supreme Brahman behind this supreme dynamic force, like the eye of a hurricane.

- Contact the point of stillness and balance behind the movement of your breath between inhalation and exhalation as one with this universal power.

- Contact the point of stillness behind the movement of your voice between speaking and listening as one with the universal power.

- Contact the point of stillness behind the movement your thoughts between learning and expressing as one with the universal power.

- Move into the ultimate point of stillness within your heart as the source of your mind, prana and speech, viewing all changes occurring within and around you as the changeless witness.

- Let everything in your field of awareness contract and dissolve into the infinitesimal point within the heart that is the ultimate origin and essence of all.

- Let that small point within the heart expand like the light of the sun to embrace the entire universe, all time and all space, beyond all boundaries.

- Hold to this immutable essence of your being throughout all the changes of life as your eternal Self. Do not be afraid of anything.

- Be the changeless being that initiates all necessary changes by being true to itself, and which needs nothing externally and need not even reveal itself.

Form is transformation, a movement in energy, a wave or vibration, not fixed objects. Transformation is ultimately a movement out of space and silence. Our outer nature of body and mind is a transformative manifestation rooted in a deeper awareness. The source of that transformative power dwells at the core of our being where no change can disturb us, where all transformations are but gentle movements in inner stillness and contentment. This is the true realm of Shiva in which we ever abide. We can step back into that realm of Shiva whenever we wish and wherever we wish, from any aspect of body and mind. It is ever present supporting all. To be Shiva is to hold to perfect peace that carries the supreme Shakti or the great universal force. By stillness within you can rule the universe and be master of all without any overt intention to do so.

Shiva and Shakti:
The Great Cosmic Duality

Duality is the dynamic of this vast and magical universe, which rests upon a myriad polarities, contraries and complementary forces. Duality is the prime power that generates energy and manifestation on all levels. Yet duality can lead to either conflict or to transformation depending upon how it is disposed. The highest dualistic forces are those that draw us back to the transcendent state of unity and peace. Shiva is present not only in that supreme unity of consciousness but also in the dualistic powers that arise from it, which consist of Shiva and his Shakti and their interrelated dance on all levels of existence.

There are many formulations of the dual powers behind the universe that different peoples have recognized over time, particularly traditional cultures that are close to nature and the Earth. The duality of Shiva and Shakti is perhaps the most important of these formations coming out of India and the best articulated. The Shiva-Shakti equation is clearly expressed and correlated in many ways, covering of all aspects of existence, personal and impersonal, manifest and unmanifest. The duality of Shiva and Shakti exists both within the universe and beyond.

- *Shiva at the first and highest level is the transcendent Absolute and Shakti is the inherent power of the Absolute to be what it is.* At this level, Shiva and Shakti are identical. Shiva is the immutable being of Brahman and Shakti is its immutable power. Both are merged into each other without any differentiation.

- *At the next and second level – from which the initial impulse of creation arises –Shiva represents the transcendent Being and Shakti sets in motion its power to create.* Shakti as the power of consciousness begins her own movement and develops the seed of creation from the reflection of Shiva as the Absolute.

In this development, Shakti rests upon Shiva as an active force upon one that is static or passive. Shiva here is the silent, immutable Absolute and Shakti is its expressive, ever changing manifestation in time and space. Shiva and Shakti at this stage represent the duality of the unmanifest and the manifest aspects of reality. Shiva is spirit and Shakti is nature. In this regard, without Shakti, Shiva has no movement, as Shankara notes:

> *Only when conjoined with Shakti does Shiva have the power to*
> *act. Otherwise the Great Lord is not even able to stir.*
>
> Shankara, Saundarya Lahiri,[25]

- *At the next and third level, there is the duality of Shiva and Shakti within the manifest universe*, with Shiva indicating the steady force and Shakti the dynamic power within the world movement. Shiva is the inherent stabilizing power that balances the creative activating power of Shakti. Shiva's presence is reflected as the being, soul, or person in the manifestation, which eventually becomes the individual creature, and Shakti is the becoming, life, or energy that it possesses.

Shiva becomes the ascending and expanding energy of creation, while Shakti becomes the descending and contracting energy that supports it. Shiva and Shakti take birth in their own creation in various ways from subatomic energies to supragalactic powers.

The entire universe is energized by the relationship between the two complimentary forces of Shiva and Shakti that exists on many levels and interpenetrate in many ways. There is an intricate play of Shiva and Shakti, with the Shakti within Shiva and the Shiva within Shakti. Each arises out of and returns to the other. It is not a rigid division but a dynamic interaction.

Cosmic Masculine and Cosmic Feminine Powers

It is perhaps easiest to understand with the duality of Shiva and Shakti as the Cosmic Masculine and Feminine powers of the universe – the great World Father and World Mother. The two are not simply biological forces, much less mere human energy, but a duality of cosmic powers on all levels, of which the sexual polarity arises as a biological counterpart.

Sexuality is the greatest polarity in the human mind and body, as well as in the biological kingdom. It is the basis of our birth and sustains the continuity of our species. It determines our physical structure, shapes our instinctual urges and emotional moods, and makes its mark strongly upon our character and personality. Sexuality dominates how we dress and is often the dominant subject that we think about or discuss. It is the foundation of our families and communities, extending into occupations and social roles. Yet sexuality is not just about procreation or pleasure. Sexuality has its deeper implications and intricacy in the realm of art and design. It has important correlations in psychic and spiritual energies and in our views of the Divine.

Sexuality reflects the Ananda or greater bliss energy behind life from which everything arises. It holds the greatest creative power, not only outwardly but also inwardly, if we can learn to redirect its power. It can reflect the highest aspect of the Shiva-Shakti relationship, which is one of love and ecstasy. The unity between Shiva-Shakti opposites, which arises from their mutual attraction, carries a portion of Divine bliss. Duality is thus ultimately the expression of a powerful and all-encompassing unity. There is ultimately no real conflict between opposing forces anywhere but a unity that holds each side of all dualities in a higher embrace.

Shiva and Shakti Correspondences

There are a number of ways that we can look at Shiva and Shakti energies. We can examine them according to electro-magnetic energies, geometrical patterns, elements, biological forces, rock formations, emotions, or higher states of consciousness. It is important to have a sense of their full range of implications. We will start at a simple level.

Shiva represents the unmoving point, the core or heart of the world. Shakti is the complimentary development of peripheral energy from and around it. Shiva is the still point and Shakti is the revolving wheel. Shiva is the center of the circle and Shakti forms its circumference. This duality applies at a transcendent level with Shiva as the immutable unmanifest and Shakti as the ever-changing manifest world. Yet this duality exists throughout all the forms and forces of nature as well and their circular movements.

We can observe this dual principle of center and circumference everywhere in the universe, starting with heavenly bodies like the Earth that both revolves on its own axis (its Shakti movement around its inner Shiva point) and yet also revolves around the Sun (its Shakti movement around its external Shiva point). In the universe every person or object is at one level a central point and at another level part of a revolution of energy around another central point beyond it. This is the Shiva within Shakti and the Shakti within Shiva.

We can recognize this Shiva-Shakti connection in the force of electro-magnetism. On one level, Shiva is the magnetic center or seat of power and Shakti is the electricity that arises as its power of action. On another level, Shakti is the magnetic power of love and attraction, and Shiva is the electric power of projection and assertion, like the female and masculine roles in nature. In the sky, the Shiva principle can be equated with the Sun as the source of light and illumination and the Shakti principle in the Moon that receives and reflects light and is also much quicker and more variable in its movement. Yet, at another level, Shakti is also the Sun as the power of heat and action and Shiva is the Moon as the power of silence and rest.

Relative to the elements, Shiva is primarily the power of fire, which is warming, ascending, illuminating, stimulating, and expanding. Shakti is primarily the power of water that is cooling, descending, nourishing, gathering, and contracting. Yet fire also has its Shakti force or power to burn, color and ripen. Water similarly has its Shiva force as its coolness and composure as in a calm lake.

We can observe this duality of Shiva and Shakti throughout the Earth, starting with the landforms on the planet. The Shiva principle is revealed by the mountain that represents stillness, expansion and ascending energy opening up to the sky. The Shakti principle is the complementary valley, mountain lake, mountain stream, or waterfall that represents dynamic and descending energy from the summits.

Relative to the kingdoms of nature, the Shiva principle of steadiness is represented in the rocks and the mineral kingdom. The honoring of sacred stones is primarily an aspect of Shiva worship. Shakti is represented by the plant kingdom with its dynamic effulgence of branches, leaves, flowers, and fruit.

However, there are Shakti ring stones, caves, crevices and grottos that have a descending energy, complimentary to the Shiva pillar stones that have an ascending force. There are Shiva plants like steady tall coniferous trees and Shakti plants like trees with abundant flowers, fragrance and fruit. Within a tree itself, Shiva is reflected in the root and trunk of the tree that hold it upwards. Shakti predominates in the branches, leaves, flowers and fruit which spread out.

On a biological level, Shiva as the male energy represents strength, warmth, steadiness, independence, and protection. Shakti as the feminine energy is receptivity, nurturing, adaptation, gathering and creativity. The male sexual organ with its erect and ascending force reflects a Shiva energy like the pillar. The female sexual organ with its capacity to receive and conceive represents the Shakti force like the ring stone. The ascending procreative power of the male, and the descending birthing power of the feminine are Shiva and Shakti formations.

All nature is a dance and interplay of Shiva and Shakti, with Shiva arising within Shakti and Shakti manifesting through Shiva. This art of Shiva-Shakti thinking requires a power of observation and adaptability of thought. It is not a matter of separate and distinct opposites but of a mutual dynamic, with shifting positions and contours. We cannot look at Shiva and Shakti in any fixed or final manner, but should understand their relative formations, energetics and transformations!

These same Shiva and Shakti forces work within our own psyche. Shiva is our inner being and Shakti is its creative and activating force. There is the Shakti side of the mind as expressive emotion and the Shiva side as reflection, reason and perception. Though emotion is usually a Shakti force and thought is a Shiva force, we can also have calm like Shiva emotions and electrical Shakti thoughts.

Shiva is the light of Prana and Shakti is its energetic movement. The ascending pranic or vital force called *udana* that governs will and effort is more a Shiva principle and the descending force called *apana*, which governs procreation and connects us to the Earth is a Shakti principle. Yet Shakti can also ascend as the power of will and Shiva can descend as the flow of grace.

The mind is more a Shiva force and speech, our main means of expression, is more a Shakti formation. Yet there are Shiva sounds like OM that are broad and ascending, and Shakti sounds like AIM that focus, descend and spread below. We will discuss these yogic factors in more detail in later chapters of the book.

Below is a table representing prime dualities of Shiva and Shakti on various levels. These are merely suggestive and not exhaustive, as the two forces are interwoven on various different levels.

Shiva and Shakti Principles

Shiva	Shakti
Light, Prakasha	Lightning, Vidyut – Vimarsha, deliberation
Being – Sat	Bliss – Ananda
Consciousness – Chit	Chit-Shakti - creative force
Self – Atman	Atma Shakti, character
Person – Purusha	Purusha Shakti, charisma
Shaktiman – will	Shakti – executive force
Eternal, timeless being	Power of time and transformation
Infinite space	Power inherent in space
Male Principle	Female Principle
Father	Mother
Symbols and Manifestations	
Linga, upholding ascending force	Yoni, supporting, nourishing, descending force
Center, point	Periphery, circle
Upward pointed triangle	Downward pointed triangle
Clear Light	Color, particularly red
Heaven, Dyaus	Earth, Prithivi
Sun, Surya – Mars	Moon, Chandra – Venus
Fire, Agni	Water, Apas
Mountain	Waterfall, Valley
Ocean	River
Rock, mineral	Plant
Tree	Herb, flower, grass
Trunk or root of tree	Branches, leaves, flowers
Manifestations in the Individual (Adhyatma)	
Presence of Prana	Power of Prana
Prana, Udana – ascending force of Prana	Apana – descending force of Prana
Yoga Purusha	Yoga Shakti
Mind, meditation	Speech, mantra
Crown chakra	Root chakra
Soma, Amrita	Kundalini
White bindu	Red bindu
OM	AIM, HRIM
Vowels	Consonants

5. Ardhanareshvara, Yogeshvara, Nataraj

Shiva and Shakti Yogas

Yoga means unification, which is first the unity of all the dualities and contraries that constitute the energies of life. Yoga philosophy teaches us to understand and transcend duality, but this rests upon harmonizing the dualities within us in a transformative state of balance.

Shiva and Shakti as the dual cosmic principles are an intrinsic part of all Yoga, which constitutes a natural process of integration and transformation. Recognition of the cosmic duality leads us into the practice of Yoga, which is their unification. All Yoga is a development of Shiva awareness and Shakti energy, the state of the seer and its energy of seeing, drawing the dual forces from their lower manifestations in the realm of division to their higher reality in pure Oneness.

The philosophy of Shiva and Shakti reveals the truth principles (dharmas), energies, and potentials of all creatures and all worlds. It is a system of higher knowledge rooted in the Cosmic Mind.

- Shiva is pure Being and Shakti is its power of becoming on all levels.
- Each world has its Shiva nature, its Self or Spirit, and its Shakti power or energy movement.
- Each creature has its Shiva nature or inner Self and its Shakti or diverse manifestation.
- Each one of us has our underlying Self or Shiva factor and our outer expressions through body and mind or Shakti factor. Shiva and Shakti form the Being and power of the individual soul.

Shiva is Being or the inherent reality that ever is what it is. Shakti is the power of action or doing arising from it. Shiva is beyond all action, while Shakti is its power of action on all levels. Being or the Divine presence has a tremendous power to act when the moment is appropriate, which is the expression of its Shakti. Shiva is the underlying unmanifest reality and Shakti generates its outer appearance.

Yet this duality of Shiva and Shakti, or being and action, occurs within the manifest realm as well. Every substance has its underlying essence or reality that is unchanging like the wetness of water, and its manifest relativity like the waves through which water moves.

Shiva is reality, that which is ever enduring, while Shakti is relativity, that which is ever fluctuating, arising and returning to the real. Shiva is unitary reality or common ground of being while Shakti is the web of multiplicity, relativity, relations, or interdependence that arises from its manifestation. Every aspect of the universe has a complementary duality of Being and its Power of Becoming.

Being and Power of the Three Lokas

Each Loka or realm of existence has its primary principle, being, light or Shiva factor and its manifestation, energy or Shakti factor.

- Shiva is the fire that exists on Earth as its Shakti or field of manifestation.
- Shiva is the lightning that exists in the atmosphere as its Shakti or field of manifestation
- Shiva is the Sun that exists in heaven or space as its Shakti or field of manifestation.

Being and Power of the Five Koshas or Five Sheaths

Each of the five *koshas* or five coverings of the soul has its primary level of being as its Shiva factor, and its different energies and power of action as its Shakti factor.

- The physical body or "food sheath" (annamaya kosha) has its overall coherence through the brain and nervous system as its Shiva factor and its diverse processes, organs or system as its Shakti.
- The energy body or "pranic sheath" (pranamaya kosha) has its ruling Prana as its Shiva factor and its diverse pranic activities through the breath, motor organs and nadis as its Shakti.
- The mind or "mental sheath" (manomaya kosha) has its ruling power of attention as its Shiva factor and its diverse sensory activities as its Shakti.
- The intelligence or "knowledge sheath" (vijnanamaya kosha) has its ruling power of discrimination as its Shiva factor and its diverse determinations and decision-making actions as its Shakti.

- The "bliss sheath" (anandamaya kosha) has its ruling power of peace and contentment as its Shiva factor and its diverse experiences of joy as its Shakti.

Being and Power of the Five Elements

Each of the five great elements has its basic nature, state of existence or Shiva factor and its diverse qualities, actions and expressions or Shakti factor.

- Shiva is reflected in the nature of the earth element as dense and steady like the mountain, with Shakti as its movement or action through Earth currents and earthquakes, and its inherent power to hold and support.

- Shiva is reflected in the nature of the water element as wet and fluid like the ocean, with Shakti as its movement through rivers, streams and rain, and its power to moisten and nurture.

- Shiva is reflected in the nature of the fire element as hot and luminous, with Shakti as its movement through various types of fire and light from the core of the Earth to the stars, particularly fire's power to burn.

- Shiva is reflected in the nature of the air element as light and mobile, with Shakti as its movement through the wind and other currents, and its power to stimulate.

- Shiva is reflected in the nature of the ether element as clear and light, with Shakti as its movement through sound and light, and its power to permeate and pervade.

Being and Power of the Eight Limbs of Yoga Practice

Each aspect of Yoga has a Shiva factor or being and an action or Shakti. The movement of Yoga is to merge Shakti back into Shiva. Generally the state of Yoga is Shiva, while the methods and practices of Yoga are Shakti.

- The yamas and niyamas or yogic principles and observances serve to cultivate a calm Shiva awareness and a corresponding Shakti force of self-control.

- Shiva is reflected in the stillness of the asana, with Shakti as the power to perform it and the energy that arises from it.

- Shiva is the nature of the Prana in its state of control or balance, with Shakti as the power to develop it. Yet overall pranayama is more a Shakti or energizing practice.

- Shiva is the principle of withdrawal or pratyahara, and Shakti the action of internalizing our energy. Yet overall pratyahara is more a Shiva or calming practice.
- Shiva is reflected in the concentrated mind, and Shakti is the directed power of concentration.
- Shiva is the meditative mind and Shakti is the power of meditation.
- Shiva is the state of absorption or samadhi and Shakti is its power of bliss.

Alignment of Shiva-Shakti

Yoga consists of the proper alignment, balance and union of the Shiva and Shakti energies within us on all levels. The more we hold to Shiva or stillness within, the stronger, higher, and subtler our Shakti or energy level naturally becomes. For example, the greater our capacity to dwell in the state of Being, the greater our capacity for transformative action in the outer world becomes and higher planes of manifestation will be revealed to us.

Shiva is the state of balance; and Shakti is the energy of transformation that naturally arises from it. The state of balance is not a mere neutral zone, like a scale held static between equal weights on either side. Whenever we reach a state of balance, the energy is naturally taken to a higher level. There are many such points of balance or equilibrium that we can cultivate in Yoga, whether it is a still asana, relaxation of the breath, or meditation and equipoise of the mind.

The path of spiritual growth does not mean to deny Shakti in favor of Shiva, but to align Shiva and Shakti together in the fullest possible manner. That affirms the essence of both Shiva and Shakti. The highest Shakti is abidance in the state of the Supreme Shiva. The still point of the Absolute, that is Shiva, naturally unfolds the full manifestation of Shakti that is the entire universe.

Shakti creates all things through the presence of Shiva. All her creations are manifestations of qualities inherent within Shiva. Shiva meanwhile is the essence or inner nature behind Shakti, not a separate principle. In our outer manifestation, we are Shiva and Shakti under limitation, with a limited understanding of Self and a limited capacity for creative action. In our inner nature ,we are Shiva and Shakti unbounded, with an unlimited understanding and unlimited capacity for creative action.

Shaktis of the Supreme Shiva

The Supreme Shiva has its special primary powers or Shaktis. The first is *Sat-Shakti*, the power of Sat or pure Being. The power of Shiva to be what he is. From that root Sat-Shakti five higher Shaktis manifest.

1. Chit-Shakti, the power of consciousness that carries the light of Shiva withdrawn into itself.

2. Ananda-Shakti, the power of bliss that reflects the nature of Shakti as the supreme creative force.

3. Iccha-Shakti, the power of will that gives ruling power to Shiva as the lord of all.

4. Jnana-Shakti, the power of knowing on all levels, that is the basis of the higher mind and intelligence in creatures.

5. Kriya-Shakti, the power of transformative action, including the Yoga Shakti, spiritual practices and the unfoldment of Kundalini.

The last three Shaktis form a triad of "Iccha, Jnana and Kriya" or "Will, Knowledge and Action" that develop in an integral manner and are reflected in the functions of various deities. They are the three manifestations of Shakti as Ananda, which is the cause of all manifestation. Shiva and Shakti Yogas work to manifest these higher powers of Shiva, through which our Shiva nature is revealed.

Will, knowledge and action also refer to Shiva as the experiencer (will), Shakti as the experience (knowledge), and the universe as the object of experience (action). They are also Shiva as the seer (will), Shakti as the power of seeing (knowledge), and the object seen (action). They form the three aspects of Shiva's triangle or Trishula his threefold spear, weapon or trident.

Shaktipat – Descent of Shakti as Grace

Both Shiva and Shakti Yogas rest upon *Shaktipat*, the descent of the power of Shakti as an awakening force to take us to Shiva as higher awareness. Shaktipat brings the energy required to guide us to Shiva consciousness, which is also the highest power of Shakti.

Shaktipat or the awakening of Shakti can occur in several ways. It can be directly transmitted by the guru to a receptive disciple by a glance, a touch or a thought. Sometimes this occurs in dream or in meditation and does not always require the physical proximity of the teacher. Shaktipat can also arise as a result of dedicated Yoga practice by the student. It can come through the good karma of previous births. It can be awakened through special pilgrimages, rituals, or even by a spontaneous descent of grace.

Shaktipat awakens the Yoga Shakti, the inner power of Yoga. The Yoga Shakti is a power of aspiration, allowing the individual to make efforts beyond what is normally possible. Yet it is also a descent of grace allowing the individual to access higher powers. The two go together. The greater the ascending power of aspiration; the greater will be the complementary descending flow of grace.

The Yoga Shakti is an electrical force of consciousness connected to the Kundalini. This subtle energy has the ability to develop our higher faculties, open the chakras and enlighten the mind. Without it, we are like a person trying to use electrical equipment without any electricity flowing to run them. Yet when the Yoga Shakti flows we can also work with that power directly and may not need to work with it indirectly through methods or techniques.

A guru dwelling in the state of Shiva consciousness or in contact with the Supreme Shakti can pass on the power of Shakti. Yet even a lesser teacher can pass on whatever degree of Shakti he or she may have realized. But this depends also upon the nature and level of the disciple. Shaktipat like artistic inspiration can be stimulated by contact with the teacher, but cannot be passed on by his mere physical presence.

Sometimes there are attempts to pass on Shaktipat to a group or en masse. Some individuals may receive something in the process. Others may, however, become disturbed because if they are not receptive to the higher force, it can irritate their minds and nervous system. Shaktipat is best done on an individual basis, as and when the need and possibility arises, or at special sacred times during the year.

The highest Shakti is transmitted in a spontaneous, unpremeditated and natural manner, like sharing of feelings of love or devotion. It cannot be owned, named, controlled or commercialized. Tantric Yoga does have formal practices of initiation and transmission of Shakti, but such general rules are guidelines that cannot be applied literally or mechanically.

Shakti is always *Svatantra* or independent. She moves where and when she wills. We must be receptive to her sacred power to receive her flow of grace. Shakti is not a force that we can personally direct, but we can ourselves learn to become a vessel for her current to flow.

Shiva-Shakti Yoga

Yogic approaches can follow primarily a Shiva orientation or what could be called *Shiva Yoga*, or a Shakti approach or what could be called *Shakti Yoga*. Or they can combine the two to various degrees as *Shiva-Shakti Yoga*. Generally Shiva and Shakti Yogas always go together to some degree. Shakti takes us to Shiva as her goal. Shiva unfolds Shakti as his power of guidance and grace.

This current book on Shiva aims primarily at a presentation of Shiva Yoga. Shakti Yoga is a topic that I have taken up in previous books relative to the different forms of the Goddess.[26] Shakti Yoga consists primarily of Yoga practices of pranayama, mantra and meditation relative to different forms and energies of the Goddess as discussed in Tantric teachings like *Sri Vidya*, *Dasha Mahavidya* (Ten Wisdom Forms of the Goddess), or *Devi Mahatmya*. Here we will examine the main factors behind Shiva and Shakti Yogas overall.

Shiva Yoga cultivates such Shiva-based qualities, attitudes, and energies as steadiness, stillness, peace, and quiescence. It emphasizes inaction, withdrawal, and silence, not as the mere cessation of energy but as its internalization for transformation. *Shiva Yoga is primarily a Yoga of being Shiva, rather than of doing something to arrive at the state of Shiva.* This allies it primarily with Jnana Yoga or the Yoga of Knowledge as a cultivation of awareness, inquiry and insight, rather than technique, method or practice. It often follows a path of world negation, renunciation or hermitage in nature. Relative to practices and techniques, Shiva Yoga involves working with Shakti as the power of action, particularly relative to Raja Yoga. Shakti is the power and process of Shiva Yoga.

Shakti Yoga cultivates Shakti energy as transformation, play, and expression. It works through creativity, bliss, and ecstasy extending into all forms of art and culture. It is primarily a Yoga of awakening the Shakti within us and letting the flow of Shakti guide us on our path. Shakti Yoga employs a variety of techniques, practices, images, and actions but emphasizing the inner energy over the outer form. Shakti Yoga does not always have fixed forms or fixed techniques, but emphasizes the adaptation of form according to and force that ultimately resides beyond all forms. It proceeds more through inspiration than through technique, though it may employ many methods. The formless inner orientation of Shakti Yoga is its Shiva point or Shiva bindu. Most forms of Hatha Yoga and Tantric Yoga have a strong Shakti orientation.

Shiva Yoga often follows the way of Self-inquiry, similar to Advaita Vedanta, diving directly into the transcendent reality of Shiva within the spiritual heart as the unitary truth. It can also develop through a devotional surrender to Shiva as the Divine essence of all.

Shakti Yoga works more through energetic techniques of Kundalini Yoga, Kriya Yoga and Mantra Yoga, as the Goddess herself is the power behind the Kundalini. It also proceeds through a devotional surrender to Shakti in various forms of the Goddess or Divine Mother.

Shakti is the way to Shiva, so Shakti Yoga or union with Shakti takes us to Shiva Yoga or union with Shiva. Shakti Yoga leads us to the state of Shiva awareness, while Shiva Yoga leads us to absorption in the highest Shakti or inherent power of Pure Being itself. As the energy of Shakti unfolds, it will take us to the state of total transformation that is the stillness of Shiva. Yoga practice is a type of empowerment or development of Shakti to take us to pure consciousness, pure light, or the state of enlightenment that is Shiva. Shiva is the Lord of Yoga, and Shakti is his power of Yoga practice.

All Yoga is ultimately Shiva-Shakti Yoga. Shiva and Shakti are present together in every aspect of existence, pervading and reflecting one another on every level. Once we recognize this all life becomes Yoga for us.

Transcendence and Descent

There is yet another way to look at Shiva and Shakti Yogas. Shiva Yoga aims at developing a direct path to transcendence and the realization of the Supreme Shiva. It sacrifices and offers everything into the fire of Shiva, giving up all other thoughts, desires, and aspirations. The simplest way is to go directly to the Supreme Shiva as one's true Self beyond all duality through the Yoga of Knowledge.[27] This is to understand oneself as Shiva. Another method is to surrender to the Supreme Shiva as the ground of all existence through the Yoga of Devotion.

As Shiva Yoga aims at a direct ascent to the Supreme Shiva for individual Self-realization, Shakti Yoga aims at the descent of Shakti as energy, grace, or wisdom in order to uplift the world and fulfill the Divine will in creation. Shakti

Yoga aims at bringing a Shakti or power of higher evolution into the world in order to uplift humanity and to reduce ignorance and sorrow in the world. It does not aim so much at individual liberation but at world transformation.[28]

Yet these two ascending and descending aspects of Shiva and Shakti Yoga also go together. The great gurus who have realized the Supreme Shiva also work to bring a higher Shakti in the world for the upliftment of humanity. This action can take many forms including teaching, writing, establishing schools, healing centers, or promoting positive trends in society. It can work through various Yoga Shaktis as *Vidya Shakti* (power of knowledge), *Prema Shakti* (power of love), *Tapas Shakti* (power of practice), or teaching and charity at an outer level. It can even proceed in silence and meditation and need not necessarily rely upon external institutions.

Shiva demands the highest knowledge beyond the world, but Shakti also requires that we work to uplift the creation that is her manifestation. Shakti demands that we take care of her children, and all creatures, however high or low, good or bad, are her offspring! *Once we realize our inner Shiva nature, we must also accept our responsibility to promote transformation in the realm of Shakti.*

Yet we should always hold to Shiva inwardly while working with Shakti outwardly. Shiva is the inner being, whereas Shakti is the natural power of transformation that we must let work through us. True Shakti accomplishes everything brilliantly without departing from the Shiva state of peace, stillness, and contentment. Shakti guides us to develop the highest human and spiritual culture, which is "the culture of Shiva."

 The true guru always has a higher knowledge that leads us to transcendence, but complemented by a sharing of that knowledge to raise the consciousness of humanity. We should pursue the knowledge of Shiva but not forget the action of Shakti. We should seek to know ourselves at an individual level but work for the good of the entire universe in our outer expression.

All Yoga is a play of Shakti, with Shiva as the goal and witness of the process. All culture is also a play of Shakti – whether art, music, dance, poetry, or philosophy. Bondage and liberation are a play of Shakti, who rules over the individual soul in its outer manifestation through the cycle of rebirth, while Shiva is the soul in his true nature that can never be bound. Yet the highest Shakti is also never bound and that power of freedom can always be directly accessed as the fundamental energy of our Shiva Self.

Assert yourself as the Supreme Shiva and the Self of all! Assert yourself through the Supreme Power that is beyond all outer needs and expectations, resting complete in its own nature. Assert your true Self, not your limited ego that needs the approval of others. This willingness to embrace the Shakti of Shiva is the prime principle of Shiva-Shakti Yoga. The inner Shiva power takes us to pure transcendence. Its Shakti allows all possible transformation and evolution of higher awareness in the universe.

6. Shiva Linga 1

The Shiva Linga:
Symbol of Transcendence

There are many hidden sacred powers in nature, from deep earth currents to the vast vibrations of space. The forces that make up the universe reflect broader cosmic laws and subtle processes of consciousness. Nature's patterns and formations reveal the play of Shiva and Shakti, consciousness and its creative power, in their wondrous myriad interactions. These are the basis of geological and biological energies on Earth as well as the heavenly powers beyond.

Shaivite philosophy is part of the greater system of *Tantra* that teaches us how to understand the energies behind the universe, extending to the highest Self-awareness. Tantra as a term refers to the weaving of cloth, and by implication means a "design" or "network." Tantra's vast array of teachings addresses the whole spectrum of forces that weave the patterns of our lives.

Tantric teachings help us understand the design of the universe on all levels of matter, energy, mind, and consciousness, including how these are linked together in a single fabric. These universal patterns extend to subtle and to causal or archetypal levels, shaping both the visible and invisible worlds.

Such primal energy patterns are mirrored in the forms and forces of nature, starting in the gestalt of fractal designs that can be found behind outer phenomena from snowflakes to gem crystals. They are part of a universal sacred geometry that extends to the chakras or energy centers of the subtle body that shape our minds and bodies from within. If we can change the deeper energy patterns behind the forms that we see, we can alter the nature of the reality we experience – and transform ourselves. There is a blueprint of forces in the Cosmic Mind that we can learn to work with in order to facilitate a higher evolution of consciousness in the world.

Linga and Yoni: Ascending and Circulating Energies

The two ultimate design forms in the universe according to Shaivite thought are the *linga* and the *yoni* as the primary ascending and descending, still and moving, progressing and circulating patterns of interdependent forces throughout all existence.

Linga is a Sanskrit term meaning a "mark" or a "determinative factor," the "chief characteristic" of an object, like the burning power of fire or the wetness of water, through which we can conclusively identify it. Yoni refers to the origin, source, or womb – the field in which an object comes into being and sustains it throughout its existence.

The linga represents the power of Shiva as stillness, fullness, expanding and ascending force, drive, and motivation. The yoni is the power of Shakti as movement, emptiness, contracting, and descending reflection and reception. The union of the linga and the yoni generates power and brings all things into manifestation. These two primal forces pervade all of nature and underlie all other forces. The linga has the power to fill and pervade. The yoni has the power of emptiness and holding. They are the positive and the negative, the reverse and the compliment of each other.

The linga has a special connection with the *bindu,* still point or particle, and the yoni with *nada* or the moving wave. The bindu point expands as a circular sphere, like that of the Sun, and becomes a linga, forming a pillar like force in its constant revolution. The linga by its power releases the bindu or drop as its expression. It presses the essence out of things. Yet the circular field is also the yoni, which has the ability to receive and hold that essence.

The yoni is sustained by the nada or vibratory force. The yoni is a force field with a magnetic nature to attract, hold, nourish, and gestate. The bindu in the nada, or the point crest of the wave, is the linga in the yoni. It is the steady focus that sustains the greater force field. The yoni is the nada or wave in its transcendent form and becomes the bija or seed of manifestation at a lower level.

The linga and yoni resemble an electrical power generator, with the linga as the power-generating pillar or rod rooted in the Yoni as the support basin and surrounded by the coils of Shakti that arise from the yoni.

Types of Shiva Lingas

Shiva is represented by a Shiva linga as the main geometrical symbol of Shiva, which comes in various forms suggesting ascending and expanding power. The linga is used for the worship of Shiva along with or instead of an image, statue, or representational form.

The Shiva linga is not just an Indian design form; it is one of the main archetypal patterns in the universe, with different appearances throughout nature, in the human being, and in the cosmic mind. As representing the characteristic feature in each thing in the universe, we cannot reduce the linga to one formal representation only. Similarly, as representing the field of manifestation for each object in the universe, the yoni also has innumerable forms and aspects.

The different types of Shiva lingas reflect an ascending energy or power of illumination like a ray of light. We can generally divide Shiva lingas into several shapes as circular, conical or triangular. Lingas can be naturally formed as in certain rocks, mountains, or plants. They occur as forces in nature like the Sun and the Moon. They can be man made, reflecting an inner artistic vision of their cosmic power. Lingas can have geometrical designs. They can be three-dimensional or two-dimensional, or they can be visualized internally. Generally, most Shiva lingas used for worship are made of stones or gems.

Many Shiva lingas are placed along with a base or a ring stone that reflects the Shakti yoni, Shakti's magnetic matrix. Complementary to the ascending Shiva force is a descending Shakti energy as a downward pointed triangle, valley, or altar in the ground. Such designs indicate the union of the linga and the yoni or Shiva and Shakti energies.

Some Shiva lingas resemble the male sexual organ and many people look upon the linga as a phallic symbol. A careful examination shows that Shiva lingas cover a wide range of energies and symbols. We find linga like designs in flowers, crystals, and atomic structures.

Throughout history, many cultures have created artistic and religious forms of standing stones, pyramids, pillars, and obelisks that indicate an honoring of the cosmic Shiva and Shakti forces. Hindu temples reflect the upward Shiva energy in their pyramidal and conical forms. Even the spires and minarets of churches and mosques reflect an ascending force that reminds us of Shiva energy.

Shiva Formations in Nature

We can identify lingas according to their different natural formations.

Round Shiva Linga

The round shape is common in nature. Round types of Shiva lingas occur in heavenly bodies, like the Sun and the Moon, but many other levels as well, including in flowers and in the shape of our own eyes. Round Shiva lingas relate to the bindu or primordial point.

Spiral Forms

The spiral represents another form of Shiva linga, particularly as a rising spiral of energy. It is an extension of the round form and is created by spheres in movement. The spiral shape shows the dance of Shiva and Shakti as the central point of Shiva and the evolving periphery or circumference of Shakti. Spirals are common in nature from water vortexes and seashells to spiral galaxies.

Mountain Forms

All mountains, with their ascending shapes, are natural Shiva lingas, particularly steeper pillar and pyramid shaped peaks. Mountains may contain special rock formations within them that are Shiva lingas. These include cliff faces and boulder fields. Yet some mountains are feminine in nature, resembling more the faces of or the breasts of women and are Shakti formations. The most famous Shiva mountain, which appears like a giant crystal, is Mount Kailas in Tibet, the legendary home of Shiva and Shakti.

Canyons

Canyon lands and desert landscapes with their mesas and large outcroppings of standing rocks are another natural type of Shiva linga. Notable in this regard are the canyons of the Southwestern United States extending to the Grand Canyon. There are similar natural pillar like rock formations in many regions in the world that carry a Shiva energy.

Rock Forms

Shiva rocks can be found in the ground or can occur on the ground. Certain rocks carry a special divine Shiva energy even if they are not large in size. Notable are Shiva linga like rocks found in various rivers in India, notably the Narmada River in the center of the country. These are sculpted by water giving them a special conical form that can carry the energy of Shiva. All river rocks contain some Shiva linga type stones. Yet Shiva rocks may be pyramidal shape stones in the ground.

Cave Forms

Stalactites and stalagmites, upward and downward facing rock formations and caves are among Mother Nature's most marvelous Shiva lingas. There are many such cave formations throughout the world.

The famous Amarnath Ice Linga in Kashmir is one of the most important Shiva pilgrimage sites in India, with a linga in a cave formed by ice alone, not a stone formation. Ice caves occur in several countries, like the famous ice caves in Austria. Yet the cave itself is a yoni or field of Shakti.

Gem Forms

Gems and crystals with their ascending shapes carry a special Shiva energy. There are many important crystal Shiva lingas in Hindu temples like the one in the Hinduism Today temple in Hawaii, one of the largest crystals in the world.[29] We now understand that crystals have powers of healing and communication as in their usage in the computer world. We can work with their energies at a psychic and yogic level to connect with the cosmic powers.

Plant Forms

Trees

All trees are forms of Shiva and reflect his ascending energy. Tall straight trees like the Deodar (Himalayan Cedar) or Redwood carry a strong Shiva energy. This extends to many conifer species. Tropical Ficus or fig trees like the Banyan hold a strong Shiva energy as well. In ancient Europe it was the sacred oak tree that was regarded as holding the strongest power. We also find Shiva forms in palm trees and in fern trees (cycads). Some trees hold womb like openings in their base like Shakti yonis. Others have outcroppings of roots that have linga like forms. Sacred groves also relate to the Shiva energy, particularly when there is one central dominant tree.

Flowers

The stamen of the flower indicates the central Shiva principle, which is formed around the pistil and ovary as the female aspect of the plant. The petals also represent the differentiating Shakti principles. Flowers serve to draw astral energies into the physical realm and carry strong Shiva and Shakti energies. Five-pointed flowers like dhatura are especially sacred to Shiva, as are flowers that are dark blue in color.

Animal Forms

Animal forms of the linga are indicated in the male sexual organs, with the yoni in the female organs. The horns of animals are another type of Shiva symbol.

Shiva in his ancient depictions is often presented as having horns, as are various other pagan deities.

Five Element Forms

There are special Shiva linga forms for all the five elements.[30]

Earth Linga	Mountains, rocks, trees
Water Linga	Crest of waves, waterfalls, ice lingas
Fire Linga	Rising flames, volcanoes, the Sun
Air Linga	Thunderclouds, lightning, rising smoke and incense
Space Linga	Space and the light forms that occur within it

Note that northeast is the main direction sacred to Shiva.

Light Forms

All light forms are types of Shiva lingas starting with the four main light forms of the Sun, Moon, Fire and Lightning. These exist not only in nature but also in the psyche.

Sun	Surya linga	Golden	Round, spiral
Moon	Soma Linga	White	Round, spiral
Fire	Agni Linga	Red	Upward facing triangle
Lightning	Vidyut Linga	Silver	Like a lightning flash

There are twelve *Jyotir Lingas* or "lingas of light" worshipped at twelve famous temples in India. These are usually made of rock, precious stones or crystals said to carry the light of Shiva. They are not actually lingas made of light.

Sound Forms

Shiva energy relates to the rhythm of the drum which holds a similar masculine force as the rock Shiva lingas. But ascending waves of sound produced in a number of ways can create a Shiva effect upon the mind. Mantras like OM convey a Shiva energy, as we have already noted. OM is the *Mantra Linga* of Lord Shiva.

Shiva Linga Forms in Temples

Most common in Hindu temples is the main conical linga form with the yoni base. This is worshipped in many temples. Some smaller shrines may just have a single linga. Certain temple complexes may contain many smaller shrines, each with its own linga. Linga shrines may be built over the buried body of a great yogi or enlightened sage.

These are often made of crystals or other gems, or rocks made into such shapes. Such are the famous rock Shiva lingas that occur naturally in rivers, particularly from the Narmada River in Central India. Many Hindu temples have Shiva lingas as natural rock forms coming out of the ground, some pyramidal like a mountain, others more conical.

Yantras and Geometrical Forms

Shiva Yantras

Yantras are special geometrical design forms. Yantras may be worshipped externally like representational forms. They can also be visualized internally as the energy body of the deity. Yantras are usually empowered by mantras and visualized along with them. Statues or lingas may contain special yantras at their base. Yantras also reflect the Shiva linga.

Triangular Forms

Shiva energy is reflected in upward facing triangles and connected to Fire. Triangles are common in nature and represent the unity behind all dualities, as well as the dynamic force that arises through their union. The ascending triangle reflects the Fire linga of Lord Shiva. The downward pointed triangle is the water vortex or yoni of the Devi.

The six-pointed star, containing both an upward pointed and a downward pointed triangle together, represents the union of Shiva and Shakti. It is the most common yantra design and generates energy at its central core point.

Five-Pointed Star

Shiva's main geometrical symbol is a five-pointed star, which we find in most Shiva yantras. Shiva's five-pointed star is a kind of Shiva linga as well. It resembles the form of the human body with the head above, and the two arms and two legs below. The five-pointed star pointing upwards shows the ascending energy coming out of the union or balancing of opposites. Pointed downward it can indicate the descent of Shiva energy.

Shiva Linga and Sri Yantra

The Sri Yantra is the ultimate yoni or vortex of Shakti energy. Yet it also has its expansion as a mountain or as a Shiva linga form. Generally, its four downward pointed triangles represent Shiva and the five upward pointed triangles indicate Shakti. It symbolizes the entire universe and the subtle body as composed of Shiva and Shakti and all the powers of sound and light. It can be portrayed in a three dimensional form as the great world mountain.

Linga Formations in the Human Being

The human being as standing upright forms a Shiva linga through the spine. This makes human beings the manifestation of Shiva or the ruling power in the animal kingdom.

There are other Shiva formations in the human being like the eyes, the nose and the head in general. Prana as the force that gives life and pervades the body is another type of linga. The power of intelligence or buddhi is yet another Shiva linga.

Yogic Forms of Shiva Lingas

There are many inner Shiva lingas in Yoga practice. Relative to asana practice, the lotus pose turns the human body into an ascending Shiva linga through the erect back with the Shakti yoni formed with the crossed legs. The bound lotus projects the upward Shiva energy yet stronger. Other sitting poses like Siddhasana and Vajrasana have a similar effect. Standing poses like the tree pose emphasize the ascending Shiva force. The spine is the Shiva linga of the body. We could say that the purpose of asana practice is to be able to comfortably hold a pose like the Shiva linga so the energy of Shiva can arise within us at a physical level. Such Shiva poses can be called the *Asana Linga*.

When we combine sitting postures with pranayama and holding of the breath, our very concentrated prana becomes another Shiva linga. The unitary prana that arises from the balancing of inhalation and exhalation and right and left or solar and lunar breaths forms the *Prana Linga* of Yoga practice, which naturally causes our awareness to ascend.

Holding the mind steady in meditation, particularly focusing on Lord Shiva, forms the *Dhyana Linga* or meditation form of the Shiva linga. We can also hold our awareness into an upward current of energy through the power of Shiva mantras. With *"OM Namah Shivaya!"* we can create the *Mantra Linga* of Yoga practice.

The subtle body is called the linga in yoga thought, and is centered around the sushumna or inner spine. Different lingas and yonis exist in the different chakras of the subtle body and are described in yogic texts.[31] In the root chakra dwells *Kamakhya Yoni*, the original downward facing triangle or altar of Divine love, along with its special linga or creative power. There are special lingas in the navel chakra and in the third eye that hold yet deeper powers. There are special lingas in the heart and in the thousand-petal lotus of the head representing the higher realizations. These lingas overall relate to the "knots" or *granthis*, where our prana or life-force is constricted in the body, and must be loosened or opened by Yoga practices.

The causal body behind the subtle body is often regarded as egg like in shape like the Shiva linga. The spiritual heart, the energy center of the causal body, holds the supreme linga and yoni holding the entire universe in its matrix of forces.

Atma Linga or the Purusha principle is the most transcendent form of the Shiva lingas, giving the transcendent view of the Supreme Self. The Purusha principle of Self-awareness that fills our being and pervades the universe is also compared to a linga.

Use of Sacred Stones and Shiva Lingas

Rocks, stones and gems can be energized with rituals, prayers and mantras. Your own empowered sacred stone can strongly carry the presence of Shiva for you. Stones hold a portion of the energy of eternity and the changeless oneness beyond all sorrow. Such Shiva stones can be gems, crystals, special river rocks or other stones in which you feel the eternal presence.

It is very auspicious to have such sacred stones and Shiva lingas on your altar, in your sacred space, or in your garden and sacred groves. Try to discover your own sacred Shiva rocks in nature, in the mountains, and learn to honor the power of Shiva through them. You can get Narmada River Shiva linga stones from India.

The main ritual for the linga is to bathe it with liquid. This liquid can be as simple as water or as complex as milk, yogurt, honey, and ghee. The liquid serves to cleanse and nourish the Shiva linga so that the power of prana can be held within it. There are special Shiva pujas or rituals that one can learn for this purpose.

Along with bathing the linga, special mantras and names of Shiva should be recited, along with the throwing of flower petals on the linga. Many Hindu rituals consist of offering flowers to the linga, each flower given along with the recitation of one of the sacred names of Shiva, usually 108 or 1008 in number.

7. Shiva's Sacred Family

Shiva's Sacred Family of Parvati, Ganesha and Skanda

Most of us have a sense of being part of a greater Divine family or universal community, which we naturally aspire to connect with in our hearts. The Divine is our Father and Mother, our inner origin and essence. Our human parents are but the source of our physical bodies, not that of our souls. They provide the body for the soul to incarnate and help educate it, but the soul comes from afar and has a mystic affinity with realms beyond time and space.

There are many ways in which our Divine parents can be thought of, visualized and approached. Shaivism presents the Divine parents in a special way, honoring both male and female aspects, as personal and impersonal, in the forms of nature and beyond – and as the two sides of our own nature. Shiva and Shakti are the Divine Father and Mother of the universe in all aspects.

Shiva is the universal father and Shakti is the universal mother, though in their higher nature they are beyond all creation. To speak of them as father or mother is symbolic and indicates a way of devotion to lead us into the Supreme Consciousness that is the most intimate part of our nature.

The reflections of the transcendent Shiva and Shakti manifest within the creation as its guiding powers and are not apart from it. From their union all creatures and all worlds come into being. The Divine couple is the center of a network of forces that extends to everything in the universe. This is symbolized by the sacred family of Shiva.

The family of Shiva is one of the most important families of Hindu deities and probably the most commonly depicted. Shiva's family indicates cosmic forces. It is a family that embraces nature and the animal kingdom as well as the human realm.

Ultimately, we are all members of Shiva's family as Shiva and Parvati reflect the Great World Father and World Mother in all their forms. We are all the children of Shiva and Shakti and partake of their being, wisdom, power and immortality. The entire universe is one family consisting of all that is animate and inanimate, creaturely and Divine.

Shiva and Parvati

First in the family of Shiva is Lord Shiva himself and his wife, the Goddess, Devi or Shakti. Shiva's wife like Shiva has a multiplicity of names, perhaps more than he does. Many are feminine forms of the names of Shiva.

As Shiva is *Mahadeva* or the Great Deity, his consort is *Mahadevi* or the Great Goddess, the Universal World Mother and the cosmic feminine energy on all levels. Mahadevi's forms embrace all aspects of existence. She is not limited merely to what human beings consider to be holy, but carries the powers and potentials of the whole of life. She is also called *Jaganmata* or *Jagadamba*, the "Mother of the Universe." Her motherhood is lauded much more than is Shiva's fatherhood, though Shiva is also called the "Father of the Universe."

The Devi's specific forms as Shiva's consort are mainly *Parvati*, *Gauri*, and *Uma* by name – and most commonly Parvati as the "daughter of the mountain." In these instances her vehicle is usually a white humped bull, Nandi, the same as Shiva's. *Girija*, the Daughter of the mountain, reflects Shiva as the mountain dweller, *Girisha*.

Devi is called *Shivā* or *Shivani* in the feminine form, as also *Shankari* and *Shambhavi*, feminine for Shankara and Shambhu. *Kali* as the Goddess of Time and eternity is the feminine form of Kala, *Bhairavi* or she who is fierce is the feminine form of Shiva as Bhairava. *Bhavani*, or the origin of all existence, is the feminine form of Bhava. While the great Mother is called Shakti, Shakti is also a general term for energy. Like Shiva, Devi is connected to cosmic sound and mantra.

When the Goddess is conceived on her own, she is usually honored as *Durga* and rides a lion or a tiger, a symbol of her royal power. This is her form as *Jagadamba* or *Jaganmata*, the great mother of the worlds. She is *Lalita* or she who plays and *Sundari* or the Goddess of cosmic beauty. She has her youthful, often militant forms, prior to her marriage with Shiva, like *Kumari*. Similarly, she has her elderly or grandmother forms like *Dhumavati*.

The depiction of the marriage of Shiva and Parvati is an important image in Hindu art and iconography. In this case Parvati usually comes riding her lion or tiger. This is usually the form of Durga. The wife empowers the man to achieve his goals in the world. In the case of Shiva and Parvati, Parvati empowers Shiva to rule the universe, as by his own nature he is transcendent and beyond desire.

Shiva, Sati and Parvati

The fact that Shiva as the Lord of the mountain marries the daughter of the mountain reinforces his mountain symbolism. The mountain is that of meditation, and the daughter of the mountain indicates the individual soul seeking the Divine through meditation.

In the original story, Shiva's first wife is named *Sati*, which literally means the "power of existence." Yet Shiva was not considered to be the ideal partner by Sati's father Daksha, who refused to honor him. Shiva with his retinue of wild animals and ghosts, and his wild and paradoxical behavior, was not acceptable to stern Daksha who represents propriety, convention and the status quo. At one point, Daksha held a great fire ceremony and invited all the Gods to attend but excluded Shiva. Offended by her Father's rebuke of her husband, his daughter Sati threw herself into the fire and immolated herself. Shiva then destroyed Daksha's sacrifice out of revenge and took his wife's Sati's burned body away.

Of course we can react against this story with our cultural morality or political correctness but it has a deeper meaning that we should not overlook. Daksha represents the outer order of society and creation bound by time and karma. He has his utilitarian correctness but is blind to the deeper spirit and consciousness. Shiva as the transcendent reality lies inherently outside of the laws of the created world and cannot be understood according to its processes. Shiva does not exist in Daksha's realm and cannot be honored within it. This is the real meaning of Daksha refusing to honor Shiva.

Sati represents the soul that takes birth in the realm of Daksha or ordinary reality, but seeks to align itself with the energy of Shiva or the transcendent truth. Sati is *Sat-Shakti* or the power of being and truth, our highest potential. To be one with Shiva, who is pure existence beyond time and manifestation, Sati must be willing to die to Daksha's limited realm and be reborn in a spiritual realm beyond it. The soul must die to the outer world, its social of times and space appearances and conventions and take a new birth in the realm of Shiva or Yoga sadhana, the mountain of Yoga practice.

After her immolation in the fire of purification, Sati is reborn as Parvati, the daughter of the mountain, symbolizing deeper Yoga practices. She arises in her pure form in the inner realms of Yoga and meditation, in which she can truly take Shiva as a husband and join in his immortal life.[32] In her tapas or yogic practice, she becomes Uma and gradually wins Shiva through her devotion and her austerities, eventually giving birth to Shiva's son as Skanda. Parvati represents the awakened soul engaged in Yoga practices to realize Shiva, which is also the grace of Shiva working inside us.

In Yogic thought, like various forms of mysticism,[33] the creator or Brahma can assume a negative role in that relating to desire, karma and creation he can indicate ignorance and attachment to the outer world. Shiva as the power of withdrawal and dissolution assumes a positive role as the bestower of liberation. In this set of views, it is the creative force that is the limited and lower force, while the power of dissolution as the power to liberate is the higher force. Such views are behind stories such as this of Daksha, himself one of the lesser creators.

Dual Forms of Shiva and Shakti

Shiva and his wife have many dual forms as Shiva/Shakti, Uma/Mahesha, Shankara/Parvati, or as the two Shivas. They are often lauded together and have several famous Sanskrit hymns to them in the dual case. Shiva is the most commonly mentioned of the Hindu deities in a dual or married form.

There are many artistic depictions of Shiva and the Goddess together, notably *Ardhaneshvara* with Shiva as the right side of the body and Shakti as the left side. Marriage forms of Shiva include *Sundareshvara*, the lord of beauty, and *Kameshvara*, the lord of love, indicating Divine beauty and Divine love.

Shiva, Kali and Chinnamasta

Kali represents the transcendent form of Shiva's energy, the supreme Shiva's own Shakti as the innate power of the Absolute, total dissolution, stillness, nirodha, and Nirvana. She is not so much Shiva's wife, as the feminine energy inherent in the Supreme Shiva. Kali takes us to Shiva in his highest nature as the Supreme Brahman, with which she is one.

Yet Kali does have an outer action to destroy all negativity. In her martial form, Kali represents the strongest purifying energy of Lord Shiva connected to his Rudra manifestation. It is Kali who destroys all ignorance and negativity, symbolized by the various demons or anti-gods that she eliminates. Kali becomes Chandi, the fierce Goddess and demon-slayer.

As a further development, Chandi becomes Chinnamasta, the Goddess who cuts off her own head, symbolizing the sacrifice of mind and ego, and the entrance into the transcendent state of Shiva. In this form she is also called *Prachanda*

Chandi or the most fierce form of Chandi. She represents Shiva's open third eye and the beyond the mind state.[34] She indicates the direct path to Shiva.

Ganesha and Skanda – the Children of Shiva and Shakti

Shiva's two children, his two sons, are Ganesha and Skanda. Yet we must not take this statement literally as mere human personifications. Ganesha has the head of an elephant and Skanda, usually depicted as a child, personifies fire. Their qualities as cosmic powers and forces of nature predominate over their human characteristics.

Both Ganesha and Skanda are manifestations of Shiva's energies, particularly as active in the material worlds. Some forms of Shiva also represent his descent to the Earth, particularly his Rudra form, which is connected to Skanda. Ganesha is also commonly known and worshipped as the Supreme Deity in his own right.

Shiva and Ganesha

I have listed the contrast between Shiva and Ganesha below. As these are important points I have highlighted them:

- Shiva is *Parameshvara* or the Supreme Lord of transcendent reality. Ganesha is the Lord (pati) of the group (gana) or lord of all the manifest powers, though with a connection to the transcendent.

- Shiva is unmanifest primordial sound, OM or Pranava. Ganesha is manifest primordial sound, OM as the power of creation. Shiva is the lord beyond the worlds. Ganesha is the lord within the worlds. Ganesha's higher form is Shiva and Shiva's manifestation is Ganesha. Shiva is OM in its transcendent nature and Ganesha is OM as it creates the universe. Ganesha is the lord of speech and has the electrical energy beyond all expression. His is the voice of Shiva. This aligns him with Shakti as well.

- Shiva is the lord of all the animals or Pashupati, who stands beyond them as the human or Yogi. Ganesha is leader of all the animals, who stands among them. The elephant is the leader or guru among the animals. Ganesha thus relates to Shiva's Pashupati form. As Pashupati is the lord of the souls, so is Ganesha. As Pashupati is the lord of perception, so is Ganesha.

Ganesha is the granter of wisdom, somewhat like Hermes in Greek esoteric thought. Ganesha is the scribe, who takes down the great teachings of the *Vedas* and *Mahabharata* from sage Vyasa. Ganesha governs calculations and numbers, particularly those relative to time. He is the background deity of Vedic astrology. He is also the deity of computers, with the mouse as his vehicle!

- Ganesha is the ruler over all karmas and teaches how to work with them in the best possible manner. Ganesha is the remover of all obstacles. He provides us with the skill to handle difficult situations. This is not just the ability to go directly through obstacles, but the wisdom to not create them or to go around them, as is best.

- Ganesha is worshipped first in all Hindu rituals and pujas and prayed to first before any classes or studies begin. Ganesha relates to that which is first or preeminent in all things, which is our connection to Shiva. As the child of Shiva and Parvati, our soul is naturally first in all things, having been empowered by our Divine father and mother to rule over and protect the entire universe. Ganesha rules over the organization of forces, but is also receptive to the needs of his followers, and symbolizes democracy or an elected leader.

- Ganesha directs the powers of Shiva and Shakti into the manifest worlds.

- He is the power of Shiva as working under and through Shakti. He directs the power of Shakti to specific levels and functions in the universe. His power of speech is also that of Shakti. Ganesha protects Shakti in the manifest worlds. One cannot approach Devi without having the grace of Lord Ganesha.

- Ganesha has many of the same functions as Lord Brahma, the third aspect of the Hindu trinity dealing with creation and with knowledge. Ganesh represents the Divine Word and the teachings that arise from it. Like Shiva he is identified with OM, but as Shiva is more OM in the transcendent sense, Ganesha is able to direct its power into specific areas or OM in the manifest sense.

As the lord of knowledge and the first among the gurus, he relates to Brihaspati of the *Vedas*. Ganesha in the *Rigveda* is lauded under the names of Ganapati, Brihaspati, and Brahmanaspati, the later two names of which are connected to Brahma.[35] Ganesha like Brahma is associated with the cosmic mind or Mahat Tattva, which is the resort of cosmic knowledge and power. Ganesha is often the lord of the Brahmins or the priestly class.

Shiva and Skanda

Skanda as the fire God is the ruler of the five elements and represents the powers of light. He is usually portrayed as a child, sometimes as an infant. While Ganesha rules over all knowledge, Skanda holds the specific and single pointed knowledge of Self-realization. Skanda symbolizes the Yogi, Sadhu or Swami who stands alone and has renounced the world. He has no group behind him but makes his own way.

Skanda is born of Uma as the fire energy of the Goddess when during her intense practice of Yoga, she surrenders herself to Lord Shiva. Parvati does the five fire tapas, with fires and four sides and the Sun above. This union of Shiva and Parvati follows the destruction of Kama Deva or the God of love and desire, showing that Skanda is the inner child born of Divine love alone. As such, Skanda is born of *Soma* (Shiva or "Sa" plus Shakti or "Uma)", representing the highest fire of bliss that can remove all negativity.

Skanda is born of the yogic power and ascetic practice of the Goddess. He takes birth in a forest of reeds (shara-vana), which represents the open channels of bliss from the thousand-petal lotus of the head. Yet he works to fulfill the work of his Father Shiva, by bringing the purifying light of knowledge into the world. Fire also symbolizes the weapon, so Skanda is the head of Shiva's army and also the its main weapon as well.

Ganesh, Skanda and Shakti

Of the two sons, Ganesha and Skanda, Ganesha is closer to Devi or Shakti in his activities and Skanda is closer to Shiva. Ganesha protects the Goddess, particularly as Durga, and serves as her attendant. Wherever there is Ganesha, the Goddess is nearby and vice versa.

Lakshmi and Sarasvati, the Goddess powers of abundance and knowledge, appear with Ganesha, particularly relative to the Hindu festival of light (Diwali or Dipavali). They relate to Ganesha's two wives as *Siddhi*, the power to accomplish or Lakshmi force, and *Buddhi*, the power of knowledge or Sarasvati force.

Skanda reflects Rudra and Agni, Shiva's fire energy that operates in the field of the Earth, and is sometimes regarded as Shiva himself. Sometimes it is Shiva or Rudra who takes birth as Skanda or as Shiva's youthful form as Dakshinamurti. Skanda's spear, his special weapon of direct insight, is called Shakti (which also means spear in Sanskrit), which connects him with the ascetic forms of the Goddess as well.

Ganesha holds and directs the energy of Shakti, allowing it to expand and express itself as power of guidance. Ganesha reflects the Indra or the ruling power of Shiva. Skanda holds and directs the Agni or immanent energy of Shiva, allowing it to ascend and focus itself to the highest truth. Skanda is Shiva's energy as a weapon. Yet Shiva's two sons have much in common and appear to have originally been a single manifestation. Both are called the head of the army (Senapati), which is the army of Shiva and Shakti.

Sometimes the *Bhairava* form of Shiva, particularly in his child form as *Batuka Bhairava*, is regarded as another son of Shiva or child form of Shiva. He is fierce and transformative. Sometimes as the child he relates to Skanda. Ganapati Muni relates Ganesha as space and manifest sound as Shiva's eldest son.[36] The Muni has Bhairava as air as the middle son. He has Skanda as Agni and the Sun as the third son.

Daughters of Shiva

The sons of Shiva have their feminine counterparts that are manifestations of Shakti. Ganesha has Siddhi and Buddhi, skill and wisdom, which also relate to Lakshmi and Sarasvati. Skanda has *Devasena* and *Valli*, who represent respectively the army of the Gods and the forces of nature, behind him. Yet the feminine form of *Kanya Kumari* or the young girl form of the Goddess also relates to Skanda in terms of her actions. In this regard, we can speak of the daughters of Shiva.

Nothing can come into being or endure without the power of both Shiva and Shakti. Shakti is nothing but Shiva looked upon in a feminine form. Shiva is similarly nothing but Shakti in a masculine form. Shiva holds the power of Shakti and Shakti rests upon the being of Shiva. The Supreme Shiva and Shakti have many forms and manifestations in the realm of time and space that can be regarded as their children. Yet Shiva consciousness and Shakti power give us the feeling of independence and transcendence, so that we feel that we are the Self of all beings. There are also both masculine and feminine orders of Shaivite devotees, priests and priestesses, Yogis and Yoginis.

Names and Forms of Shiva

The Supreme reality both transcends all names and forms, and underlies all names and forms. All names and forms are but symbols and expressions of that which is beyond words and concepts. Yet if we understand what names and forms indicate, rather than taking them literally, we can follow them as gateways to the transcendent.

Shiva is not a deity that can be reduced to a single name, historical incarnation, or book of revelation. Nothing in the human world can encompass him, or anything in the realm of words and ideas. Shiva has many names and forms through which his different aspects and attributes are worshipped and can be brought into our lives.

As Shiva personifies the Divine Word and sound current, the names of Shiva are among the most important Divine names – and all Divine names are ultimately names of Shiva. Shiva has many expressions relative to his qualities and action, as well as his transcendence of these. Contemplating these aspects of Shiva widens our horizons and draws us into the infinite.

The Name Shiva

The mantra *Namah Shivaya*, which first emphasizes the name Shiva for this great deity, occurs in the famous *Rudram* chant of the *Krishna Yajurveda*.[37] Along with it are over a hundred important names of Shiva, including the great majority of his most famous names. The same section of the Rudram that teaches *Nama Shivaya* begins with the names of Soma and Rudra, harking back to primary Vedic deities, as well as Aruna, Pashupati, Bhima, and Ugra that are also important names for Shiva. Along with Namah Shiva directly are the following names. I have added the transliterated Sanskrit on the right:

> Tara – the one who takes us across – *Namas Tārāya*
>
> Shambhu – the dispenser of blessings – *Namaḥ Śambhave*
>
> Mayobhu – the dispenser of harmony – *Nama Mayobhave*
>
> Shankara – the maker of blessings – *Namaḥ Śankarāya*
>
> Mayaskara – the maker of harmony – *Nama Mayaskarāya*
>
> Shiva – the auspicious one – *Namaḥ Śivāya*
>
> Shivatara – the most auspicious one – *Namaḥ Śivatarāya*[38]

Yet prior to teaching of the *Namah Shivaya* chant, the same Rudram section of the *Yajurveda* at its very beginning calls upon Rudra, who is generally regarded as a fierce deity and form of fire and lightning, to assume his auspicious or Shiva form, *with the term Shiva occurring numerous times*. The term Shiva has a more generic meaning in the *Vedas* up to this point as indicating that which is auspicious, but its application is so frequent here to Rudra that we can see the term becoming a name for him.

> *OM! Reverence to Bhagavan Rudra! OM! Reverence, Rudra, to your wrath and to your arrow. Reverence to your bow and to your arms.*
>
> *That which is your most auspicious (Shivatama) arrow, and that which is your auspicious bow (Shiva Dhanu), and your pointed arrow that is auspicious (Shiva), with that O Rudra, be compassionate to us.*
>
> *That which, O Rudra, is your auspicious form (Shiva Tanu), not fierce and not harming those who are impure, by that peaceful form, O dweller on the mountain, look over us.*
>
> *The arrow, dweller on the mountain, which you carry in your hand, make that auspicious (Shivam), O mountain lord! Do not harm any person or creature. With an auspicious speech (Shivena Vachasa), O mountain lord, may we speak to you.*[39]

Rudra's arrow is symbolic of the powers of time and karma. It relates to his higher perceptual power through the third eye, whose lighting arrow is the weapon of the Gods.

The Rudram ends with the Tryambakam mantra followed by an important lauding of this Supreme Divinity. Rudra is not only the fiery form that demands purification, he is also the watery Soma form that rules over the plants and grants all medicines.

> *Which Rudra is in the Fire (Agni) and in the waters, which has entered into all the plants. Which Rudra has entered into the entire universe, to that Rudra we offer our reverence!*
>
> *Adore him who has a good arrow and a good bow, and who rules over all medicines. May we worship Rudra for an auspicious mind; honor with surrender the Divine almighty power.*

Bhagavan Rudra, your hand which is most full of blessings, with that grant me all healing medicines, with that hand touch me with the auspicious powers.[40]

Rudra is not only the power of life but also the power of death. He rules over death and can take us beyond death.

The bondages that are a thousand and ten thousand, O Death, which you have to strike the mortal, with the magic wisdom power of the sacrifice, we offer all these away.

Reverence to Death! Reverence to death.

OM, reverence to Bhagavan Rudra and Vishnu; may Death protect me.

Rudra, you are the knot of the Prana. Do not enter into me as death. By that Prana fill my being, Sadashiva OM![41]

Eight Traditional Names of Shiva

Shiva has a group of eight primary names in ancient texts from the *Shiva Mahimna Stotra*[42] to the *Yajurveda*. Curiously, the name Shiva is not among these.

1. Bhava – the raw power of existence

2. Sharva – the one who has the arrow or the power of focus, purification and karmic rectification

3. Rudra – the fiery one, he who is fierce, demanding purification, humility and self-abnegation

4. Mahadeva – the greatest of the deities, the lord of the gods

5. Pashupati – the lord of the animals and of all souls in the state of bondage

6. Bhima – he who is fierce like the wind

7. Ugra – he who is awesome and powerful

8. Ishana – the supreme lord and ruling power over all

Shatapatha Brahmana adds a ninth name to these, which is *Kumara* (the child, a name of Agni or Skanda) and makes these into names of Agni.[43]

Names of the Five Faces of Shiva

The Five Faces of Shiva first occur in the *Brahmanas* and the *Mahanarayana Upanishad*[44] as part of the ancient *Shivopasan*a or worship of Shiva. They also can refer to the body as a whole.

Name	Directions	Cosmic Process	Element	Shakti	Limb
Sadyojata	West	Creation	Earth	Kriya	Entire body
Vamadeva	North	Preservation	Water	Jnana	Sex organs
Aghora	South	Dissolution	Fire	Iccha	Heart
Tatpurusha	East	Concealment	Air	Ananda	Mouth
Ishana	Northeast	Liberation	Ether	Chit	Head

Each name also has its own significance. *Sadyojata* means "the one who is born or manifests quickly or instantaneously." Shiva is known for his quick action. *Vamadeva* means the "blissful deity" or "the deity who has Shakti on his left side (Vama)." Vamadeva is a common general name for Shiva. *Aghora* means "the one who is not fierce." Aghora Shaivites are branch of sadhus known for their unorthodox action. *Ishana* is related to Ishvara as the ruling power. He is a deity of the northeastern direction in all directional formulations. Northeast is regarded as the most auspicious direction to face and is the region of a dwelling given to the altar or puja room or the main deity in a temple. Northeast is the direction of Shiva.

Trimurti, the Three Heads of Shiva

Shiva is often portrayed with three heads. These are associated with Brahma (creation), Vishnu (preservation) and Shiva/Rudra (dissolution). Shiva governs over all three as the power of time and eternity. In some Shiva Trimurti forms the heads of Brahma, Vishnu and Shiva are used. These three are the basis of the five forms of Shiva immediately below.

Shiva and His Five Functions Relative to the Five Elements and Five Lower Chakras

Deity	Process	Element	Chakra
Brahma	Creation	Earth	Root chakra
Vishnu	Preservation	Water	Water chakra
Rudra	Dissolution	Fire	Navel chakra
Maheshvara	Concealment/bondage	Air	Heart chakra
Sadashiva	Liberation	Ether	Throat chakra

Deities like Brahma and Vishnu can also be regarded as manifestations of Shiva as the Supreme Consciousness behind all deity forms. Bondage and Liberation refer to Shiva as ruling over the bondage and liberation of the soul, through which it comes under the three phases of time.

Other Common Names and Forms of Shiva

There are many other forms of Shiva, which may be worshipped at special temples or pilgrimage sites.

- Nataraja, the great lord of the cosmic dance of ecstatic dissolution, who consumes the entire universe in the all-pervasive cosmic fire.
- Dakshinamurti, the enlightened youth who sitting beneath a banyan tree teaches through silence even the most senior of the sages.
- Chandrashekhara, who holds the crescent Moon on his head as an ornament and has the power to control the mind.
- Nilakantha, the blue-throated deity who can transform all poison into bliss.
- Gangadhara who holds the Ganga River on his head, allowing the cosmic waters to stream into the Earth.
- Sadashiva, ever auspicious.
- Hara, the one who captivates or carries away.
- Mahakala, the great lord of time.
- Bhairava, he who is fierce and awesome.

Shiva has human forms, nature forms, light forms, plant forms, rock forms, symbolic forms, geometrical forms, and abstract forms. There are special forms of Shiva for all the five directions, five elements and seven chakras, which refer to their inner ruling powers. Everything in the universe has its Shiva or spirit, through which we can connect to the cosmic energy.

Iconography and Representative Forms

Yogic iconography represents a universal language of form, color, gesture, and symbol. It is not merely a cultural expression or formality. The deeper mind, including the subconscious, thinks more in terms of images than in ordinary language or abstract ideas, much as what we experience in the dream state, mystical visions and inner journeys. All religious and artistic traditions employ some degree of iconography whether as a painting, a statue, geometrical symbols, or calligraphy. In India these have all been explored to a great degree.

The Hindu tradition allows for and encourages the full range of iconographical representation both form-based and abstract, allowing a full spiritual unfoldment of all artistic and creative expression. It has created what can appear to be a bewildering number of Divine names, images, attributes, actions, appearances, and functions. It is perhaps relative to Shiva that we find the greatest diversity of these.

If we learn to read this symbolic language then we can understand the reality of Shiva at a deeper level. Many different images of Shiva exist in human or semi-human form depicted long with various vestments, adornments and weapons, assuming certain poses and postures, and making certain gestures or mudras. These forms, either sculptural or painted, are called *murtis* in Sanskrit, which implies a formal, yet symbolic and artistic representation.

All forms of Shiva are but appearances in the greater dance of Shiva that is both behind and beyond all forms. Different depictions of Shiva in different temples have their special features. Some forms of Shiva appear like the image of a physical person. Some scholars believe that Shiva was originally a person, perhaps a great Yogi who lived long ago. Yet even those who hold that Shiva is transcendent recognize that he can descend and appear in the human realm and work through various great teachers and gurus.

Shiva's depictions contain supernatural factors in order to indicate his higher powers. For example, Shiva is often portrayed with three eyes, three heads, and garlanded with serpents. There are various forms of Shiva as Yogeshvara, Nataraja, Nilakantha, and Dakshinamurti, with their particular symbolisms. Shiva is associated with various plants, animals, rocks, landforms or celestial phenomena that can enter into his iconographic representations as well.

Such representations of Shiva can be extremely powerful tools for visualization and contemplation. They provide us a symbolic image of Shiva to imagine and contemplate in order to bring higher energies into our minds and sensory fields. They reflect aesthetic concerns and are indicative of Shiva's Divine and cosmic powers and qualities. Such meditation images help the mind to withdraw from images of the mundane world into a receptivity to the Divine.

Yet one should not look upon images of Shiva merely as tools for concentration. One can use them to communicate directly with Shiva, particularly in his manifestations in the subtle realms, and to draw his power into the physical world. They are particularly important for Bhakti Yoga that orients us to see the Divine Beloved as form and person, albeit cosmic form and cosmic person. Seeing the transcendent in form also has its power to help us understand that everything, even in the material worlds, is also a manifestation of Shiva.

Such images of Shiva do not represent the full reality of Shiva, nor are they the only focus of Shaivite practices. One does not need to worship or visualize images of Shiva in order to appreciate the Divine reality that he reflects. But images have their place and need not be excluded or looked down upon as an inferior approach.

Shiva temples usually contain specially consecrated images of Shiva, particularly in the form of stone-carved statues. These are usually in granite or black granite in South India. From Rajasthan and in the north of India, they may be made of marble. Bronze sculptures are also common, like the beautiful Chola bronzes in South India. Shiva temples also have symbolic representations of Shiva, notably Shiva lingas or trishulas. Both images and lingas are often used together.

Relative to colors, Shiva is usually portrayed as dark blue (Nila) like the color of infinite space, or as white (Shveta), the color the Moon. Yet he is sometimes worshipped through gold. Other times he is regarded as transparent. Shakti is more commonly red in color, either as relating to her beauty or to her martial power, but she can be white or dark blue as well. White is her pure form and dark blue is her unmanifest conditions. The different colors of the Shiva and Shakti reflect their diverse qualities, which ultimately cover all of existence.

Relative to animals, Shiva's main vehicle or vahana is a white humped bull called *Nandi* or the "joyous." The bull is a symbol of the spirit or Purusha and is the dominant animal symbol in India going back to ancient Harappan times. As Pashupati, he is the lord of all the wild animals. The deer is also sacred to him and he is often portrayed as wearing a deerskin. As *Ahipati*, Shiva is lord of the serpents. His special serpent is called *Vasuki,* which he wears around his neck. In his Bhairava form, Shiva's sacred animal is a dog, generally black in color.

Shiva has his special sacred rivers as the Ganga, the main river of the Himalayas, which flows down upon his head. The Narmada River in Central India is also sacred to him and famous for the special stone lingas fashioned by its waters. All mountains are sacred to him, particularly the Himalayas in Uttar Khand by the sources of the Ganga and the great Mount Kailas to the north in Tibet.

Shiva's supreme weapon is the *Trishula* – his trident or three pointed spear. It symbolizes the three gunas of sattva, rajas and tamas, and the three processes of creation, maintenance and dissolution, the three powers of will, knowledge and action, and the cosmic lightning force as the supreme weapon. Yet Shiva is also famous for his bow, particularly in his Pashupati form. This shoots the arrows of karma but also those of liberating knowledge.

8. Nataraj

Part IV

Shiva's Cosmic Raja Yoga

Victory to Shankara, the lord of Parvati! May Shambhu be compassionate, who wears the crescent Moon, who is the destroyer of the God of desire, who is gentle for his devotees, who delights in Mount Kailas, and who is an ocean of the nectar of compassion.

Shiva, all pervasive, Sharva, the giver of peace, surrendering before you, O Deity, grant me mercy.

Reverence to Ishvara, the Lord, the ruler of all directions of space; again and again let there be reverence to you!

I take refuge in he who wears the crescent Moon and I take refuge in the youthful daughter of the Mountain. I again take refuge in the two of you. For refuge I do not go to any other deity.

Upamanyu Shiva Stotra 1, 17-18

The following section presents Yoga according the tradition of Shaivite Yoga. It shows the relevance of Shiva and Shiva Yoga to every Yoga student at every level of practice from the most basic asana to the highest Samadhi, particularly relative to the higher domains of Raja Yoga, the royal path of Self-realization, and deep meditation. May Lord Shiva take you to your highest yogic potential!

Yogeshvara Shiva
Shiva, the Great Lord of Yoga

The great secrets of Yoga on all levels of body, mind, prana and consciousness can be understood through the figure, symbolism and teachings about Lord Shiva. Shiva is the essence of Yoga and guides us to the highest yogic reality according to our degree of attunement with him.

Let us explore Shiva's vast yogic connections, but first place Yoga overall in the perspective of Shiva Dharma. Classical Yoga, such is the basis of Shiva Yoga, is a sacred path of arriving at the Supreme Reality, which is our inmost Self and the essence of all existence. This distinguishes it from current popular Yoga in the West, which often neglects this spiritual dimension, though can lead to it.

Classical Yoga is not about the physical body, though it includes the body as part of the greater reality of consciousness. The human body and brain can be molded into an ideal vehicle for the realization of the universal truth, but this requires a radical change in how we look upon ourselves. To reach a higher awareness, we must move beyond body consciousness and give up our belief in physical reality. This means removing our attachment to the physical body – and being able to consciously withdraw both our prana and mind out of it.

Classical Yoga is also not about personal healing, as is much of modern Yoga, and was not intended to be a medical system, which is the place of Ayurveda that examines all aspects of health and wellness in terms of both diagnosis and treatment. However, Yoga does teach us how to remove all suffering – which requires that we give up our identification with the body bound by time and death and learn to embrace the entire universe within our own hearts.

Classical Yoga is not something usually done en masse like modern Yoga classes, though group Yoga and meditation practices can have their value. Yoga is about aligning our individual being with the universal being, which requires a good deal of time spent alone, in silence, and in nature. This is the basis of true Yoga practice or *sadhana*, prescribed on an individual basis. Yoga is about spiritual experience at an individual, existential, and cognitive level. It can be described as a science or way of knowledge, and as an art or means of contacting the essential beauty and bliss behind all existence.

Yoga is not simply something that we do, an action among other actions that we do in our personal lives. Yoga requires opening to a higher flow of grace, energy, and awareness that rests upon the surrender of the personal self. Yoga also has its theory, goal, and worldview and requires the right orientation to practice, and cannot be done mechanically.

The greater Yoga tradition encompasses all helpful tools and attitudes helpful to arrive at a realization of the universal being. Yoga is our means of transcending ourselves in order to reach that great Unknown, Infinite, and Eternal beyond all names, forms and actions, yet whose presence, guidance, and help is available at all times. A deeper study of Yoga takes us to the teachings about Lord Shiva. If we want to symbolize all that Yoga is and represents, Shiva is the best place for us both to start and to end.

Shiva as the Great Yogi

If there were one deity who could best represent the Yoga tradition in all of its facets, it would be Lord Shiva. Shiva is the deity most commonly lauded as the great "Lord of Yoga," *Yogeshvara,* and as the great guru and teacher of Yoga behind all Yoga teachers, lineages, and branches. Shiva is the main deity of the Yogis who have renounced the world for a life in the mountains of the jungles.

Lord Krishna, perhaps the most important avatar of Lord Vishnu, is also honored as the avatar of Yoga, with every chapter of his *Bhagavad Gita* reflecting a different aspect of Yoga, including knowledge, devotion and action. His Yoga power on a human level is exalted and unparalleled. In addition, Lord Vishnu has his *Yogamaya* or yogic power at a cosmic level, from which the Goddess Lakshmi arises, who fulfills all the desires of the soul, worldly and spiritual.

Shiva has a closer connection to Yoga in all of its forms than probably any other deity form. While many other deities – including Brahma, Ganesha, Skanda, Rama, and Hanuman – have profound yogic implications, Shiva best personifies Yoga as a whole, including both Hatha and Raja Yogas. Several other yogic deity powers like Skanda, Ganesha, and Hanuman are lauded as manifestations of Shiva. Different forms of Shiva have special relevance for different aspects of Yoga practice. The stories about Shiva that occur in Shaivite and Puranic literature are often metaphors for Yoga practice.

Shiva's feminine counterpart as Shakti or Devi similarly is the main Yoga Shakti or power of Yoga and works along with him. Shakti is the basis of Kundalini, and the powers of knowledge, devotion, and service through which the inner yogic process proceeds. Shakti's different forms as Parvati, Uma, Sundari, Durga, Tara, and Kali indicate various aspects of Yoga practice and stages of Yoga Sadhana. Her "Ten Wisdom Forms" (Dasha Mahavidya) are especially relevant in this manner for their secret yogic applications.[45]

Traditionally in India there are several lines of Yoga practice, of which three are probably most important as noted in the *Mahabharata* and *Shiva Mahimna Stotra*:[46]

- *Samkhya-Yoga* is represented by *Hiranyagarbha* as the founder of Yoga Darshana, *Kapila* as the founder of the Samkhya system, the *Yoga Sutras* as the main Yoga Darshana text, *Samkhya Karika* as the main Samkhya text, but also the *Mahabharata*, the *Vedas*, and Lord Brahma.

- *Vaishnava Yoga* is represented by Yogeshvara Krishna, Vishnu and Narayana, the *Mahabharata*, *Bhagavad Gita* and Srimad Bhagavatam as the main texts, and emphasizes devotion or Bhakti Yoga.

- *Shaivite (or Pashupata) Yoga* is represented by Yogeshvara Shiva, the Nath Yogis and Shiva Babas, Shiva and the *Agama Shastras*,[47] and cultivates all aspects of Yoga, including Hatha and Raja Yoga.

The line of Shaivite Yoga is probably the largest of the yogic lines in terms of the number of teachings, practices and followers. Most of the yogis and sadhus in the Himalayas up to today follow Lord Shiva. Yet all three lines are connected to each other, just as Brahma, Vishnu, and Shiva are the three powers of creation, preservation and dissolution. The three overlap in several ways.

The Shiva Principle of Yoga Practice

Shiva represents the original essence and power of Yoga. All existing Yoga practices and teachings are reflections of the unbounded consciousness of Shiva that dwells behind all yogic energies and potentials. Yet that supreme reality of Shiva cannot be limited even to yogic teachings and practices, which are but expedient methods of approaching him.

We can easily define the "state of Yoga" as the "state of Shiva," with the term Shiva indicating balance, silence, steadiness, awareness, calm, and presence – the main factors that constitute the essence of all Yoga practices. All forms of Yoga involve emulating certain qualities associated with Shiva and his energies of stillness and transformation. Shiva indicates the principle of non-doing or reduction of unnecessary action that is the power of Yoga to undo all the karmic compulsions of life, relieve all stress, and let go of all attachments.

Classical Yoga as defined in the *Yoga Sutras* aims at the realization of the Purusha or cosmic person, the seer of all. [48] The Purusha as the goal of Yoga can be defined as the state of being Shiva, which is the supreme state of detachment and observation. Shiva symbolizes the Supreme Purusha that is the silent and inactive witness beyond all fluctuations of the body and mind internally, and all disturbances of the gunas or qualities of nature externally.

Yoga is a process of Self-realization, and Shiva indicates the Supreme Self beyond all the worlds. Yoga is the process of becoming Shiva, of merging into the state of Shiva of perfect peace, which is auspicious to all. To discover Shiva within oneself is to know the heart of Yoga. To awaken the consciousness of Shiva within oneself is to awaken the inner power of Yoga.

Shiva is the seer whose nature is pure light, who is the witness of all, beyond birth and death. Yoga works through developing this seer-power. This requires calming of the mind and developing the state of Samadhi or the yogic state of absorption, which is the main means of Yoga practice. The *Yoga Sutras* defines Yoga as Samadhi.[49] Samadhi as the state of mergence into bliss is the mind that is one with Shiva as the state of ecstasy and discerns the delight of Shiva everywhere. Samadhi, which means equanimity, is the nature of Shiva, for whom everything is serene and quiescent. The image of Shiva is the main depiction of the Yogi in a sitting posture withdrawn into his own consciousness in Samadhi.

Shiva is the prime deity governing stillness and silence that is the state of nirodha or nirvana in which all the disturbances of the mind and heart are dissolved. "Chitta Vritti Nirodha" or calming the disturbances of the mind arises through the power of Shiva to create calm, balance, and detachment.[50] Nirodha is the Shiva principle of peace and stillness in Yoga. Shiva is that immutable state in which all movement is back into oneself.

Shiva is the deity most commonly called Ishvara or the Lord in yogic thought. He is also called *Maheshvara*, the great lord, and *Parameshvara* or the Supreme Lord. When the *Yoga Sutras* call Ishvara the original guru of Yoga, they are suggesting Shiva.[51]

Natha is a similar term to Ishvara in Sanskrit. Shiva as *Adi Natha* or the original lord is the primordial guru of the Nath Yogi traditions of Hatha Yoga mentioned in the *Hatha Yoga Pradipika*,[52] and of Siddha Yoga, a kind of Raja Yoga, mentioned by Gorakhnath.

> *We honor Adi Natha, conjoined with his Shakti, the Lord of the*
> *World.*[53]

The *Yoga Sutras* states that "surrender to Ishvara or *Ishvara pranidhana*" is one of the best means of going into Samadhi.[54] The *Yoga Sutras* states that the main means of contacting Ishvara is through Pranava or primordial sound vibration, which is the origin of the *Vedas*, and is indicated by the seed mantra OM.[55] This suggests a Vedic basis for Yoga and the *Yoga Sutras*.

More specifically, Shiva is the deity of Omkara and Pranava, and the origin of the Sanskrit alphabet that is the basis of all mantras, which arise from the beating of his drum. All mantras are the manifestation of the sounds of Shiva, which are the sounds of silence. As Patanjali, the compiler of the *Yoga Sutras* was also a grammarian, a further suggestion of Shiva, the Lord of Sound, arises here. Yoga as the language of mantra is the language of Shiva, which is the cosmic language of the Divine Word.

In addition, the Yoga Sutra tradition rests upon Hiranyagarbha as its founder.[56] Rudra-Shiva is said to be Hiranyagarbha's progenitor:

> *Who is the origin and arising of the Devas, the ruler of all, Rudra,*
> *the great seer. Who generated Hiranyagarbha in the beginning,*
> *may he develop for us an auspicious intelligence.*[57]

Yoga practice or Sadhana is said to be one as Pranava, primal sound,[58] Mantra Yoga or OM that is the indicator of Ishvara. All the different Vedic teachings including Samkhya, Yoga and Veda are identified with OM, including the figure of Hiranyagarbha himself.

Yoga in the *Bhagavad Gita* has several definitions, notable among which is the state of balance or *samatva*.[59] Shiva represents the balance of opposites and the transformational point between them. So the Shiva principle in Yoga can be equated beyond the boundaries of Shiva as a deity.

Shiva and the Eight Limbs of Yoga
The eight limbs of Yoga can be interpreted according to Shiva and his qualities.

Yamas are the principles of dharma that allow us to develop the calm Shiva consciousness within us. They consist of principles of self-control of non-violence (ahimsa), truthfulness (satya), non-stealing (asteya), and non-coveting (aparigraha), which allow us to develop peace and stillness as our natural state of awareness. The Yamas are "Shiva self-control principles" that afford us inner peace. *Yama*, the deity of death and Self-control, is a form of Shiva, particularly as the lord of time. Time is the greater teacher who teaches us all the lessons of life and death.

1. Niyamas are means of cultivating and developing self-control, stillness, and balance, what can be defined as the actions and attitudes of Shiva within us. These including tapas, Self-study (svadhyaya), Ishvara pranidhana (surrender to God), purity and contentment (saucha and santosha). Shiva is often defined with tapas as the transforming power of heat and fire, particularly as Rudra and Agni. Shiva as svadhyaya is self-study and the recitation of mantras. Surrender to Ishvara is also surrender to Shiva.

2. Asana; Shiva is the primary deity of asana practice, with asanas being best described in Shaivite Tantric texts.[60] All asanas are regarded as Shiva's poses and movements, but that is just the beginning of his yogic connections. Asana is defined as steady (sthira) and pleasant (sukha), which are other synonyms for Shiva's nature. Asana is the main means for developing the body of Shiva. Shiva is the inventor of 84 lakhs (8,400,000) asanas. Shiva is the Lord of all the asanas, particularly the seated poses that are the most important of all the asanas. He is usually portrayed in either Siddhasana or Padmasana (lotus pose). As Pashupati Shiva or the Lord of the Animals, he is also the lord of the asanas that each animal represents. Shiva is the lord of the dance or Nataraja, which includes the gestures of mudras and the movements of vinyasas.

3. Pranayama; as the great lord of Prana, Shiva is the main deity in the practice of pranayama. Pranayama means developing the Prana or immortal energy of Shiva, who is the great Prana or Mahaprana. Shiva is the breath of God that creates everything and yet holds everything within itself. Shiva represents the holding of the breath in the state of retention, and the ultimate cessation of the breath in the state of Samadhi. Khechari mudra, or holding one's awareness at the soft palate of the mouth, refers to moving in the space of Shiva. Kevala Kumbhaka as the unitary breath behind inhalation and exhalation is the unitary breath that is the life of Shiva. Shiva is the breathless breath that breathes without duality in the stillness of the mind and heart.

4. Pratyahara refers to developing Shiva energy or the power of stillness within ourselves. It is turning inward to embrace the silence, energy, and grace of Shiva. Shiva is sometimes called the related term of Shava or a corpse, symbolizing the one whose senses are turned within. Shiva is dead to the outer world, its noise, chatter, and gossip. Shiva is the state in which the mind is dead or dissolved and no longer interested in pursuing any external reality. Shiva is the deity of Yoga Nidra or yogic wakeful sleep. This is also the supreme state of Nirvana.

5. Dharana – Shiva relates to the bindu, the still point of concentration and its flow. Shiva is the state of pure concentration that upholds the mind and heart, develops the prana and keeps the spine straight. He holds the powers of steadiness, firmness, focus, and wisdom that uphold the practice of Dharana. Shiva gives us back our own power of attention and removes us from any fascination with external sensations. Shiva reveals the supreme wonder of being and consciousness taking us beyond the need for sensation.

6. Dhyana – As the original light of awareness or Prakasha, Shiva is the supreme meditator. Meditation is developing the stillness of the mind of Shiva. Meditation is the mind of Shiva, which is still like a mirror and has a power of endless contemplation and reflection. Meditation is the essence of being Shiva, which is the coolness and calmness of awareness. Meditation is the supreme action of Shiva that constitutes his life. In meditation, we naturally become Shiva and let all that is not auspicious fade away.

7. Samadhi is the ecstasy of Shiva that takes us beyond the mind (the unmada state). Samadhi is the nature of Shiva, who represents the original reality into which everything is merged. Shiva is the being and consciousness of Samadhi that finds bliss and delight in everything.

8. Samyama is the combination of the three higher aspects of Yoga as Dharana, Dhyana and Samadhi. It is the ultimate focus of awareness, which is the supreme state of the Shiva mind.

Shiva and the Branches of Classical Yoga
Shiva relates to all the branches of classical Yoga. We will summarize the main points here.

- Shiva and Jnana Yoga, the Yoga of Knowledge. Shiva is the main deity honored in non-dualistic Advaita Vedanta and non-dualistic Shaivite systems like Siddha Yoga, as he indicates the Supreme Self and its direct realization. Shiva in his youthful form as Dakshinamurti teaches the reality of the Supreme Brahman through silence alone, who is popular in Advaitic temples, schools, and ashrams. Ramana Maharshi, perhaps the greatest modern exponent of the Yoga of knowledge, is regarded as a manifestation of Dakshinamurti. Shankaracharya, the greater philosopher and teacher of Advaita Vedanta is regarded as another manifestation of Dakshinamurti.

- Shiva and Bhakti Yoga, the Yoga of Devotion. Shiva has many devotional forms, and most systems of Shaivism are primarily devotional in nature. Bhakti remains the most popular, simple, and direct form of Yoga with a wide and enduring appeal. Shiva has specific bliss and beauty forms like *Kameshvara* and *Sundareshvara* that are particularly important. Shiva's connection with mantra, chanting, music, and dance is integral to Bhakti Yoga. Shaivite Bhakti Yoga overlaps with the Shakta Bhakti Yoga and the worship of dual forms of Shiva-Shakti as the Divine Father and Divine Mother. The worship of the Divine as Father and Mother in the Yoga tradition occurs mainly through Shiva and Shakti forms. Shiva Bhakti Yoga contains a Yoga of worshipping the Divine in nature through sacred stones, plants, flower rituals, and fire rituals, which is also part of Karma Yoga.

- Shiva and Karma Yoga. Much of traditional Karma Yoga revolves around rituals. These include Vedic fire rituals, of which Shiva, who is frequently identified with Fire or Agni, is commonly the prime deity, particularly in his Rudra form, as in the Mahamrityunjaya Homas and the Rudram. There are also many pujas or devotional rituals to Shiva. Relative to Karma Yoga as seva or service, its second important aspect has an important place in Shaivism also. Shiva has commonly been a deity of the warrior class in India and of political and social action to protect the Dharma.

- Shiva and Raja Yoga. Shiva Yoga is primarily a Raja Yoga, an integral path that emphasizes meditation but acknowledges support practices of asana, pranayama, mantra, and concentration. There are special Shaivite systems of Raja Yoga, particularly in the traditions of Siddha Yoga, using specific texts and teachings that can be a little different than the

Yoga Sutras. Shiva is the king or raja of all the yogis. Shiva represents the power of will that is emphasized in Raja Yoga. As the overall deity of Yoga in all of its approaches, Shiva easily relates to Raja Yoga that combines many other Yoga approaches within itself.

- Shiva and Hatha Yoga. Shiva is the original guru or Adi Natha of the Hatha Yoga tradition.[61] Asana, pranayama, mantra and mudra of Hatha Yoga are integral parts of Shiva Yoga. Shiva relates to self-effort oriented and warrior approaches, such as traditional Hatha Yoga. Shiva holds the supreme power behind all forms of true power Yoga, which is about the inner power of awareness.

Shiva Yoga and Tantra

Most Shaivite Yoga is Tantric and most Tantric Yoga is Shaivite. Shakti based Tantric Yoga rests upon the power of Lord Shiva as its foundation. Tantra broadly speaking consists of a large body of texts, mainly from the medieval period, which developed out of the older *Puranas, Agamas* and *Vedas*, in which there are many teachings about Shiva and Shakti as the dual cosmic powers.

Contrary to modern portrayals, sexual *Tantras* comprise only a small portion of Tantric literature, and are not the focus of most Tantric teachings. While there are Shaivite teachings about sacred sexuality in the form of Shiva and Shakti, Shiva is also the deity of ascetics, renunciates, and celibates. Shakti is the deity of the great Mother Goddess who is best approached by honoring her as the mother of all. While we can recognize Tantric teachings on sacred sexuality, we should not use these to characterize Tantra or Shaivism as a whole.

The *Puranas* are great encyclopedias of Hindu and Vedic lore, encompassing all traditional arts and sciences, history, all aspects of life, religious worship and various philosophies including Yoga, Samkhya, and Vedanta. There are twenty *Puranas* of more than five hundred pages each, making them the largest branch of Hindu and Yogic literature. Owing to their strong devotional nature and emphasis on iconic worship, academics tend to ignore them, though the *Puranas* are quite sophisticated in their philosophy, emphasizing the Supreme deity according to various names, who transcends all duality, including that of Purusha and Prakriti.

Tantras are often encyclopedic in nature and often follow the model of the *Puranas*, on which several of them are based. Yet they are usually not as long or as detailed as the *Puranas*. Like the *Puranas*, the *Tantras* address both rules of outer worship and of inner worship, with the inner worship as Yoga. *Tantras* like *Puranas* have rules for dharma or right action for the different classes of people and stages of life. *Tantras* reflect the same deities, iconography, forms of temple worship, and philosophies as the *Puranas*.

Many Tantric teachings arise from the *Puranas*. The main mantras for worship of the Goddess in the *Devi Mahatmya* derive from the *Devi Bhagavata Purana* to the Goddess. Shiva worship and the practices of Shiva Yoga occur in Shiva *Puranas*, like the *Agni, Vayu, Skanda*, and *Linga Puranas*, which have special sections related to Yoga including mantra, pranayama, and meditation. Yet Shiva is commonly mentioned in all the *Puranas*.

The *Agamas* are a diverse literature like the *Puranas* but of a similar antiquity, and cover similar topics, including rules of iconography and temple worship. Most temple worship in South India, for Shiva, Vishnu and Devi, is Agamic. *Tantras* are often rooted in the *Agamas*. Like the *Puranas*, *Agamas* are in Sanskrit and are rooted in older Vedic texts but have their own special teachings. Shaiva and Shakti *Agamas* are quite extensive and numerous, with much philosophical depth.

There are many specific Tantric texts apart from the *Puranas* and *Agamas* but usually of a later date and Yoga is a common topic to them as well. In addition, there are special Shaivite Yoga texts, extending to commentaries on Vedic teachings. The Hatha Yoga texts of Shaivism include the main texts on Hatha Yoga including the *Hatha Yoga Pradipika, Gherunda Samhita*, and *Shiva Samhita*. The Raja Yoga texts of Shaivism include works of Abhinavagupta like *Tantra Loka*, and special meditative texts like *Vijnana Bhairava* as part of the literature of Kashmir Shaivism. They include Shankara's works and poems on Shiva and Shakti, like *Shivananda Lahiri* and *Saundarya Lahiri*.

Tantric texts emphasize the mysticism of the Sanskrit alphabet and the use of Sanskrit bija and name mantras. Tantric texts bring in Vedic mantras like Gayatri and Tryambakam as well. Tantric Yoga, including ritual, mantra, pranayama and meditation is primarily a form of Raja Yoga, following an integral approach combining devotion and knowledge, Bhakti and Jnana.

Traditional Tantric texts are worthy of a deeper study, especially by modern Tantrics who are not always aware of the roots of their tradition. Tantra is not a license to do anything in the name of spirituality. Rather it emphasizes developing the network of energy and awareness in all aspects of life in order to lead us to the supreme reality.

The Body of Shiva

The Yogi seeks to develop what could be a called the "body of Shiva." *The body of Shiva is the body of Yoga.* The body of Shiva is first of all a physical body purified by the practice of Yoga, adept in asana, and filled with light and prana, having gone through the fire of Shiva. It is a physical body permeated with the power of stillness and peace, in which the sense and motor organs are turned within and held in a state of silence. The body of Shiva is not just a body good at asanas or with the flexibility of a gymnast. It is a body that can endure tapas, austerity, and endurance, and which reflects control over all bodily urges and impulses, including bringing a higher consciousness and bliss into the very cells of the body.

Yet the body of Shiva is not just the physical body. The ultimate body of Shiva is the subtle body and its chakra centers, which allows our deeper Shiva consciousness to develop and manifest. The subtle body holds the energy of Shiva as the power of Prana. It requires a strong physical body in order to hold its high vibratory frequency. The subtle body of Shiva when fully developed merges into the body of the Shiva Linga, which is the causal body of Shiva, the Shiva force that rules over all.

The Mind of Shiva

The "mind of Shiva" is the silent meditative mind – the mind that is cool and serene like a mountain lake, beyond all agitation and disturbance.

- In the mind of Shiva, the *chitta* or core level is deconditioned and free of all karmic patterns and their currents, like the silence at the depths of the sea.
- *Buddhi* or the perceptive part of the mind is clear, sharp, and discriminating like lightning, functioning as a weapon of truth consciousness.
- *Manas* or the outer aspect of the mind is attentive, calm, under control, and non-reactive, not swayed by the sense organs or driven by the motor organs.
- *Ahamkara* or the ego aspect of the mind is merged into the Divine I am, the pure I of Shiva consciousness. There is no separate Self but rather a recognition of all as the Self.

Meditation is a process of cultivating the mind of Shiva by merging our distracted thoughts into the all-pervading consciousness of Shiva that constitutes our core awareness. The mind of Shiva is the mind of peace, in which the whole of reality is mirrored without any personal choice or effort. It is the unitary mind that ever remains in a state of perfect concentration. This mind of Shiva is "no-mind" or beyond our ordinary thought patterns as the detached witness of all that is, outside of any sense of bodily identity.

The Eye of Shiva

The "eye of Shiva" is the awakened and open third eye, through which unitary perception occurs beyond the duality of the outer mind and senses. The eye of Shiva is ever awake and perceiving the truth, though all states of waking, dream, and deep sleep and the entire process of birth and death.

Drishti Yoga or the "Yoga of seeing" requires developing the eye of Shiva and its inner light. The eye of Shiva is the basis of true discrimination through which we can move from darkness to light. It has the power to overcome all desires and fears, and can burn up all negativity in an instant. The Yogi cultivates the eye of Shiva, which is the power of samadhi, the vision of bliss that knows the essence of all. When the eye of Shiva is open within us we perceive all things as full of light. Yet we can also direct that light to remove negativity and bring about self-purification.

Our Shiva Essence

- Shiva sees without an eye. He is the eye of the eye, the inner power of vision.

- Shiva hears without an ear. He is the ear of the ear, the inner power of listening.

- Shiva breathes without the breath. He is the prana of prana, the inner power of existence.

- Shiva speaks without a voice. He is the word behind the word, the supreme word of silence.

- Shiva knows without a mind. He is the mind behind the mind, the awareness that perceives beyond thought.

Shiva is the singular essence of all, the one that makes all things possible and yet stands beyond all. We can return to that essence of Shiva in all that we do and in all that we see, if we but shift our awareness within, through the inner power of peace.

Nada and Bindu
The Cosmic Approach of Shiva Yoga:

The seed imperishable sound (bija) is the supreme bindu (point)
with the wave (nada) above. When the sound in the imperishable
syllable is dissolved, the soundless is the supreme state.

Dhyana Bindu Upanishad 2

When the mind becomes of the nature of the Nada, it no longer
desires anything in the realm of the senses.

Everything dissolves in a state of mergence, in the Nada of the
Divine Word. Liberated from all states, beyond all thought and
imagination.

Nada Bindu Upanishad

Shiva Yoga leads us to a profound cosmic experience of unity and transformation beyond the boundaries of language, mind and thought. It enables us to understand the entire universe, known and unknown, within our own minds and hearts as a single yet unbounded and unending event.

Shiva Yoga is an internalized cosmic knowledge, resembling a higher meditative form of physics and cosmology. It examines the process of cosmogenesis as the natural expression of our consciousness, not simply as an external phenomenon. Shiva Yoga allows us to experience the unfoldment of the entire universe as the very root of our own existence and as a continual state of bliss.

Shiva Yoga rests upon a recognition of the primary cosmic principles through which the universe develops out of the seed state of pure awareness. These powers of higher intelligence form special meditation practices through which we can realize the universal consciousness within ourselves, culminating in the state of the Supreme Shiva behind and beyond all.

In the following chapter, we will focus on the cosmic nature of Shiva Yoga and how it helps us understand the universe within ourselves. We will introduce the key principles of Shaivite cosmology and show how these can unlock the subtle energies of life and consciousness beyond all charted horizons.

Psychology and Cosmology

Modern culture, extending to new forms of healing and spirituality, is largely psychological in nature, emphasizing human joys and sorrows in the realm of time. It aims at helping us gain harmony in our personal existence by removing any emotional trauma or pain that we may be holding from the past. Psychology focuses on uncovering suppressed memories of the present life but does not posit a reincarnating soul beyond the ego of the current birth or understand the movement of karma. It looks at our human relationships as the primary factors in our lives, and does not properly examine our soul connection to cosmic realities.

Psychology, we should note, does have a place in Shiva Yoga but in a secondary manner. Shaivism teaches us how to move from ordinary human emotions, which inevitably involve suffering, into Divine bliss that is beyond ordinary joy or sorrow. In Shiva Yoga, our personal psychology is dissolved into a universal sense of Self, which finds the same life, being and energy in all existence. Shiva Yoga, like classical Yoga and Vedanta on which it is based, follows a philosophical, ontological, and cosmic approach. Its concern is not with personal feelings, which are usually self-centered, but with the greater universe that exists as an all-embracing Being and Consciousness. It directs us from human action and personal becoming to universal Being and unbounded awareness. It orients us to cosmic principles rather than personal considerations, taking us beyond the mind.

Shiva Yoga teaches us that one of the best ways to transcend our personal suffering and human ego – and to purify the mind and heart – is to contemplate the greater universe of consciousness. Bringing in a universal view reduces our psychological problems, which are based upon affording too much attention to the physical self and physical happiness, which is always problematic.

Shiva and Shakti Tattvas:

Pure Consciousness and its Unbounded Energy

Beyond all outer and inner manifestation, gross, subtle and causal that constitutes the known universe of matter, energy and mind dwells the supreme Shiva and Shakti, united, immutable, and full, resting in a single unitary nature. This is the supreme reality out of which all creation in time, space, and action is but a ripple at the surface of its boundless sea. The Supreme Shiva, with its Supreme Shakti merged within it, is the supreme Brahman or impersonal Being-Consciousness-Bliss. Shiva is its light and Shakti is its power of illumination, which in essence are the same.

The two form *Shiva Tattva* or the Shiva Principle and *Shakti Tattva* or the Shakti principle as the two highest tattvas or principles of Shaivite philosophy. They constitute the substratum of creation or the universal manifestation, though in their own nature they are transcendent. The consciousness in the universe rests ultimately upon Shiva and the power of manifestation has its higher basis in Shakti as the power of consciousness.

Nada and Bindu: the Primordial Wave and Particle

Wave and particle theory, are prominent concepts in modern physics, particularly in Quantum Mechanics. There is a debate whether the wave or the particle is primary – whether the entire universe rests at the level of the wave or at the level of a particle. At a quantum level, one cannot measure the wave and particle at the same time. If motion is considered, it is a wave. If location is considered it is a particle. A particular energy can be identified as a wave or as a particle but not as both at the same time. The point is an identification of location. The wave is an identification of movement.

The entire universe, as modern science has revealed, consists of a dynamic twofold interplay of waves and particles. Everything that we see is made up of waves or particles of energy that are interrelated. Waves consist of particles and particles create waves. Neither can be strictly differentiated from the other.

The fixed physical world that we take for granted as real in our ordinary lives is illusory. The boundaries of name and form that appear through our senses are not final, but are as much created by the limitations of our senses as part of any definite external reality. The objects that we perceive in life are but vibratory wavelike appearances of subtler forces, which may have very different qualities. All objects are composed of smaller particles down to subatomic levels that occupy only a minute fragment of the space in which the object appears. Objects are force fields created by subtle particles, not solid in nature.

We can observe this process of particle formation throughout the universe that consists of atoms at material level, or in the human body that consists of cells, the prime building blocks of the body. We can observe the universal process of wave formation, whether it is in the ocean, in the wind, in electromagnetic currents in space, or in the movement of prana within our own bodies and minds. The particle is the steady and form based factor, while the wave is the moving energy, but the two constantly overlap.

Ancient Shaivite Yogis clearly understood the nature of the universe as consciousness and energy, wave and particle, flow and focus simultaneously. In deep meditation they learned how to change the vibratory levels of their own minds and hearts, and directed their awareness into a unitary point of transformation that could take them into new realms of consciousness beyond the known world, as well as bring new powers of transformation into it.

Nada and Bindu and Transcendent Reality

Nada comes from the root "nad" meaning to vibrate or to make sound. Nada also refers to a reed or a channel, through which a vibratory force flows, implying music, like that played through a hollow bamboo flute. As a channel, Nada is connected to the idea of a river, current, or channel, *nadi. Bindu*, which literally means a "drop," is the point focus, the particle, the atom, or monad. It can be any liquid drops like rain, but drop formation on many other levels as well.

As terms like Shiva and Shakti, Nada and Bindu cannot be entirely translated into English. The closest approximation is wave or "wavelike vibration" for Nada and particle or "point-awareness or particle" for Bindu. Nada represents wave motion in all of its manifestations back to the silent Self-sustaining vibration of the Supreme Brahman. Bindu represents the drop or point in all of its manifestations back to the ultimate state of singularity that is the Supreme Brahman.

Nada and Bindu are intertwined as subtle energies beyond the limited boundaries of form that we know of in familiar material objects. Bindu in Yoga is a point of focus on the inside, not merely a place of location on the outside. Nada is a vibratory nexus internally that can take different forms in manifestation. When we throw a rock into water it creates a point of entry or bindu from which a wave like motion occurs or nada. Stars and planets are points or bindus but create nada or vibratory fields in their movement. The bindu point as it moves creates a nada wave. Nada in its inner essence is the bindu point. For another example, we can relate the bindu to the bead on a rosary or mala and the nada to the thread or sutra that holds them together.

Bindu is more the male principle and can relate to the semen, which is discharged in drops. Nada relates more to the female principle that holds and receives. Yet there are masculine waves and feminine points. The body similarly has its *mar-*

mas or "sensitive points" and its currents or waves, including channels that connect the marmas.

Nada relates to our sense of wholeness, completion, and allness. It is the wave that holds the ocean. Bindu reflects our sense of the one, the single, and the unique. It is the one that is all, the drop that is the entire sea. In the Supreme Brahman or Supreme Shiva, Nada and Bindu or wave and particle are one. Bindu and Nada or point and circle, center and periphery are simultaneous and all-pervading.

Bindu is the point that is smaller than the smallest (aniyor aniyam), the ultimate singularity, monad or atom. Nada is the wave that is larger than the largest (mahato mahiyan).[62] We can relate bindu with Shiva or the central still point and nada with Shakti or the peripheral display of energy. The Bindu is the Shiva singularity and nada is its Shakti expansion. We can see the bindu as the spiritual heart and the nada is the thousand-petal lotus of the head.

In the process of manifestation, nada relates to Prana or vital energy that has a wave like motion through the rhythms of life. Bindu relates to the mind that has a point based movement, though the focus of attention. Wherever we direct the mind, a point or Bindu is created. By resolving all our energies and faculties back into nada and bindu, we can return to the supreme reality, the Supreme Shiva, as the unity of Prana and mind, energy and awareness.

It is through nada and bindu that the cosmic manifestation proceeds, though first at an ideal level. The entire universe consists of nada and bindu, which in turn reflects the primordial Shiva and Shakti. One can identify Shiva as the ultimate point of stillness with the primordial point or bindu, and Shakti as the supreme movement with the primordial wave, vibration, or nada – though there are bindu and nada aspects of both Shiva and Shakti. *Bindu Shakti* is literally the point of power or power point. *Nada Shakti* is the field of infinite energy that arises from it.

Nada is sometimes said to produce the bindu, which is the point focus of the nada or vibration. Nada creates the bindu as the wave creates a, or as a cloud creates lightning or rain. Energized nada results in Bindu. Nada is thus not simply a spread out vibration but a vortex or matrix, which creates points of convergence and transformation. Meanwhile the Bindu is always vibrating, carrying and generating a force of Nada or vibration, just as light radiates from the disc of the Sun, or just as stars and planets are ever revolving in a wave like motion in space. The curvature of the wave eventually results in a circle of bindu.

We can compare the unity of Nada and Bindu with a spiraling movement. The spiral has a focus or Bindu and a curving wave like motion from it like a Nada. There are two complementary movements in life of ascension and return. The ascending force of inner evolution is more the Shiva force and the returning cycles, the Shakti force, with the two ever intertwined.

The Nada flowing through the nadi, or the current flowing through the channel, creates a Bindu at its point of opening or its orifice. In fact the energy channel is like a tube created by the point or Bindu. The Bindu allows the energy of the current or Nada to be channeled and spread onto a new plane of manifestation.

Our consciousness has a point focus or Bindu and a vibratory field or Nada. This point focus or Bindu is reflected in the eyes, in visual perception that focuses on one point at a time. The vibratory field or Nada is reflected in hearing, which is omnidirectional and provides a sense of space. The opening of the Third Eye is the awakening of our inner Bindu of higher perception. The opening of our corresponding inner ear is the awakening of the inner Nada of higher revelation. Bindu relates to the higher mind or buddhi focused in perception through the Third Eye, as Nada relates to Prana or the energizing power.

Generally speaking, our power of attention and concentration has a point like focus, while awareness suggests a field. Nada as wave relates more to the power of sound, while Bindu as particle relates more to the energy of light. Yet we can further relate Nada with the idea of a spectrum, as a spectrum of light, with the point of light being the Bindu. Similarly, musical notes are Bindus, while their resonance and melodies are Nada. The interplay of Nada and Bindu creates the universe as a gradual stage-by-stage unfoldment, with point like existence and wave like expression.

Tantric philosophy usually makes the Nada subtler than the Bindu as a cosmic principle.[63] The entire universe arises from a single point that is the Bindu. Yet behind that Bindu there is a subtler Nada or vibration that the Bindu concentrates. The Bindu is a contraction of this primordial Nada of pure potentiality and serves to orient it in a specific direction towards a particular set of actualities.

However, according to other accounts there is a yet higher Bindu behind even the highest Nada, which is the singular state of the supreme Shiva. In this regard, the Bindu is subtler than the Nada and indicates the Self of all. In this regard, the highest Bindu or point focus is Shiva and the highest Nada is its vibratory power or Shakti.[64] This is the Nada Bindu or the Bindu, singularity, of the Nada, wave.

Nada – Vibration, Wave

Nada as a Tantric philosophical term indicates vibration that is the basis of all manifestation through light and sound, time and space, which are all vibratory in nature. Yet Nada is most closely connected to sound, which is the most primal of the sensory potentials, as the sensory quality that relates to the element of space. Nada relates to Prana at the highest level as the unmanifest Prana underlying manifestation, which itself is the root of sound, space and time. Nada similarly is like an electrical current or an electro-magnetic force of an expansive and pro-pulsive nature. One could call electro-magnetism in its various wave like forms as the movement of Nada.

Nada in Yoga also refers an inner sound vibration that one can hear with the inner ear and which arises and expands in the mind during the practice of med-itation. It constitutes an entire branch of Yoga called *Laya Yoga* or the "Yoga of Mergence" that is connected to music overall. This Nada or inner music relates to the music of the nadis and chakras internally, and to the music of the spheres, stars, and planets externally.

Different types of Nadas are mentioned in yogic literature with sounds like that of a drum, a flute, a bell, and an oboe. The OM current is part of these and said to resemble the roaring of the ocean. The practice of Laya Yoga consists of merging the mind into the Nada and tracing the outer Nadas or vibrations back into their origin in the inner supreme Nada behind the mind and Prana. The inner Nada is the Divine Word, the voice of the guru, and Cosmic Sound, OM and Pranava.

Nada as a wave is associated with the idea of the cosmic waters and cosmic ocean of space, with the idea that space has its own vibration. These cosmic wa-ters of space are further identified with Prana as air currents arising from space. Water makes a sound as it flows. Cosmic space is ether that has a wave like vi-bration, currents, eddies and vortexes.

Nada vibrations can resemble clouds swirling in various strata or levels that gives rise to different shapes, forms, and colors. Spiral galaxies suggest such currents of cosmic vibration or Nada. The *Dharma Megha Samadhi* of the *Yoga Sutras*, the "rain cloud of Dharma" that is the highest Samadhi, can be defined as dwelling in the original state of pure Nada, in which all Dharmas or all powers of truth and law are held together and arise through the power of the Divine Word from within.[65]

Tantric philosophy holds that everything in the universe consists of various types and levels of vibration, referred to variously as Nada, *Shabda* (sound vibration), or *Spanda* (vibration of mind or Prana). This Nada weaves everything together into various networks, force fields or *Tantras*, which are fields of feeling, knowledge and seeing inwardly, and fields of energy, action, and transformation externally.

Nada relates Nadis or channels of the subtle body, and to any vibration flowing in a channel. Wherever there is Nada or vibratory current, there must be a Nadi or channel to carry the current. These are not just the Nadis or channels of the subtle body but pervade the entire universe, like the wormholes of modern physics that pervade all of space.

Each object has its own Nada or vibratory level. By changing that level or vibration, the nature of the object can be changed. Matter, energy, light, life, and mind are but different vibratory frequencies of the same force or substance, which is subtler than any manifest object. Nada is thus ultimately the higher Nature or Para Prakriti behind the forms and forces of nature externally, which is the Supreme Shakti. Prakriti as the power of nature is the expression of Nada, which connects us to the vibration of consciousness or the Purusha that holds all vibrations together in a single point.

Great Yogis learn how to change the vibratory patterns of their prana for greater energy and healing, revitalizing body and mind. By merging into a single point or Bindu, they can expand out as a new wave or Nada into a new Loka or realm of perception with its own distant horizons. By changing vibratory rates, we can change the structure, nature, and movement of everything in the universe. Most important is to learn to raise the vibratory rate of our own being, through working on the vibratory powers of speech, breath and mind through Yoga practice.

Nada is said to be the union of Shiva and Shakti and to indicate their relationship, the unity of pure consciousness and its power, from which all energy and vibration arises. It relates primarily to *Sadashiva Tattva*, the third Tattva, also called *Sadakhya*, among the 36 Tantric Tattvas,[66] though it is present to some degree in all the tattvas. Sadashiva Tattva holds the universal manifestation below and takes us to the unmanifest Brahman above. It represents the power of Divine will, the original ruling and guiding vibration.

Bindu – Point, Particle, Singularity

The Bindu is the sizeless point from which all manifestation occurs, the original singularity as in modern physics, which is behind the Big Bang at the beginning of the universe. Bindu is the sense of oneness, aloneness, self-contentment, and inner fullness that relates to our sense of Self, the pure I or Purusha. Bindu is the One as Nada is the Infinite.

Bindus exist on the minutest as well as vastest levels of the universe like quantum particles behind the atom and the quasars behind the galaxies. This Bindu or point/drop singularity occurs throughout nature. Each creature has its Bindus or circular concentrations. We can observe this as the round shape of our heads and of the round eyes placed within. Every force of nature has a Bindu focus through its guiding or transformative power.

The Bindu is a round object or ball. We know how much human beings and even animals like to play with balls. We have games like basketball that involve putting a round ball in a hole. We often eat our food in round balls or shape medicines into round pills. We shape things with our hands in round forms, reflecting the Bindu or round shape in the palm of the hands. We spend much of our lives watching or playing with various balls or Bindus.

The Sun and Moon are Bindus, points, or spheres of light from which light radiates outwardly. All stars and planets are Bindus or round points, which shape is sustained by the circularity of their movement. Water flows in drops or Bindus, particularly as the rain. The blood in the body flows in drops. The Bindu relates to the essence of delight hidden in things, Ananda, which is extracted as drops. This is the Soma Bindu that the *Vedas* speak of, the drops of nectar in the lotus of the head.

Bindu relates to the one-pointed mind or *ekagra chitta* of Yoga practice. Each of these points of mental focus, like drops of fragrant oils, have the power to permeate the entire mental field down to the subconscious mind. Bindus are of various types in higher Yoga practice through the chakras, with three being most important:[67]

White Bindu	Moon, Soma	Mind	Thousand-petal Lotus	Male seed	Shiva	Iccha, will
Red Bindu,	Fire, Agni	Speech	Root chakra	Menstrual fluid	Shakti	Jnana, knowledge
Golden Bindu	Sun, Surya	Prana	Heart	Child[68]	Union	Kriya, action

Bindu relates to *Ahamkara* or to the "I-principle." Our sense of I or Self is singular, though full of power and motivation. The ego is the source of all differentiation and division, yet reintegration or Yoga can be facilitated by the return to the Bindu as one's guiding awareness, the Self behind the ego, prior to its identification with the body and mind.

The Cosmic Ahamkara Bindu, or the seed of Cosmic Ego, is the seed of Prana and sound, the Bindu that holds the entire alphabet, comprising all the sounds from the vowel-a to the consonant-h.[69] These seed sounds give rise to the wave like expressions of speech.

In Tantric philosophy, the Bindu relates to the fourth Tattva, *Ishvara Tattva*, the cosmic lord who rules the universe through his power of knowledge, though the Bindu also exists in various forms on all levels of reality, manifest and unmanifest. The secrets and interrelationships of Nada and Bindu are endless and profound, and can only be touched in words and ideas. We need to experience them in our Yoga practice through pranayama, mantra and deep meditation.

Bija – Seed Mantra

Mantra is the primary practice of Shiva-Shakti Yoga, the teachings of which arise from the mantra as well. Mantra holds the unity of Nada and Bindu, or vibration and point-focus. This occurs not only in human speech but also throughout the universe as the Divine Word or cosmic mantra. Bija or seed mantras are special combinations of Nada and Bindu in their primal states. Sound vibration unites wave and particle as energy and focus or sound and meaning.

Bija, which means a "seed," refers to Bija, seed mantra or *Akshara*, the prime sounds from which the Sanskrit alphabet arises. Bija Mantras are often called "Shakti mantras," as they reverberate the universal power of Shakti. Each Bija mantra contains both Nada and Bindu or vibration and focus. In Sanskrit, this is indicated by the crescent (Nada) and dot (Bindu) written above the *Anusvara* or nasal vowel utterance. *Visarga* or Sanskrit breath sound is also indicated by two dots or two Bindus.

Bindu is the basis of meaning and intention behind the mantra or word, which is its focus. Nada is the basis of sound and power, including the Prana and vitality moving through the mantra. Bija contains not only Nada as sound, but also its focus as Bindu and their specific energization, which is the particular Bija mantra. The Bija Mantra is Nada-Bindu in expression and diversification, starting with OM.

Bija as the place of origin is Shakti as the womb or basis of manifestation, while Nada is Shakti as the higher space or pure potentiality prior to manifestation. Bija is not only the seed but also its field of growth. Bija mantras represent the manifest Nada-Bindu that becomes the basis of particular sounds and letters, yet still at a very subtle level. *As Nada is Prana and Bindu is mind, Bija is speech.* Yet Bija is also a kind of Nada but with the beginnings of a more overt differentiation. While Nada is mainly heard, Bija must be spoken or articulated.

Every force of nature has its own mantric sounds. We can sense these in the sound of the wind or in the sounds of space through radio waves. Every creature has its own mantric sounds. We can sense these yet indistinct bijas or seed sounds in the sounds of insects (crickets, for example) and birds. Bija is thus a more evident subtle form of Nada, as the Nada begins to develop specificity through its connection with the Bindu. From Bija mantras the alphabet or field of verbal sound potentials arises and with it language in all of its forms. From these sounds, ideas and names, through which we can recognize the world of form gradually take shape and arises.

In the cosmic mind, Bija mantras form the main ideals, archetypes, or prototypes behind outer forms and creatures, their inner law or dynamic essence. In the human being, the seed sounds of the alphabet are the basis of the main types of meaning, value, or principles that we follow and organize our lives according to. It is according to our ideas shaped by language that we function in the world, with speech as the ruling power of all our motor organs.

Through the causal power of bija mantras, one can gain the knowledge and the power behind all creation, the cosmic tattvas and elements. Yet for this to occur one must first become a mantric being – a being in whom the mantra predominates, united to the Bindu point of focus and the Nada cosmic vibration. In this state of mantric existence, there can be no ego that can try to use the mantras for personal gain or enjoyment! Then one's thought, speech and breath become Bija mantras.

Bija Mantra relates to *Shuddha Vidya Tattva*, which is the fifth Tattva, meaning pure knowledge, which is the basis for transformative action (kriya) on all levels. The bija mantra contains knowledge but is also able to project it into action as the ruling processes of the universe.

Developing the Power of Nada, Bindu, and Bija Mantra

To truly awaken a bija mantra at its original level of energy, one should first develop the powers of Nada and Bindu within oneself. One gains the power of Nada by the awakening of the inner sound current in the mind, specifically in the central channel or Sushumna, which vibrates with the Nada as the highest of the nadis or channels. This requires cultivating a sense of receptivity and listening both to the inner truth and the sounds of nature and, most importantly, being able to listen to the truth without any resistance. Nada is also awakened by chanting, Pranayama, pranic movements or dance, particularly the unitary prana or the breath held within.

One gains the power of the Bindu by awakening the inner light, particularly at the Third Eye, but also other centers like the base of the spine, navel, heart, top of head, palms of the hands, and soles of feet. Bindu is also developed by deep perception and *trataka* or "fixing of the gaze," including by *Shambhavi Mudra*, focusing the gaze within while the eyes remain open externally. Deep introspection or Self-examination also allows the Bindu to develop.

Both the inner Nada and Bindu arise through dharana, yogic concentration, pure attention, the one-pointed mind. The mind itself becomes the Bindu flowing with the Nada. One can hear these Nadas or inner sound vibrations and see and feel the Bindus pulsating in one's awareness. The Bija mantra is their unified power and expression.

The bija mantra takes the mind back into the Bindu or unitary point and then dissolves it into Nada or pure all pervasive vibration, returning us to Parashiva, which is pure being, the Supreme Brahman. Or, by a complimentary view, the Nada behind the mantra takes us back to the primordial One as the supreme Bindu. This Nada Bindu of OM or Pranava is the supreme vibratory state that dissolves into transcendence.

Kalā – the Cosmic Gestalt or Cosmic Design

Kalā is another important concept of Tantric thought, through which we can understand the design of the universe. Kalā refers to an aspect, portion, approach, or manifestation. Kalā implies division and formation. Division is originally a division of the one into many, which is a replication with the one repeatedly giving rise to larger numbers. This process of repetition begins with the one becoming two, which then multiplies into infinity through all the other numbers. The basic forces behind the universe are dualistic, consisting of input and outtake, reception and expression, inhalation and exhalation. These two multiply on various levels. In other words, all outer division in the universe is only apparent and consists of additional formations of oneness and unity as a greater Self-manifestation.

Kala is primarily a spatial division of which Kāla is the division of time, though each reflects the other. Both terms arising from the root "kal" meaning to count, energize, desire, imagine or set in motion.

Kalā is the basis of all the mathematics, gestalts, patterns, and forms of nature starting with the triangle, which is the most basic of shapes and yantras. While natural forces are usually two, their unity and combined energy in manifestation is three. We cannot make a design with two points only. For that we need at least three points. Kala is the basis of all the designs of nature such as we see particularly in crystals and in flowers.

Kalā is the primal geometry that arises from Nada and Bindu, as point and line creating various patterns. Kalā is the design of the universe and the inner mathematics through which all things develop and can be comprehended. Kalā is the essence of art, reflecting right proportion and proper alignment, through which the underlying idea or meaning behind the form can be understood and expressed.

Kalā is not only division in space but also division in time. It also reflects movement, rhythm, and dance. Time has its seasons and movements though the day, the month and the year. Each season forms and colors the events that occur under its predominance. Soft shapes prevail in the springtime, while nature's lines draw harsh and sharp in the autumn and winter.

Kalā as design indicates the *rasa* or "essence" of each object. Each one of us has our own design or unique energy pattern as a soul. Kalā as the beauty of design allows one to perceive the Ananda, bliss, and Soma reverberating behind all things. It imparts a certain grace and artistry to one's thoughts and expressions. When our minds are aware of the level of Kala, there is precision, beauty and order in our expressions. Kalā relates to complementarity, with the Kalātra, or means of Kala being the wife or partner, allowing us to grasp the universal harmony of apparently opposing forces.

Kalā reveals the forms of the Devatas or Divine powers, both as *Murti* and *Yantra*, manifest form and subtle energy pattern. Kalā as cosmic design is the root of the chakras or subtle energy centers. It is the basis of both the subtle and causal bodies. The causal body is the ideal design pattern behind the subtle body, which in turn is the design pattern of energy for the physical body, which all adhere to a similar pattern of cosmic powers and principles. The Tattvas or cosmic principles are different Kalās, each having its own particular orientation, impetus, and design. Kala as the design of the world is the body of the Goddess, the expression of Shakti, which is the form principle created by Nada and Bindu.

Kalās are generally said to be sixteen in number, reflecting the digits (Kalās) of the Moon – the fifteen lunar phases of waxing and waning, along with the sixteenth or immortal phase, *Amrita Kalā*, which never changes and holds the power of renewal. These sixteen Kalās are reflected in the sixteen vowels of the Sanskrit alphabet. The Kalās as types of art are said to be sixty-four, which is a fourfold extension of the number sixteen.

Kala is the basis of the meters in Sanskrit poetry. Each meter has its particular rhythm or design, its mathematical variation of long and short syllables. Sanskrit meters reflect complex mathematical designs, through which various energies and moods are conveyed. Sanskrit meters are primarily in groups of four syllables, reflecting music and dance.

Kalā is the basis of planning, strategy, vision, and imagination. Kalā is the art of dividing space, and the design of objects placed in space. It is how we define our space and the stage of our lives. We do this through our desires and goals, the things that we want and how we plan to get them. Kalā implies creating a sacred space and Divine design in our lives.

From Kala desire and vision arise. To return to unity, one must turn multiplicity around, which is to discover the One that the many are manifesting from at their origin. Yoga merges all the different principles and kalās of life into the primordial Divine love from which the entire universe arises as an overflowing of grace.

The Supreme Kalā is the One reality or the Bindu that is the basis of all multiplicity. Everything we see is a replication or multiplication of the One Being that is the Supreme Shiva. Yet Kala as Bindu in its rhythmic unfoldment becomes Nada. It holds the Bija or seed of all forms.

Kalā is the designing power of the Supreme Intelligence from which the Universe through Nada, Bindu, Bija, Mantra, and Tantra is the great fabric and design that is created. In Shaivite philosophy it is the first power created by Maya, the creative force in manifestation. Yet its essence transcends Maya as well.

Kamakalā is the design of Divine Love that unites everything together. It is regarded as the original triangle of forces through which everything is created. Kamakalā, the primordial Kalā, is formed by the three Bindus (white, red and mixed or golden) or by Nada, Bindu and Bija together. Returning to the Kamakalā resolves all diversity into unity. At the center of the Kamakalā is the *Parabindu*, which connects us to the *Paranada*, the supreme point and supreme vibration.

Yoga practices develop the design of the subtle body that holds the design of the entire universe. Each chakra center is a center of cosmic design through its related elements, sense, and motor organs that are the main structuring powers in the universe. In Shiva and Shakti Yogas we strive to perceive this underlying design of life and attune our vibrations to it, which links us with the cosmic order of wisdom and delight. That is what Tantra means as the network of forces within, behind and beyond everything.

Spanda or Vibratory Reverberation

Shaivite thought looks at the world as having the nature of vibration or *spanda*. Spanda is a little different in meaning than Nada. While Nada implies a wave or flow, Spanda indicates a reverberation or beat, a pulsation, in which one can sense both Nada and Bindu.

Everything in the universe consists of vibrations. No object or creature is fixed. The boundaries between objects are those of vibrational fields only. This is the field of their Spanda. As vibratory rates change, so does the nature of the object. This is their type of Spanda. Similarly as the spanda of the subject changes, so does the nature of the subject change and what it is able to perceive, including the worlds of experience it can access.

Spanda is something we can all easily understand in the modern world where we work with many vibratory levels of energy through electricity, computers, electro-magnetic fields and radio waves. Spanda as a concept is close to Nada in meaning but even the Bindu or particle has its own spanda or vibration. Kalā also is a design born of vibration, which creates various patterns. The five elements are nothing but five rates of vibration from the slower earth element to the more subtle and dynamic ether. The chakras have different rates of vibration. To move from one chakra to another occurs simply by developing a higher vibration. Yoga practices develop the pulsation that raises our vibrations to the next level.

Each thing in the universe is vibrating with space, time and energy. Each thing is spinning and moving in various waves that create specific vibrations. Vibration or spanda is not a closed field. It is part of a process of drawing in and giving out that eventually extends to the universe as a whole. All vibrations are eventually linked together.

Within the individual the two dominant vibrations are those of prana and mind, or *Prana-spanda* and *Chitta-spanda*. Prana spanda or the vibration of the breath and life-force and Chitta spanda or the vibration of the mind and its thoughts reflect one another. We can use one to adjust the other. Meditation changes the movement of our vital energy, for example, and pranayama can be used to control the mind. Generally speaking, it is easier to alter the movement of the mind through changing the movement of Prana than it is to change the mind to alter the movement of Prana.

Mantra, however, can change the vibratory rate of both prana and mind. The *Mantra spanda* is the root vibration of our being and the easiest to change to bring about transformation. That is why Shiva and Shakti Yogas are strongly rooted in mantra practice.

The purpose of Yoga practice is to develop higher levels of vibration that align us with higher realities and expanded awareness. Yoga works through developing higher vibratory frequencies of mind, speech, and prana, which are interrelated vibratory fields in the reflection of consciousness as the highest vibration. The highest spanda, which is the energization of the consciousness of "I am all" takes us back to the reality of the Supreme Shiva. This is the *Jnana-spanda* or the spanda of the highest knowledge.

Such higher spandas bring about quantum vibrational leaps in awareness. They dawn suddenly and are transformative in their effects. We should note that these quantum leaps are not merely quantitative leaps but, more accurately speaking, qualitative in nature, opening us up to new dimensions of awareness.

Our yoga practice sets in motion various forces that when they reach a certain threshold create the Yo*ga Spanda* or transforming vibration of higher awareness through body, prana, senses, and mind. Out of stillness and balance arises a spanda that takes us to a new level of our being.

This spanda teaching has its practical side. Our spanda or vibration consists of the energies that we regularly set in motion in our lives, through our daily, seasonal and yearly activities. These vibrations both affect ourselves and other people, just as we are affected by our surrounding electrical fields.

We must learn to carefully monitor our vibratory rate and become aware of the forces – sensory, emotional, mental, and intuitive – that we are allowing to move within us. There is no machine or computer that can do this for us. We must learn to monitor our own awareness and its levels of vibration. We need to develop the "vibration of consciousness "or the "vibration of Shiva "within ourselves. Each one of us is vibrating at a certain level and rate that we can consciously learn to alter in order to take our lives to a higher level. We can attune our vibration to the higher forces of Shiva and Shakti. By aligning with the spanda of Lord Shiva and his great gurus we can transcend all vibratory rates and limitations.

Shiva is ultimately the state beyond all outer vibration and Shakti constitutes its inner vibration, through which the entire universe comes into being. To go beyond spanda as mind and prana, we must develop the spanda or vibration of unity and bliss, which absorbs all other vibrations into itself. This *Ananda Spanda* or "reverberation of bliss" is the supreme and enduring transformative energy.

Shiva Yoga, Kundalini and the Chakras:

The Secret of the Hamsa

Kundalini is well known as the inner power of Yoga, through which the chakras are activated and higher states of consciousness can be accessed. It is one of the most visionary and fascinating topics in spiritual thinking today. Yet Kundalini is often misunderstood and scaled down into lesser powers and formations, as are the chakras. Kundalini is ultimately the great Shakti of Lord Shiva working in the individual soul and the basis of all higher consciousness.

Kundalini means "what is coiled" or "what dwells in an altar or a cavity in the ground." It is symbolically regarded, like all pranic forces, as a serpent energy. Kundalini as a specific term is most emphasized in Tantric Yoga, though it reflects a higher energy of consciousness that has many names throughout history and many angles of approach.

Some equivalent to Kundalini can be found in all branches of Yoga going back to the *Vedas* as a higher power of mantra, prana, or awareness. All aspects of Yoga rest upon an energy of Yoga or "Yoga Shakti" that can be defined in terms of knowledge, devotion, concentration, or samadhi, each of which implies the other. Kundalini is closely connected to the Divine Word and power of mantra, with wisdom as a feminine principle, and with the Word as the source of will-power and energy in the universe. Classical Kundalini Yoga in India is an integral part of Tantric Yoga and Shiva Yoga, with approaches in both Raja and Hatha Yogas. New Age thinking in the West has brought in another angle of looking upon it that reveals its healing energies but can obscure some of its higher potentials.

Kundalini and the Physical Body

The basis of most misunderstandings about Kundalini rests upon looking at Kundalini primarily in physical terms. While Kundalini as the root energy of consciousness has ramifications down to the nervous system, it is subtle in nature and dwells on a higher level of existence than either body or mind. It is ultimately a power that pervades all of existence, a portion of the universal Shakti.

The physical reduction of Kundalini is part of modern Yoga approaches that look at Yoga primarily from a physical standpoint as an asana practice. Yet just as modern physics is teaching us how to deconstruct physical reality and see physical objects as but force fields existing in space, Tantric Yoga shows us that behind our apparent dense physical body are subtle energy fields that transcend all physical boundaries of time, place and person. This is what Kundalini is really about.

Classical Yoga aims at developing the subtle or energy body (sukshma sharira). The subtle body relates to the inner nature of the mind (chitta) and is sometimes regarded as a synonym for the mind. The subtle body is the field created by mind and prana that exists around the physical body, but is not limited to physical matter. Yogic concepts like Kundalini and the chakras are energetic rather than physical in nature and apply primarily to the subtle body, to energies and processes rather than to physical formations.

The subtle body relates to the dream body, which is its manifestation. It is a creation of thought and so is much lighter, more malleable, and changeable than the gross physical body. We cannot locate the dream body in physical time and space, or precisely define its specific organs and structures. The dream body can transform suddenly in many ways that the physical body cannot. The same is true of Kundalini and the chakras, their actions, appearances, and experiences.

Kundalini can be compared to a force like electricity that has no fixed form or location. The same electricity in our house can run a heater or a refrigerator, a fan, a sewing machine, or a computer. We cannot identify the nature, form or location of the electrical energy according to that of the different machines that it operates. Though there are electrical circuits in the house, the electricity itself can operate other houses and has an existence apart from anything that runs under its power.

In Tantric Yoga, one energizes the subtle body that has a similar appearance but different nature than the physical, being composed of energy and light only. One works with the subtle body in order to go beyond the physical body. One should view the subtle body as the body of the divine presence within us, not as our own personal body.

The Tantric practitioner is asked to visualize his or her own body in the form of the deity in order to remove our attachment to our existing physical structure. One should visualize the subtle body, though appearing like the physical body, as made of energy, light and consciousness, not of flesh or physical matter. This helps us purify both body and mind. One looks at ones own body as the body of Shiva and Shakti, transparent and filled with bliss and awareness. One can visualize this energy body in different sizes and locations, most commonly in a miniature form placed in the lotus of the spiritual heart.

Kundalini as Shiva's Shakti in the Individual Soul

Kundalini in its true nature is the Shakti or power of the individual soul (Jivatman) that seeks to unite with Shiva or the supreme Self (Paramatman). Kundalini reflects our highest aspiration, which is our soul's search for immortality and eternal life. Kundalini does this by rising out of its state of latency in the subconscious mind and root chakra, and ascending the central channel or sushumna up to the thousand petal lotus of the head that is the abode of Shiva and the highest awareness.

For this to occur the Kundalini must first be awakened from its ordinary state of latency. This requires that we move beyond any physical idea of reality of bodily identity to recognizing the supreme power of consciousness, of which all forms are but shadows or waves. We must remember our own immortal nature and the many births of our soul in its Godward journey.

Kundalini, though energetic in nature, is no mere unconscious or inanimate force like electricity. Kundalini is a higher power of Prana and awareness. In this regard, Kundalini is a manifestation of Devi, the Goddess or Shakti, the consort and feminine counterpart of Lord Shiva. Kundalini is Parvati, the wife of Shiva, seeking to return to her abode with him. Kundalini is *Chit-Shakti*, the energy of consciousness that complements *Chit-Jyoti* or the light of consciousness that is Shiva. Kundalini is a sacred power that we must approach with humility and respect, not like electricity, a power that is inanimate and can be controlled from the outside.

Kundalini is the power and the grace of the Divine Mother and carries the higher evolutionary potential of Mother Nature. She relates to the Uma form of Shiva's wife that is the fiery power of tapas or the fire of Yoga. Kundalini is the wife of Shiva that we must honor in order to reach Shiva. Kundalini is no mere inert force that we can manipulate for our own personal benefit. It is the power of God or the Divine reality within us. To honor Devi or Shakti as sacred is the foundation of all authentic Kundalini Sadhana, for which she is the inner power and guide.

Serpents symbolize electrical and pranic energy in yogic thought, what is called *Vidyut Shakti*, the power of lightning, which moves in various channels in both the external world and in our own bodies and minds. Shiva as the lord of serpents has the awareness to handle the Kundalini force. In order to work with such serpentine energies and their potential poisons, we need the equipoise of Shiva, which only arises by surrendering to the peace, calm and fearlessness of Shiva within ourselves.

Kundalini Shakti is Shiva's Shakti inherent within us at an individual level. It is the portion of *Mahashakti*, the great consort of Shiva within us. Kundalini is a manifestation of Shiva's Shakti and requires the consciousness of Shiva in order to control its great power that extends to the universe as a whole.

Kundalini contains within herself all potentials for the higher evolution of consciousness. This means outwardly promoting a higher development of the brain and nervous system, particularly the neocortex of the brain. Inwardly it means going beyond the physical and personal state altogether. Once awakened, Kundalini takes the soul from its individualized or Jiva state to its transcendent or Shiva state. Kundalini is our potential to become Shiva at the core of our being.

Kundalini: Prana and Pranava, Breath and Mantra

Kundalini as the pranic energy behind the individual soul sustains it through the entire process of reincarnation, propelling it to eventual Self-realization. Kundalini carries our memories and aspirations as a soul as it strives to grow in consciousness from one life to another. Often its awakening brings out higher past life tendencies within us, allowing us to feel our enduring existence in time. Kundalini is the life that exists even in death, and which allows us to cross over death into a new birth into eternity.

This higher Prana of Kundalini is a manifestation of primal sound or Pranava, the Divine Word. Kundalini is said to be composed of the garland of the fifty letters of the Sanskrit alphabet that are prime seed mantras that arise from OM. Kundalini as sound is a manifestation of all mantras. Shiva as the origin of sound and mantra is the spirit behind Kundalini, which is his power of Shakti in the individual soul. That is one reason why chanting helps awaken the Kundalini.

Kundalini is defined as the force of Pranava or primal sound vibration and its wave like expression as Nada. Nada is like the body of the serpent while the Bindu, the still point, is like its head. The serpent when at rest is like the Shakti

Yoni or coiled in the womb, when in action it is like the Shiva Linga or straight like a pillar. The Shiva Linga symbolizes the awakened Kundalini and its union with Shiva.

- Kundalini is the energy of the voice of Shiva that is primordial sound. Kundalini as primal sound is Omkara. Its three and a half coils are the three and a half syllables of OM, as A, U, M, and Bindu or point. Kundalini is the power of OM as it moves upward.
- Nada relates to the *Paravak* or supreme level of sound in the root chakra, while the Bindu relates to the point awareness, the drop of the Moon and the nectar of Shiva in the thousand petal lotus of the head.

Kundalini as an electrical force of Prana, light and sound contains Nada and Bindu, or the wave and the point, as well as all Bija Mantras. She dwells in Kamakhya, the womb or altar of the Earth or root chakra, which is also Kamakalā, the triangle of the root chakra, which holds the threefold law of all manifestation. She unfolds all the Kalās and Tattvas, the factors of cosmic structure and design, in her ascension. Her movement reveals all the secrets of cosmogenesis and helps us understand the inner workings of nature as a play of consciousness.

Types of Serpents

There are many different types of serpents in Vedic thought, generally divided into those of the three worlds of the Earth, the Atmosphere and Heaven. Most commonly serpents as powers of lightning relate to the Atmosphere. Higher types of serpents or *Nagas* are known for their wisdom and are similar to dragons.

Vishnu's serpent *Ananta* upholds the entire universe as the unlimited power and potential for creation. He gives us the power of asana or steady and comfortable posture. Shiva wears his serpent *Vasuki* around his neck, symbolizing his power of speech and mantra.

Kundalini encompasses all three types of serpents. Her dwelling in her dormant state is in the Earth (Muladhara). Yet she has the power to rise through the atmosphere (Prana) and ascend to Heaven (the lotus of the head). Ultimately, Kundalini is a serpent or electrical energy of space, specifically the space of consciousness, which is the highest form of serpent. The liberation of the individual soul implies the liberation of its energy or creative power as the Kundalini to move anywhere and pervade the entire universe.

The Chakras as Energy Centers

The chakras are not simply physiological or psychological centers; they are centers of the Tattvas and Shaktis, cosmic principles and their related powers. The physical and psychological aspects of the chakras are but outer workings of the inner chakras that are spiritual in nature. Kundalini Shakti as it ascends and expands energizes the chakras, which is symbolized by the petals of the chakras opening and turning upward. This ascent implies a condition of unitary prana and unitary mind, a state of samadhi, inner balance and equipoise. The inner chakras can be experienced only to the extent that we let go of our ego consciousness and identification with body and mind.

In the ordinary person, the chakras, like Kundalini, exist in a latent state and function on reserve energy only. The chakras work indirectly through their physical reflections in the nervous system. The connection of the chakras with cosmic consciousness is not developed. In Shaivite Yoga, this higher opening of the chakras occurs as part of Yoga sadhana or inner Yoga practice. It is not something that can be induced from the outside in a mechanical manner, though we can use the outer chakras to improve our physical well-being without necessarily awakening their inner potentials.

Each chakra is a center of Shiva-Shakti energies, a blending of the two cosmic powers. The central point of each chakra, its bindu, relates to Shiva and its peripheral unfoldment through its petals or nada relates to Shakti. The chakras are not literally lotuses or chakras (wheels). They are force fields and dynamic centers through which energy is generated according to various geometrical patterns of cosmic law.

The chakras are patterns of cosmic sound and light. The chakras are yantras, geometrical energy matrixes, and manifestations of Kalā, or the cosmic design principle. The chakras are branches on the tree of the spine and subtle body that develops from Nada, Bindu and Bija, from vibration, point focus, and mantric seed energy.

The chakras arise from the energy patterns of the cosmic alphabet of sound vibration, which is reflected in structure of the Sanskrit alphabet. They are the prime vibratory codes behind all manifest existence, and reflect the unfoldment of the sound patterns inherent in the Kundalini.

While we can access the chakras more easily at certain locations by the spine, they are not actually located in the physical body and are not limited to any physical locations. To enter into the chakras at the level of consciousness, we must move beyond time and space, from localized appearance to non-localized essence. We must eventually merge the subtle body with all of its chakras into the spiritual heart, which is the "heart of Shiva" and the seat of the higher Self.

The chakras are not located in the body, but the body is an expression of the chakras. The chakras as energetic formations can have different forms and aspects. For example, in Tibetan Vajrayana Yoga, the navel chakra has sixty-four petals, while in Hindu Tantric Yoga it has only ten. One might think that this is a sign that the chakras are purely imaginary and have no reality. The ten petals of the navel chakra reflects its pranic connection to the five sensory and five motor organs. The navel as having sixty-four petals reflects the many subtle nadis that radiate from it, governing all the dualistic forces of life.

Kundalini and Soma (Amrita)

Shiva primarily relates to the Soma principle, the amrit or nectar of the thousand petal lotus of the head, which is called the "region of the Moon" in Tantric thought. Kundalini Shakti is the Agni, fire, or electrical energy arising from the root chakra. Kundalini rises to drink the Soma, which drops upon her ascending energy as a nourishing food or nectar in order to allow her to climb step by step, strata by strata, level by level, Loka by Loka, which are developments of her vibratory power.

Soma as Divine love awakens the Kundalini at a deep and calm level. The best and safest way to arouse the Kundalini consists of first developing our own inner Soma of peace, devotion, and concentration – to learn to flow in harmony with the beauty and bliss of life. Without Soma we cannot truly access Kundalini or understand her power.

In the majority of Tantric Yoga teachings, Agni or fire relates to the Shakti force and Soma or the Moon is the Shiva force. Yet in Devi Tantric teachings the duality of Agni and Soma is represented the fiery and water aspects of Shakti herself as *Tripura Bhairavi* and *Tripura Sundari*, the triple forces of fiery purification, on one hand, and of watery delight on the other. In other Tantric teachings, Agni and Soma are regarded as the fiery and watery or harsh and soft aspects of Shiva himself, what are called Rudra and Shankara, with Rudra meaning fierce and Shankara as the bestower of blessings.

The Secret of the Hamsa (Hamsa Rahasya)

Shiva Yoga and Hamsa

The Hamsa as a bird is portrayed in later Sanskrit literature as a swan, which is a symbol for Prana and the inner Self that is the highest Prana. The Hamsa in Puranic thought is the vehicle for Lord Brahma, the Creator, and his consort Sarasvati Devi as the bringers of knowledge. Yet Hamsa has other meanings and there are many forms of Hamsas back to the *Rigveda* where the Hamsa is primarily a solar symbol, the bird of light. Hamsa is also the *shyena*, the hawk or falcon that steals the Soma and takes it up from the Earth to enjoy it in the freedom of the highest Heaven.

The Hamsa in Tantric thought represents the individual soul or Jiva, whose life is governed by the breath, and all the dualities that arise from it. This is because Ha and Sa are the natural sounds of the breath through inhalation and exhalation. Many forms of Pranayama follow these sounds accordingly.

Yet at a higher level beyond duality, Ha and Sa are the natural sounds of the Self, which is the inner breath of awareness, the unitary Prana that is Self-existent and immortal. Ha is the Self as I (aham) and Sa is the Self as that or the inner Being. Hamsa also refers to the supreme or *Paramahamsa*, which is the liberated soul that dwells in the state of the Supreme Shiva. In this regard, Hamsa teachings are an integral part of Shiva Yoga and Shiva is also Hamsa. Hamsa as sound and prana vibration is also OM or Pranava.

Hamsa represents the union of Shiva and Shakti, which are Ha and Sa, Sun and Moon, Prana and Apana, the incoming and outgoing vital energies. All dualities, starting with the breath, are a reflection of the greater two-in-one power of Shiva and Shakti.

In terms of Tantric Yoga practices, the Hamsa represents the Shiva principle as the Kundalini, the Shakti principle. Hamsa and Kundalini must unite and move together. It is the Kundalini that carries the Hamsa up the spine. At the same time, it is the Hamsa or soul energy that turns the Kundalini into a force of spiritual aspiration and ascent.

As Kundalini is the serpent power or Shakti of the soul, Hamsa is like the bird or Shiva/Purusha of the soul, whose two wings are prana and mind. Hamsa is the Jiva that seeks to fly upward to heaven, the thousand petal lotus of the head.

Together Kundalini and Hamsa are the feathered serpent, or the bird that flies upward holding the serpent. Yet Kundalini is not always a serpent, it is sometimes a bird, the Hamsa. Similarly, the Hamsa is not always a bird; sometimes it is also a serpent. Both serpent and bird indicate electrical and ascending energy. The Hamsa is an extension or expansion of the bindu or the point-focus in its movement and expansion. Yet the Nada or vibratory principle forms its wings.

Without this soul awakening or *Hamsa Chaitanya*, the "consciousness of the Hamsa," one cannot work with Kundalini Shakti in a completely harmonious manner. If the Kundalini moves without the Hamsa, it is likely to disturb our physical and subtle bodies. It is Shakti without Shiva. First one must awaken the Hamsa in order to effectively awaken the Kundalini, though both tend to manifest together. This means to awaken as an individual soul in its perennial pursuit of the Godhead.

The Hamsa is the Jiva or individual soul that must take its journey back through the chakras guided by Shakti, to realize the supreme Shiva above in the thousand petal lotus of the head. The Hamsa is propelled in its ascending movement by Nada (vibration), Bindu (concentration) and Bija (mantras). It moves through the energies of the Lingas (powers of stillness) and Yonis (powers of receptivity) along the way. The Hamsa carries the Soma or nectar of delight up from the lower chakras to the thousand petal lotus of the head, where it can release it in a thousand streams.

Yet there are several types and colors of Hamsa, reflecting the cosmic energies that it is working with:

- Nila Hamsa – Dark blue Hamsa, power of electrical energy or lightning, the Vidyut Hamsa, represented by the bija mantra *Krīm*. Here the dark blue is that of a rain cloud from which the streak of lightning arises.

- Suvarna Hamsa – Golden Hamsa, the expansive power of the Sun and the heart, Surya Hamsa, represented by the bija mantra *Hrīm*.

- Shveta Hamsa – White Hamsa, the expansive power of the Moon, the Soma Hamsa, represented by the bija mantra *Shrīm*.

- Rakta Hamsa – Red Hamsa, the ascending force of Fire, Agni Hamsa, represented by the bija mantra *Hūm*.

These different types of Hamsas are manifestation of the same Hamsa that is the soul in all of its manifestations.

Hamsa Yoga: Shiva Hamsa Mantras

Hamsa as the sounds of Prana combines mantra and Prana in various forms of Hamsa Yoga. Hamsa mantras serve to awaken the inner consciousness and aid the soul in its ascension to Divinity. They are perhaps unparalleled in this regard. They are commonly used to promote Shiva awareness, to stimulate the Kundalini, and open the chakras. Below are a few examples. *Hamsa* – used as the natural sound of the breath, particularly Ham as inhalation through the right nostril and Sa as exhalation through the left; relates to the day or solar breath.

- *So'ham* – also used as the natural sound of the breath, particularly So as inhalation through the left nostril and Ham as exhalation through the right; relates to the night or lunar breath.

- *Hamsa Soham* – combines both, and reflects the balanced movement of the unitary prana, through the unity of the Sun and Moon.

- *Shivoham* – the natural resonance of the prana and mind as "I am Shiva," the supreme Self-aware Prana.

- *Hamsa Soham Shivoham* – Combined meaning of "I am he, he am I, I am Shiva." This is the "Shiva Hamsa mantra."

- *OM Hūm Hamsa* – Adds the fiery mantra Hum with Hamsa as the solar breath to arouse the Kundalini, the Agni Hamsa Mantra. For example, *OM Lam Hūm Hamsa* stimulates the Kundalini in the root chakra.[70]

- *OM Hrīm Hamsa Soham Svaha* – Mantra to the Supreme Light, uses the solar mantra Hrīm and the fire offering mantra Svaha. It is a Surya or Solar Hamsa mantra.[71] Many other mantras can be added to this. Using the lunar mantra Shrim instead of Hrīm, it becomes a Soma or lunar Hamsa mantra.

- *OM Hūm Hamsa Soham Svāhā* – Mantra to the Supreme Light emphasizing Kundalini and Agni; Agni Hamsa mantra.

The Hamsa is the all-pervasive cosmic power of prana, sound, light, and Self-awareness. The main seer of the Hamsa and So'ham mantras is the Vedic Rishi Vamadeva. He recognizes these different forms of the Hamsa in a special verse from the *Rigveda*, explained below, which shows the intricacy of the Vedic Yoga.[72]

1. Light form in Heaven – Sun or Surya – Śuci – light of the higher mind or buddhi.

2. Pervasive power in the Atmosphere – Wind or Vayu – Vasu – light of inner prana.

3. Invoking power on Earth – Agni – Hota□ – light of illumined speech.

4. Inner and timeless guest – Atithi – timeless divine light of the witness.

5. The Hamsa that dwells in the soul – Nṛ – light of the individual soul or Jivatman.

6. Hamsa that dwells in the supreme – Vara – light of the supreme Self or Paramatman.

7. Hamsa that dwells in the truth – Ṛta – light of the cosmic truth, Tattva Hamsa.

8. Hamsa that dwells in space (the inner space of the heart) – Vyoma Hamsa – light of the space of awareness in the heart, Akasha Hamsa.

9. Hamsa born of the cosmic waters – Abjā – light of the cosmic space and the power of bliss.

10. Hamsa born of the milk of light – Gojā – light of the creative and nurturing power of consciousness.

11. Hamsa born of the cosmic mountain – Adrijā – light of the power of Being.

12. Hamsa born of the supreme truth – Ṛtam Bṛhat – light of the Absolute, Satya Hamsa.

Levels of Approaching Shiva:
Shiva Yoga and Shiva Sadhana

Shiva reflects the multileveled universe that manifests from transcendent Being-Consciousness-Bliss and unfolds organically to the very Earth on which we stand. There is a pure and absolute unity at the higher levels that develops into a unity-in-multiplicity below, which becomes almost entirely obscured in the separate forms of our material world.

The same forces that occur on one level of the universe occur in different ways on the others. Yet what are forces of integration in the higher worlds become forces of division and separation in the lower worlds. Divine forces become obscured in the lower levels as mechanical, unconscious forces - or anti-Divine or Asuric energies that appear as the opposite to the Divine powers above and compete with them.

The human embodiment provides the individual soul with a brain and intelligence that is capable of realizing our universal Shiva nature. Yet this is only possible through sustained and deep spiritual practices over many births. It is not a given state for humanity as we know it, but the highest development of our human potential that only a few rare individuals can ever hope to entirely realize in their current incarnation. We are all Shiva in manifestation, only the manifestation of our Shiva nature is as yet incomplete. The purpose of human evolution is to manifest the awareness of Shiva and his universal power and knowledge within his own creation. We must all move on the path to Shiva to develop the higher potentials of our species. For these to manifest on a mass level could take thousands of years to come, however, and is not at all imminent!

Yet our human nature has a dual potential and can also develop in a way that allows undivine powers to come into the world, the very forces that oppose the power of Shiva. The human being can work to undermine the spiritual force in the world rather than to facilitate it. This has become the condition of humanity today, in which powers of ignorance and violence rule over the planet, often with great cruelty or indifference to the pain of others. The only antidote for this world crisis is to bring in the power of Shiva, the Supreme Lord of all, to whom even the forces and principalities of darkness must bow down to and surrender.

Going Beyond Physical Reality

Our minds are habituated into dealing with only one level of interpretation of what we observe, outward in view, in which we look at things according to fixed parameters of person, object, date and location. Our minds reflect our involvement in physical reality, whose rigid boundaries we project on reality as a whole, including into the spiritual realm - thinking in terms of name and form, number and quantity, even relative to the infinite and eternal.

While such a time-space specific way of looking at things can help us understand the practicalities of the physical world, where these distinctions seem definitive, it is inaccurate and inappropriate relative to yogic realities, in which the normal rules of time, place, and person, form and function do not apply. To develop the inner practices of Shiva Yoga, we must learn to see the One in the many and the many in the One, eternity in an instant, and infinity in every point. A major shift in vision is required, which means a deeper level of perception of a non-physical, non-localized and non-linear type that cuts through the appearances of the external world to their underlying laws and energies that in turn dissolve like waves into a deeper awareness.

Shiva Sadhana

Shiva Yoga consists of various *sadhanas* or sets of yogic practices, performed to help us realize the state of Shiva or to gain his grace for our various needs in life. Sadhanas can be simple in nature like repeating a single mantra like *OM Nama Shivaya*, or meditating upon Shiva as the Self within the heart.

Sadhanas can be comprehensive and intricate, taking a great deal of time or the use of various external factors. Broader sadhanas involve rituals, use of representational forms (statues and lingas), mantras, yantras, nyasas (consecrations), mudras (gestures), pranayama, concentration, and meditation. They include all eight limbs of Yoga, along with other factors of worship, including temple worship and pilgrimages. All aspects of the spiritual life are explored to which art, philosophy and science may also be included.

Ignorance and the Three Malas

The individual Soul is subject to ignorance, karma and suffering by its lack of knowledge of the higher tattvas. There are three aspects of this root "impurity" called *malas* in Sanskrit, by which the individual soul is bound and held in various limitations leading to suffering. Our problem in life is not sin or even karma but impurity that consists largely of clouded perception. This gets us caught in external bondage. Shiva Sadhana is designed to remove these malas.

1. Anava Mala: This is the primal ignorance of the individual soul, consisting of the identification of Self and consciousness with external factors. The individual considers himself to be a separate entity apart from the universal consciousness. He is unaware of the higher Tattvas in which unity prevails and loses his sense of his eternal nature. This external projection of Self is the root of ignorance. Our true sense of "I am" is not a separate state but our reflection of the universal I am of the Supreme Self. Knowing that we go beyond all ignorance.

2. Mayiya Mala: This refers to the impurity arising from Maya or illusion. Confused by the external realm of appearances, the individual soul takes the external world to be real in itself apart from consciousness or Shiva. He also perceives the objects of the world as separate and different. He sees himself as a body. This mala is like the trunk of the tree of illusion developing from the root of ignorance. All that we see is Shiva in various names and forms energized by his Shakti. Once we realize this we go beyond all Maya, seeing it as no more than a creative play.

3. Karma Mala: This is the impurity arising from karma, which entrenches us in the realm of ignorance and illusion. The individual soul considers itself the agent or doer and comes under the bondage of various types of karmas and samskaras. He assumes a separate power of action, which in turn binds him to the limited results of his own karmas. This mala is the full development of the tree of ignorance with its branches, flowers and fruit. Note that whatever we do is only through the power of Shiva, not through anything that belongs to us as a separate individual. Once we realize this and give up our sense of doership we can go beyond all karmas.

The Four Levels of Shiva Initiation

There are four primary levels of Shiva Sadhana, as outlined below. I have presented this material in a simple way. There are many details of the different factors that occur at each of these levels.

1. Anupaya – Direct Realization Beyond All Methods

Anupaya means "without any *Upaya* or method." It is the method of no method, the practice of no practice. Anupaya is the direct realization of Shiva as the Self, *Shivoham* or "I am Shiva." It is much like the direct Self-realization of Advaita Vedanta given through the *Mahavakyas* or Great Sayings of the *Upanishads* such as *Aham Brahmasmi* or "I am Brahman." The Anupaya approach relates to the highest level of aspirant, who can immediately realize the truth when pointed out to him by a realized Guru.

The realized teacher imparts this knowledge through a word, a glance, a gesture, or an indication. The ripe disciple reaches the realization of Shiva consciousness immediately without any additional effort. There is an immediate dawning of Shiva consciousness, a recognition of the pure light of Shiva, and the understanding of Shiva Tattva as ones true nature and true reality from which there is no subsequent departure.

The Anupaya level is obviously only for very advanced souls who are prepared to merge into Shiva consciousness, which is extremely rare, particularly in the modern age in which our minds are dulled by the mass media and our intellects lack humility. It can also occur when students of the lower levels rise to the point at which they are ready for the direct knowledge. This is more commonly the case.

Yet this direct knowledge that ones true nature is Shiva should be taught to everyone, so that they can gradually become receptive to it. All followers of Shiva Yoga should recognize that the true knowledge of Shiva is ultimately beyond all methods and approaches, which are only outer aids and preparatory in nature.

One should continue to follow all helpful means and methods along with the direct teaching until the full and steady realization dawns. A true guru never recommends a disciple to give up any helpful practices until their fruit is gained and one is ready to transcend. If a student gives up helpful practices prematurely, his ability to reach or abide in the supreme truth may be severely compromised.

2. Shambhava Upaya – The Path of Continuous Awareness

Shambhava means what relates to the nature of Shiva as *Shambhu* or the giver of grace. This is the highest Upaya or method, the most direct method that can quickly result in realization. It is the method of recognizing Shiva as existing in all things.

Shambhava Upaya involves the concentrated use of the mind and will as directed to Shiva consciousness, whereas the Anupaya approach happens spontaneously and immediately. The Shambhava Upaya requires holding to a state of awareness that everything in the universe is Shiva – letting go of the mind's outer activities so that it can dissolve into its inner focus. It is still a very advanced state and is non-conceptual in nature, a cultivation of insight.

According to the great teacher Abhinavagupta, Shambhava Upaya occurs when those who cannot enter into the light of Shiva Tattva directly, by recognizing the independent power of Shakti can then enter into it.[73] One recognizes the entire universe as a reflection (pratibimba) in the space of the Supreme Shiva created by Shakti as the power of consciousness. "All this universe is a reflection in the space of consciousness." [74] It is a way of entering into Shakti Tattva from which Shiva Tattva can be easily accessed.

Abhinavagupta explains the Shambhava Upaya relative to a special Mantra Sadhana through the letters of the Sanskrit alphabet, which indicate the prime powers of Shakti. The mantra serves as a mirror in order to reveal the Shiva nature inherent in all things. Each object in the universe is a manifestation of mantra Shakti that manifests in the consciousness space of Shiva.[75] Once one sees this one then can immediately recognize the presence of Shiva everywhere.

3. Shakta Upaya – The Path of Deeper Meditational Practices

Shakta Upaya relates to the power of Shakti, with the term here meaning "determined effort," implying a greater exertion at the level of the mind and the practice of meditation. It requires a degree of imagination, thinking, or mental activity (vikalpa). It has a conceptual component, but an inner examination that takes us beyond ordinary mechanical thoughts, such as dominate our mind from the subconscious, to a state of higher yogic contemplation. Here one trains the mind to constantly think of Shiva as the Self and identify with it.

The Shakta Upaya can involve direct statements like *Shivo'ham* or *Aham Brahmasmi* like the higher methods, but meditated upon as affirmations to gradually draw us to the realization, not yet a direct experience of the truth of these profound statements. It also involves cultivating detachment and discrimination, the *vairagya* and *viveka* of Yoga and Vedanta. One purifies ones mind from worldly thoughts to spiritual thoughts in order to take the mind eventually to the state beyond thought and duality. Shakta Upaya is mainly the level of meditational or psychological practice.

Some may regard this stage as an unnecessary development as it sets in motion additional thinking, but it is very difficult to move from the attached state of mind to the direct perception of Shiva, without first cultivating a deeper level of thought and contemplation. Shakta Upaya involves replacing lower samskaras with higher samskaras, refining the mind by sattvic mental activity in order to eventually reach the thought free state. By the mind constantly contemplating the Self within, it gradually becomes merged into the Self. It is more a path of inner meditation than outer methods, a Yoga of Knowledge or Jnana Yoga, or a Raja Yoga or Yoga of Will power.

4. Anava Upaya – The Path of Individual Effort through Yoga

Anava Upaya is the primary level of practices that relates to the full range of Yoga methods, rituals, asana, pranayama, mantra and meditation. Detailed sadhanas occur here and most of yoga practice, extending to all the methods of Hatha Yoga as well as outer forms of worship.

One begins at this stage knowing oneself as an individual aspirant caught in the world of duality, karma and ignorance and gradually strives to evolve beyond it. This is always the condition of the great majority of people. Not only psychological and meditational methods can be done at this stage, but also physical and pranic efforts. Often a good deal of outer purification is required here, including relative to the physical body, like Ayurvedic practices. Performance of good karmas may be necessary first to help neutralize the effects of difficult karmas from the past.

Sometimes people object to this level of defined practices stating that since the Self or Shiva state is naturally realized, such outer practices are not necessary and may breed confusion or distraction. We must remember that such Yoga practices are not meant to realize the Self, which is self-effulgent, but to remove the impurities in body and mind, which abound in human beings, particularly in our non-spiritual era today, so that this natural state of realization can manifest itself. That is why this level of practice is always most relevant to the largest number of people.

Generally students move from the lower to the higher Upayas, from fixed regular practice to the spontaneous realization state. This can take years or lifetimes owing to the strength of our samskaras or past life karmas. One should not give up helpful practices until one has realized their fruit, which may require a recognition of such by the guru. The final realization will dawn of itself but not unless the foundation is created in this or in previous lives. One need not be in a hurry to reach the highest state, as such an expectation usually reflects an undeveloped mind. The higher realizations dawn from the state of enduring peace.

Once the Shakti of practice (Sadhana Shakti) is awakened it will lead the student through whatever practices may be necessary. The role of the true teacher is to help unfold that inner Sadhana power that leads us to Shiva. We should aim at developing that power of practice and not try to rush any results or project any experiences. That Yoga Shakti often works through the unexpected, unplanned, spontaneous, and natural; thus helping us understand the Shiva-Shakti powers and qualities at work already within and around us, and how to access their higher potentials.

Fire Rituals and Bhasma

Fire rituals (havans and homas) are common in Shiva worship owing to the ancient connection of Shiva with Agni, the Cosmic Fire principle in the *Vedas*. Many Shiva temples have fire altars along with images and lingas. Shaivite yogis often keep a perpetual fire burning at their place of sadhana. External fire altars reflect internal fire altars like the altar of the heart, in which inner offerings of speech, prana and mind can be made to Shiva in his Rudra form as the inner fire of consciousness (Chidagni).

The *bhasma* or sacred ash of Shiva is very important in his worship, and commonly used to anoint the linga or the murti of Shiva. Sometimes sandalwood powder and kumkum (red turmeric powder) is used along with the bhasma. Some gurus give initiation with their specially empowered bhasma and give some to the student to use regularly, particularly applying on the Third Eye, as the basis of their meditation practices. The bhasma symbols our immortal Shiva essence purified by fire. Through the bhasma we can go beyond darkness and death. Once we are purified in the inner fire of Shiva we become that immortal essence or bhasma.

Shiva Puja

Devotional ritualistic worship of Shiva is important relative to Shiva images and lingas, offering incense, ghee lamps, fragrances, flowers or liquids, or pouring liquids over the forms. Such devotional worship draws the spirit or Prana into the form, which is otherwise regarded as merely inert and having no inherent value of its own. Puja may also be only mental in nature in which Shiva and the offerings to him are done by mind alone.

Rituals may be performed to Shiva Lingas as to statues of Shiva. Shaivite Hindus may have a statue of Shiva or a Shiva linga in the home. Certain Shaivite sects require wearing a small Shiva linga around the neck. Generally it is made of crystal and kept in a small golden casket.[76]

Sacred Stories of Shiva

There are many sacred stories about Shiva found in such texts as *Puranas* and *Agamas*, extending to various local temple stories, which can be quite dramatic, fascinating and miraculous. These stories are symbolic in nature and reflect deeper truths about cosmic reality and Yoga practice, like artistic images. They often employ paradoxical events that are not easy to understand as their purpose is to take us beyond the mind.

Modern scholarship tends to label such sacred stores as "mythology." But mythology can be a demeaning term and suggests falsehood or superstition. Under the guise of mythology there is a tendency to reduce such sacred stories to mere psychological metaphors or cultural statements, particularly when a Freudian approach is used. Such intellectual approaches cannot reveal the deeper truth of such yogic teachings and can be both insensitive and disrespectful. To understand the sacred stories of Lord Shiva, we must have our Third Eye or deeper perception open, which requires Yoga and meditation on a regular basis!

Actually it is the outer world that is a myth and the inner realm of Shiva that is the true reality. The intellect weaves its conceptual interpretations of life that are illusory. Yet the true reality being beyond form is often easier revealed in an indirect manner through image, metaphor or story.

My Encounter with Lord Shiva and His Great Gurus

It is extraordinarily difficult to speak of one's encounter with the reality of Shiva. It is an encounter beyond time, space, and person and the outer reality that we reside in as human beings. It occurs in a different type of awareness, in which ordinary rules, boundaries and appearances do not hold. It occurs on several levels and different dimensions at the same time.

This encounter with Shiva can arise through the world of nature, but requires contacting a subtler and vaster realm of nature than what our senses ordinarily perceive. In these immersions into the presence of Shiva the ordinary self is suspended while the inanimate world of nature comes to life as the expression of a greater being and consciousness. One communes with the stone, the mountain, and the sky as Shiva's aspects. One merges ones awareness into the forest and its vast canopy, but as a current of endlessly unfolding and expanding energy beyond any particular boundaries, not merely as a plant rooted in the ground.

In *Shiva Chaitanya* or the "consciousness of Shiva" all forms are transparent and glow with an inner light of gem like radiance. The immersion into Shiva is a movement into a deeper space and silence that holds all things but has no form or action of its own. The world becomes turned inside out as it were, with the outer world becoming a diaphanous shadow cast by luminous currents of etheric vibrations from within.

One's encounter with Shiva is a powerful perceptual experience, with the large becoming small and the small becoming large, the near becoming far and the far becoming near. The infinitesimal and the infinite merge into one. Within and without merge and cross dimensions, as do different levels of time, with a sense of the most distant past and the most distant future uniting like the two arcs of a circle.

These Shiva transformations happen spontaneously and at unexpected moments. The current of experience arises from a deeper awareness that illumines things from within and absorbs the world into a single effulgence. The human factor becomes minute. Everything reflects a mystic face moving in a dance of inner music lit by an internal sun, with knower, knowing and known reflecting upon one another. Once these experiences dawn they remain in the periphery of the mind, long after they appear to be over as a residual inner pull, a background glow that is ever increasing.

Personal and Impersonal Aspects of Divinity

My primary inclination has always been to the impersonal aspect of deity – the Supreme Brahman that is eternal and infinite, the Supreme Self in which there is nothing other or different than what it is. One cannot speak of that state of pure consciousness as an experience in the ordinary sense of the world. It occurs beyond any event horizon, and outside of any localized coordinates. It is not an encounter with something external but an absorption into a deeper awareness of being that breaks through all boundaries. To reach it requires a deep forgetfulness in which one remembers the soul's secrets that are not of time or of this world.

Dwelling in that transcendent reality has been my primary focus in meditation, though not in an exclusive manner. I have always accepted the reality of various deities along with the impersonal and do not find any contradiction between these two levels of divinity. The Supreme unity displays various aspects of itself like the brilliant feathers of a peacock, sparks from a fire, or waves on the sea. The impersonal reality can manifest in personal ways as it works behind the multifarious forces of life. These deities can be of different types and levels from supernatural beings to personifications of transcendent truths.

And what is most strange and wonderful is that one can experience the whole of the Absolute in every part, in every cell, every atom, and in every instant. The One is present completely in each of its diverse manifestations, though standing in the background and not interfering with the outer movement of karmas. Similarly, one can withdraw into the Supreme consciousness from any point in the body and mind, prana, or senses. It requires a simple art of stepping back into the awareness of the witness and seer, which is present at every level. One can discover the supreme consciousness and light behind every event, but particularly in what is small, silent or inconsequential like a falling leaf or the glow of a distant star.

Devi and Shakti

My main inclination to the personal form of divinity has always been to Devi, Shakti or the Divine Mother, discovering her different aspects personal and impersonal, in nature and in the spirit, in the universe and beyond. With her I have had a more personal relationship than with Lord Shiva, and many experiences in the realms of waking and in the astral sphere.

I began at a young age with the image and power of *Ma Kali*, marking the great unknown and world negation, the doorway to realms beyond death and limitation, with her dark blue currents opening higher dimensions of awareness as a sky beyond the sky. Kali over time revealed herself as *Durga*, the great protectress, particularly as her form of *Mahishasura Mardini*, the destroyer of the powers of darkness and the demon hordes, who brought me her many weapons and her golden grace.

Ma Durga's form developed further into *Tripura Sundari*, the blissful beauty of the three worlds who represents the vision of everything as Brahman, Shiva's blissful counterpart in the luminous lunar thousand petal lotus of the head. Her Tripura Sundari form has been predominant for me over the last twenty years, but as connected to Uma, Parvati and Gauri, her mountain forms as Shiva's consort, as well as Lalita and Rajarajeshvari, the great Mother of bliss.

The Devi came to me in the form of certain great women teachers. Most important was Anandamayi Ma (the bliss permeated mother), who I corresponded with for several years in my twenties and who encouraged me in my sadhana in many ways. Anandamayi Ma holds the Himalayan Yoga Shakti and the Lalita-Sundari energies. Her letters to me were always preceded by an electrical current through my body and mind. Sharada Devi, the wife of Ramakrishna has been powerful as well as the spiritual mother of the New Age or Yuga, along with her husband Paramahansa Ramakrishna. The Mother of the Sri Aurobindo ashram, Mira Alfassa, came to me as the White Tara of a New World manifestation hidden in the jasmine flower, with connections to Tripura Sundari as well. She remains nearby at all times and guides me in secret ways

I am primarily a Devi worshipper and Shiva has come through her, according to her grace, as her background presence. To the extent that my devotion has been towards a masculine symbol of divinity, it has always been to Shiva, and behind my worship of Devi or Shakti I have always sensed the power of Shiva. Shakti inevitably leads us to Shiva. With Tripura Sundari, Shiva manifested as Dakshinamurti, the youthful silent sage teaching the elder rishis beneath the vast Banyan tree. Yet for me Shiva has primarily been Yogeshvara, the great lord of Yoga on whose head Ma Ganga flows.

Overall I have viewed Shiva as the impersonal and formless aspect of Deity, with the Devi representing the personal and form aspect. Nature is the play of the Goddess through her display of colors and fragrances, though the silent and still essence of Shiva marks the contours of her dance. Devi as the personal aspect is accessible as a mother or a muse, while Shiva as the impersonal formless beyond can only be accessed in the abandonment of the known.

The Devi has the form of all nature and is only vaguely anthropomorphic in her expression. She is not a mere personification of human qualities and emotions, however sublime, but is interwoven throughout all existence from the Earth to the stars. Her Shakti works to draw one to Shiva, and to make his awesome unknown presence more gentle and kind.

The Light of Awareness

At a young age an inner light dawned in my mind that has steadily increased over the years. This vibrating light has many colors, starting with earthly tones, almost like the colors of lava gushing forth from a volcano or like a liquid rolling mass of liquid iron streaked with lines of gold and silver. It is more like a glowing vibrating mass, than a single point, though it can have a reverberating focus or take the shape of an eye.

This inner light follows its own sound vibration or nada, in which various musical tones arise from high-pitched streams to deep oceanic currents and the beatings of the cosmic drum. The light includes a certain pressure, which conveys an implicit demand for continual change and transformation of body and mind. It reflects an increasing power of concentration, almost like a weight pulling from within, a kind of magnetic force or gravitational pull. It draws one deeper within, a continual immersion, like a tunnel into a secret realm of cosmic mystery. It is generally formless or wavelike in nature but sometimes assumes specific forms and patterns. Sometimes it forms circular patterns or is like a display of fireworks, expanding out in multiple dimensions.

Sometimes one senses certain deities or gurus through this inner light, as it assumes various faces or forms. But these usually move into a deeper space and silence and are not held long in form. A deeper prana and knowledge readily flows and expands out of this light, a flow of healing grace and wisdom insight. It brings in an intuitive sense and psychic knowledge of people, events, and nature around one. Yet its overall impetus is not towards any subtle or occult worlds but to the formless Divine. Sometimes it is like the light of the dawn and suggests the rising of an inner Sun. Sometimes it is like a fire hidden deep within the Earth.

This inner light continues to grow through all the circumstances of life, good and bad, friendly or adverse. Out of it arises various inner experiences as heightened states of its energy, as it erupts into dynamic forms and patterns. This light began in the region of the third eye and usually remains centered there but is not limited to any particular region of body or mind. It can extend downward into the heart, upward to the top of the head, and beyond into space. It can pervade my entire body or move into my entire field of perception and most distant horizon. It can assume the shape or energies of any of the chakras, which spin and vibrate under its influence. It is often connected to the breath and is energized by pranayama and retention of the breath. One can let go of the breath and merge into its force, as a kind of natural ongoing retention and mergence into the cosmic life. It frequently has a kind of knocking, clicking or bursting sound like a breaking down of barriers in the mind.

Sometimes this inner light merges into certain external objects or informs certain outer events, coming alive as it were from the inside of things like a person emerging out from behind a mask. Other times it unfolds certain names, forms or qualities within the mind, providing guidance and knowledge on various subjects, mantras and cosmic powers. Yet it is not so much a light that one can see as it is an inner light of seeing and consciousness.

When people ask me questions, I withdraw into this light and the answers come immediately from within according to its powers. It can become a conduit for communication with great gurus in the world today or from previous eras. It can take one into different lokas altogether, moving out through the top of the head, where the Earth realm is all but forgotten and no boundaries or divisions exist. Sometimes the light functions like a channel or nadi into another realm, though one can also remain in that tunnel as a vortex of energy.

Whatever I deeply wish to know or learn about, if I concentrate on it through the inner light, the secrets of that subject will gradually become revealed. Wherever I may be located in at any particular time, if I focus on that inner light, the secrets of that place both today and in the past will emerge. My writings arise primarily from holding the focus of that inner light and letting its voice come forth, while in my mind I endeavor to be respectfully silent and observant and not interfere with its movements or messages. From it the teaching becomes a continual flow like great river.

This inner light provides its own motivation and impetus, with its own indomitable will power. The Shiva force knows who it is and where it is going. It pressures one to evolve in life and can sometimes harshly demand purification. It can take one in various directions as may be required by a higher law, the logic of which may become clear only much later on in life. One needs to tune into this inner force and strive to follow its latest impulses with a calm acceptance. It has an irresistible power that one cannot go against. It holds steady as a witness but can be a dynamic active force in special circumstances.

Shiva as the Supreme Brahman

That inner light is my original and ongoing experience of what one could call Shiva, not as a particular deity but as a conduit to the Supreme Brahman or highest Godhead, as the Cosmic Self and Person, the Atman and Purusha. This mass of light often assumes the form of a Shiva linga or pillar of light, vibrating in various dimensions, standing from the heart to the head.

This light of Shiva has led me to various mergings into Brahman. Sometimes the outer world appears to stop all together, held by an immutable force. Other times one becomes distant from the world as if located in a space above and beyond it. Sometimes one becomes a silent witness, and life's movement becomes a curiosity or even irrelevant to a deeper stillness.

One experiences that Supreme Brahman as beyond experience - beyond all sensation, emotion, or concept. In that presence, time, space, action, and person are suspended and dissolved, or simply lose any significance. You as a person fade and disappear into a greater light. No one remains there to be the experiencing subject and there is no other and no object to experience. Yet what is experienced is most sublime and transformative, beyond the descriptions and ideas of the known world.

When one is in that state of Shiva, one can function to some degree in the external world, but everything has a different meaning, starting with oneself. You realize that you are not the body or the mind. You do not have sense organs, motor organs or any kind of organs. These organs belong to the body, which is a formation of physical matter, not to your true nature. You do not have thoughts, emotions and sensations. These are but energies of the mind that is rooted in memories, with your awareness standing ever beyond. Body and mind are instruments you can use, but you can also withdraw from them and forget about them altogether.

You do not do anything. It is the body, organs and mind that act, while you observe the process. You do not have any definitive name, nor does anything else. All things are vibrations of the same nameless presence. All apparent knowledge becomes illusory and inconsequential. There is nothing to know and no one who could know anything. All is self-existent and self-illuming as the light of Shiva, in which all truth is self-evident and not in need of any explanation or description.

There is a reality, being, consciousness, presence, power, light, vibration, and continuity of Self-awareness that is vast, endless, and beyond all limitation. Dwelling in that we discover a perpetual peace in which there is no possibility of sorrow, no dilemma, duality, or desire. It is a state that is empty of any other mark or condition, yet full, overflowing into itself, a self-contentment that holds an unbounded beauty and grace.

Coming out of that experience of Brahman there is no sense of having experienced something, or having done anything at all. There is no sense of having left it. There is no specific event to describe, where mind has been set aside. There is a kind of black hole in time and space in which one transcends to a level of pure Self-awareness. Yet this inner experience lends a deeper light and beauty to all that one experiences and continues in the background at a stronger rate of vibration. That presence dwells at the core of the mind and heart, an ineffable, great unknown that draws us beyond all boundaries, and flows through all divisions with an irresistible power.

That *Brahma Bhava* or state of Brahman as the Supreme Self is the reality of *Parashiva*, the Supreme Shiva, the being of peace, dissolution, and endless transformation. I have always sensed Lord Shiva as the indicator of that supreme Reality and the highest form of deity for my spiritual unfoldment. There has never been any doubt about it. Yet it has more often been Shiva as the formless Supreme Self rather than Shiva as a personal form for devotion.

Shiva Loka

In recent years, higher realms of Shiva have been gradually dawning in my awareness, often unexpectedly. These include the higher astral Shiva Loka that is the one of the main goals of Shiva based Bhakti Yoga, as well as formless causal realms. Yet the experience is not so much of the outer aspect of these realms as it is of these subtler realms as places of worship and meditation, with a more direct connection with the Supreme Shiva beyond all manifestation than can be found in this limited physical world. The lights, colors, patterns, flowers and nature forms of these subtle realms are quite magical and hold the essence of all creation.[77]

Today we pride ourselves in being able to access more of our physical world through the internet and social media. We should also learn how to access the higher worlds through Yoga and meditation. What we will find there extends far beyond anything that we can experience in this material world. The objectivity of our physical realm is an illusion born of collective karma. The subtler realms are much more free and fluid. We can work wonders of vision and delight within them and fulfill all the wishes of the heart. All is Shiva's dream, with our Earth a realm of challenge to the soul to search out a deeper transformation. Yet Shiva himself is the origin of the dream and stands beyond even these subtle dream worlds.

My Worship of Shiva

Integrating the presence of Shiva into my life has been a long journey with many surprises and wonderful events, as well as facing and overcoming a number of dangers and fears. We do not live in a world that recognizes Shiva. We live in a realm that is trying to avoid his power and shuns his grace, but Shiva looms overall nevertheless, awesome in the distance but blissful when close.

Shiva as a form for worship has been most important for me as the great mountain lord. I have generally lived in mountain areas, seeing mountains out of my windows, frequently hiking in them, and taking pilgrimage in the Himalayas and into the mountains of North America. Alone in the heights of nature, letting go of all thoughts of the world, one can touch the Supreme Shiva and open up to the cosmic sphere of consciousness. The power of Shiva moves through nature and is connected to the impersonal Brahman as the pinnacle of space at the top of the world mountain.

Shiva as the mountain lord is Yogeshvara or the Lord of Yoga. The mountain has always been the prime symbol and ideal locale for Yoga practice. Shiva as the mountain lord and lord of Yoga is the supreme guru, the greater teacher and guide. Shiva is the guiding presence of the mountain. His energy is particularly strong in the rocks and in the glacial lakes and rock fronts in the high mountains that resemble natural Shiva lingas.

I do not read many books apart from certain Vedic and Yoga classics in the original Sanskrit, which I continually go back over in a contemplative manner. I have always cultivated memory over any efforts to compile references, lists, or databases. This began with a focus on poetry when young and gradually extended into mantras and Vedic verses.

In my work translating Vedic hymns or working with Ayurveda and Vedic astrology, the presence of Shiva has always been there. Vedic knowledge and its mantras are the sound body of Shiva and reflect his wisdom. This sound form of Shiva helps develop the light of Shiva. Every day I cultivate this light of sound in one way or another and it continues to expand, sometimes in quantum leaps, integrating various levels of knowledge, including subjects that I have not studied and am not supposed to know. This inner knowledge is always clear, rational in its own way, yet full of depth, hidden nuances, and multiple levels of meaning.

Mantra, pranayama and meditation have been my main ways of Shiva Sadhana, leading to silencing the mind, negating all appearances and moving into the realm of pure consciousness. Yet that pure awareness then pours down as a stream of knowledge and teachings to bring into the world. Sometimes one has to shut the stream down and return to the pure silence so as not to be overwhelmed.

Shiva as the Supreme Guru

Lord Shiva, Mahadeva, Adi Nath is the supreme Guru, the guru of all gurus. He is Ishvara, God as the Cosmic Guru drawing us back to our true Self. Shiva manifests through the *Guru Tattva* or the cosmic guru principle. All human gurus are but representatives of the Supreme Shiva, channels for his higher wisdom and grace. We should not regard the guru as existing apart from Shiva, nor will the true guru ever place himself above Shiva. The presence of Shiva, in some energy or aspect, will always be there in any truly great guru, ancient or modern.

My primary gurus have carried the power of Shiva in several ways. This includes both the human teachers I have met in this life, and the sages whose books I have studied and whose minds I have communed with.

Shankaracharya

Shankaracharya or "Shankara the teacher (acharya)" is the greatest of the Vedantic gurus and philosophers of the Advaitic or non-dualistic line. I came in contact with his teachings at a young age through his commentaries and his shorter works on Self-knowledge. Shankara came to me in a personal way, a youthful form of Shiva like Dakshinamurti. His face would appear guiding me, drawing me into the teachings of Vedanta out of the many spiritual philosophical systems of the world I was examining at the time. His presence has remained throughout the years.

Perhaps my most notable contact with Shankara was at the famous Himalayan temple of Kedarnath, the main Shiva shrine in the Himalayas and Shankara's place of disappearance, where he left his body. There I could feel the presence of Shankara and his Himalayan Shakti of clarity and Self-realization, like the melting snow waters. I also felt his presence as a great teacher at nearby Joshi Math, particularly near the giant mulberry tree that he was reputed to have meditated by.

I discovered Shankara's power through the many other temples and maths he established, particularly the Char Dham (the four main Himalayan temples of the Hindus). I felt his power at the Sringeri Math, where I also had a discussion with the current Shankaracharya, and Kaladi, Shankara's birthplace in Kerala. His is the supreme rational and yet intuitive path of higher perception.

Over time, I developed my own view of the great guru and realized that he did not teach Jnana Yoga or direct Self-realization alone, but shared all the main Yoga paths, including Bhakti Yoga in his wonderful hymns to various Hindu deities, Raja Yoga in his works on the Goddess that reveal all the secrets of Kundalini and the chakras, and Karma Yoga in his establishment of temples and ashrams throughout the country. He wrote, traveled, taught, developed commentaries on the ancient texts and founded new institutions. I drew inspiration from the full scope of his activities.

Bhagavan Ramana Maharshi

Ramana Maharshi has always been the supreme Sadguru or spiritual master, particularly in regard to the Yoga of knowledge, since I first saw his picture and studied his simple yet profound teachings of direct Self-realization in the heart. Ramana reflects Shiva's son Lord Skanda, the deity of Fire, purification and transformation that I experienced strongly at his ashram in Tiruvannamalai and at the nearby hill of Arunachala. I had an experience of spiritual death and rebirth in the fire of Skanda at a visit to the ashram in 1988, followed by many other experiences there in my visits during later years.

Arunachala is the mountain form of Shiva and his fire linga. It is the mountain of the dawn, the rising Sun and the Aruna Ketava Rishis of the *Taittiriya Aranyaka*, among the ancient Siddhas.[78] There is a wonderful chant to Ramana and the mountain:

OM Namo Bhagavate Sri Ramanaya! Arunachala Shivaya Namah!

Ramana is also connected to the youthful Dakshinamurti form of Shiva who teaches through silence. As a lad of mere sixteen years, Raman had the full realization in a Self-inquiry phase of less than an hour, a feat that few even of the greatest masters have anything comparable with. Ramana taught that silence was the highest teaching, though if asked a question about the most esoteric topics, he always had the answer, however profound the subject. Ramana's presence remains strong for me, sometimes reflecting Shankara or Ganapati Muni, other times taking one beyond all form or teachings.

Kavyakantha Ganapati Muni

Kavyakantha Ganapati Muni, the chief disciple of Ramana, whose line I also follow, relates to the energy of Ganesha, the second son of Shiva and Parvati, in his individual nature, as a master of the mantra and all fields of knowledge and culture. Ganapati was also a great devotee of Shiva and teacher of Shiva Dharma. He began as a devotee of Shiva but through the grace of Ramana Maharshi's mother, Saundaryamba, particularly at the time of her death, the greater Devi Shakti came to dominate his thought, taking the form of Uma, the ascetic form of Shiva's wife.

Ganapati remains as a special inner connection for me and his teachings on Shakti draw one to the Supreme Shiva. I have tried to carry on his legacy in various fields of Yoga and Vedic studies. He taught the unity of Vedic Indra with Shiva, providing a clear basis for Vedic Shaivism. He wrote wonderful verses in praise of Ramana as Lord Skanda, Shiva's second son, his spiritual brother. Ganapati's teachings reflect Shaivite philosophy like that of Kashmiri Shaivism. He was a great teacher of Raja Yoga and connected to the great Siddhas as well.

Mahavatar Babaji

Paramahansa Yogananda's famous Babaji, the great immortal Yogavatara, is also called *Shiva Baba* and *Tryambakam Baba*, which are names of Shiva. He resembles the immortal human form of Shiva as the Supreme Guru of Yoga. His presence is particularly strong at Babaji's cave in Dunagiri in the Kumaon

Himalayas, with Babaji as the power of Shiva. I have had several visits and long meditations in the cave in which Babaji has appeared to me along with Lahiri Mahashaya, whom he taught there, unfolding the Himalayan message of Yogeshvara Shiva for the centuries to come. I have felt Babaji as Shiva and Babaji as the Himalayas, not so much as a person.

I have visited Babaji's cave several times in March when the large rhododendron trees that dominate the hillsides are full of massive red flowers, carrying the power of Shakti. One can sense the presence of Babaji in the trees and flowers, as he would have seen them often during his sojourns in the area. His presence extends to the nearly Dunagiri Durga temple of Shailaputri a few kilometers from the cave.

Babaji and Shiva Yogeshvara relate to the Shiva temple of Jageshwar (which I believe relates to Yogeshwar), located not far from Dunagiri past Almora. Babaji also relates to great ancient Shiva teachers like Lakulish and Gorakhnath. We have had many visits and powerful experiences at Jageshwar with the powerful Shiva lingas and Deodar trees, massive in size almost like Redwoods, several with dual trunks in the Shiva-Shakti form.

I have sensed Babaji's energies above Badrinath in the Garhwal Himalayas by the source of the Alakananda, the largest branch of the river Ganga. His energy is strong above Vasundhara falls. It seems that he and his group of great Yogis still wander and play in the area!

Sadguru Sivaya Subramuniya Swami

Subramuniya Swami of *Hinduism Today* magazine and its Kauai monastery has probably been the most important exponent of Shiva Dharma in the western world in recent decades. He has boldly and proudly proclaimed the presence, power and universality of Lord Shiva, while honoring all aspects of Hindu Dharma. His influence has been crucial to me over the years relative to all aspects of my teachings and sadhana. I visited with him a number of times at his Hawaii temple, with its stunning beauty of flowers, trees, mountains and waterfalls like a heavenly abode.

Swamiji has brought the presence of Shiva, particularly in his Dakshinamurti form, to the West and embodied it in a powerful crystal and granite temple for generations to come. His Shaivite teachings reflect the tropical paradise of the Hawaiian Islands that is much like the astral heavens of Shiva his devotees can easily reach. His teachings are broad, comprehensive and designed for all levels of aspirants and all levels of society. He was as great communicator and has left many important books and courses. The Hinduism Today temple complex remains perhaps the most important Shiva shrine in the West and their publication the main voice of Shiva Dharma as well as Hindu Dharma in the West.

Sri Sadguru Sivananda Murty

Sivananda Murty is a great Yoga and Vedanta guru of Andhra Pradesh in South India, though known throughout the country and has traveled to the West as well. One can feel within him the presence of Shiva, yet in a very accessible and fatherly form. Whenever he gives his blessings he chants "Mahadev." Whenever he speaks of gurus, he always states that Shiva is the only true guru in all gurus.

Sivananda Murty has been my main Shiva guru over the last twenty years and brings the guidance and blessings of Shiva to all. Along with my wife, Yogini Shambhavi Devi, we joined his *Shaiva Mahapeetham* order and have taken up the wearing of a small crystal Shiva linga personally from him, along with the *Namah Shivaya* mantra. Sivananda Murty is associated with Trailanga Swami, a famous nineteenth century Yogi, and with Bhagavan Ramana Maharshi, whose teachings he deeply understands and conveys.

Over time I have had many conversations with Guruji on many profound subjects and he has unfolded for us the secrets of Shiva. His teachings are remarkable in that he can bring the presence of Shiva into every person, at any level or stage of life, and into every aspect of human life, culture and knowledge. He provides important guidance for India and for all humanity. He has a special deep insight into the secrets of the Puranas and into Vedic astrology, though there is hardly a Vedic or Yogic subject that he does not know from within. He has long gone beyond our ordinary consciousness bound by time and space, birth and death.

Guruji has many powers like that of the Siddhas. These are not powers that he has cultivated or tried to use but which occur naturally and spontaneously around him, as many people have reported, extending to powers over the forces of nature like the great Rishis of old. After one trip to India when I visited with him, I remembered that I had not brought back enough Shiva Bhasma or sacred ash to sustain my daily practices, nor had I brought back enough sacred threads for the regular practices I am required to do. Yet when I opened my altar area where I had kept such special items, I found a large pack of bhasma and another of dozens of sacred threads that I had not brought back from India.

Shiva and the *Vedas*

Early in my studies I learned that most scholars regarded Shiva as a non-Vedic deity, representing teachings outside of the Vedic texts. This caused some doubts in my mind because I always felt that my path was Vedic, and my main work was a Vedic mission to bring out the deeper teachings and Vedic Yoga going back to the *Rigveda*. This dichotomy between Shiva and the *Vedas* extended to a greater dichotomy of Vedic and Tantric teachings that certain scholars also proposed, with many feeling that Tantra represented a pre-Vedic or non-Vedic tradition.

However, I always felt that Shiva and the *Vedas* had a deep connection, as did Veda and Tantra. My main gurus through the lines of Ramana Maharshi, Sri Aurobindo, Ramakrishna, and Yogananda confirmed these views, as has Sivananda Murty, whose Shaiva Mahapeetham is a branch of Vedic Shaivism. I experienced Shiva as the all-Vedic deity consisting of Agni, Soma, Indra and Surya, the four Vedic light forms of fire, Moon, Lightning and Sun, as related in this book.

I also developed a special recognition of Lakulish, the great teacher of the ancient Pashupata Yoga, particularly in his Jageshwar Himalayan shrine that Sivananda Murty also honors. Of the shorter *Upanishad*s, I was most moved by the *Shvetashvatara Upanishad*, which was said to have been composed in the same area of the Himalayas, and is primarily to Shiva.

The Rishi Vamadeva

Vamadeva is both one of the main Rishis of the *Rigveda* and an important name for Shiva. I have taken his name, originally from the Vedic Rishi, and spent much time meditating on his hymns and mantras, particularly those to Agni and Indra. These hymns of Vamadeva contain a strong sense of Shiva or the cosmic I am and are honored in the *Upanishads*. Later I came in contact with the Vamadeva form of Shiva, which is his form that includes Shakti, with Shakti being the left side (Vama) of Shiva as the deity (Deva). Vamadeva is the Soma aspect of Shiva that also holds the grace of the ancient Rishis, of which he is the foremost.

9. Trimurti: Brahma, Vishnu and Shiva

Part V

Subtleties of Shaivism

In this section we will explore the relationship of Shaivism with Ayurveda and Vedic astrology, as well as examining its philosophy in detail, including its relationship with other schools of thought and Yoga approaches. The depth and intricacy of such considerations can help us understand the presence of Shiva in all aspects of life and culture.

Shiva as the Great Healer
Shiva Ayurveda

Ayurveda is an integral part of Tantric Shaivism, which uses all branches of Vedic knowledge and all the Vedic sciences. Ayurveda plays an important role in Shiva Yoga, particular the Shaivite Prana Yoga and Hatha Yoga traditions that rest upon an Ayurvedic view of body and Prana. Shiva is the deity of the cosmic Prana, which is the supreme healing force that can help us energize all healing practices. All forms of Pranic healing and Ayurveda connect to him.

Shiva as *Mrityunjaya*, the great lord who takes us beyond death and suffering and grants immortality, naturally has strong connections to Ayurveda as a healing practice for body, mind and spirit. Shiva himself is called Ayur or longevity, which is a synonym for Prana. The Vedic *Ayushsukta* for longevity is directed first to Rudra Shiva reflecting the antiquity of these connections.[79]

Shiva represents the state of grace, blessing, and healing. Healing can be described as bringing the power of Shiva into our lives. Shiva also indicates the state of balance, which includes the balance of the doshas or biological humors of Ayurveda that is the basis for health and well-being for body and mind.

Generally in Ayurvedic thought, Dhanvantari, an incarnation of Lord Vishnu, is looked upon as the deity of Ayurveda, with his image found in most Ayurvedic books and institutions. This may cause us not to look into the role of Shiva in Ayurveda. Yet if we study the history going back to the *Vedas*, it is Rudra Shiva who is most honored as the great deity of healing. Shiva as Rudra is lauded as the great doctor in the *Vedas* reflecting the greater antiquity of this connection.

The *Rigveda* lauds Rudra as the greatest of doctors and the giver of blessings and balm.

> *Who holds wonderful medicines in his hands.*[80]
> *We lauded you as the greatest of all doctors.*[81]

The Rudram chant says the same:

> *He speaks as the guide, the first Divine Doctor.*[82] *O Rudra, with your auspicious form and your auspicious universal medicine; With that auspicious medicine of Rudra by that grant us compassion for our longevity.*[83]

Shiva as the deity of doctors, is known as *Vaidyanath* or the Lord (Natha) of all Ayurvedic physicians (Vaidyas). A true doctor imparts the healing power of peace that Shiva indicates.

Soma and Rudra

There are two related deities of healing most commonly honored in the *Rigveda*, Soma and Rudra. Rudra usually indicates Shiva in his harsh or protective Agni form. Soma is Shiva in his soft or nourishing form.

In this regard, Shiva is associated with both reduction and tonification, detox-ification and rejuvenation therapies, the two main aspects of Ayurvedic heal-ing. Shiva as fiery Rudra helps us overcome febrile and infectious diseases and brings about purification through heat and light. Yet as watery Soma, Shiva also holds the powers of nourishment, rejuvenation and revitalization, including spe-cial healing powers of the plants contained in their juices. Shiva is the supreme healer, eliminating all disease causing pathogens, strengthening our bodily fluids and tissues, calming our emotions, and bringing rest, peace, and rejuvenation to body, mind and heart.

> *Soma and Rudra, grant to our bodies all the medicines that you have.*[84]

Soma is the lord of the plants, connecting Shiva with herbal healing, not surpris-ing for a mountain deity. All herbal remedies are through Soma as the healing power of the plants. In the Rigveda, all plants spread on Earth are called "queens of the Soma,"[85] identifying them also with the Shakti principle.

The Maruts or Rudras

The Maruts or Rudras in the Rigveda are the sons of Rudra.[86] They represent the powers of the wind and storm, the pranic forces of Rudra-Shiva. The famous Tryambakam mantra to Rudra-Shiva occurs in a *Rigveda* hymn to the Maruts.[87] The Maruts are also referred to as Hamsas, further connecting them to Prana.[88] The Maruts are also famous for their healing powers.

The Ashvins

The Ashvins, the twin Vedic horsemen, are additional important Vedic deities of healing and the original teachers of Ayurveda. The horse itself is a symbol of Prana. These magical twins represent Prana and its state of balance. They are referred to as Rudras in the *Rigveda*, indicating their connection with Rudra's healing force and move by the "path of Rudra."[89] The Ashwins hold the knowledge of the honey bliss (Madhu Vidya), which grants immortality, lauded in the *Upanishads* as the supreme power of bliss.[90] The Ashwins have all magic powers of healing, including resurrection of the dead. Rejuvenation is under their power as well. We can perhaps equate the two Ashwins with Soma and Rudra. They are also called Hamsas, connecting them with the mantras for the breath.[91]

Nilakantha

Nilakantha is a form of Shiva who drinks the cosmic poison that arose from the original churning of the cosmic ocean, which turns his throat (Kantha) blue (Nila), but does not penetrate further to harm him. Shiva grants us resistance to both disease-causing pathogens and to negative thoughts. He helps strengthen both physical and psychological immunity, so that nothing can disturb or imbalance us.

Nilakantha is a deity of detoxification, and helps us eliminate poisons and toxins of all types. Such forms of Shiva are very important in this time when our food, air and water are often polluted.

Shiva and Hanuman

Hanuman is the great monkey God and companion of Lord Rama, the seventh incarnation of Lord Vishnu. Hanuman is said to be the son of Vayu or the Wind God. He possesses all the pranic healing powers of nature and of yoga practice. Hanuman is regarded as an incarnation of Shiva as both are connected to Vayu or the wind. Hanuman has the ability to find all the healing plants as well. He is also the ideal warrior and represents the highest and most focused devotion.

Shiva and Nandi

Shiva's vehicle is a bull, which also represents vigor and vitality. His bull is called Nandi, meaning "the joyous." Shiva increases our vital energy and strengthens our Ojas, which is the primary vigor of the body in Ayurveda.

Shaivite Ayurvedic Traditions

There are special Shaivite Ayurvedic traditions, particularly from the Himalayas and also reflected in Shaivite Tantric lore. Shaivite Ayurveda brings in alchemy, ritual, mantra, astrology, Yoga and meditation, and is not limited to a physical or doshic model of disease. In Ayurvedic alchemy the two primary substances used are purified mercury, which represents Shiva, and purified sulfur, which represents Shakti. These two are the basis of many special Ayurvedic alchemical preparations.[92]

Shiva and Psychological Healing

As well as healing the body, Shiva also has the power to heal the mind and heart. Shiva is the lord of the mind and the great psychologist, showing us how to deal with the mind from the standpoint of a higher consciousness. He is the master of observation, detachment, calm, and composure through which the emotions can be settled and the mind made clear.

Shiva is the ruler over all the Bhutas or Pretas, the ghosts and negative spirits that symbolically indicate disturbed thoughts and emotions which afflict the mind. He is the lord of the animals that includes our instincts that need to be controlled by a higher force. He is the lord of the serpents, which on a lower level indicate toxic energy and agitated prana that can poison us. Shiva controls the astral spirits or subtle negative energies that can afflict the psyche, including false imagination and bad dreams. He helps clear negative memories and traumas even from the deepest level of the psyche. He enables us to overcome all obsessions, compulsions and addictions and strengthens our will power.

Chanting *OM Namah Shivaya!* is one of the simplest and most powerful methods for calming the mind, clearing out deep-seated emotions, and dealing with severe psychological unrest. The silence and peace of the Shiva state of consciousness heals the mind and heart. Invoking and honoring Shiva is a direct way of removing all that ails the mind and heart. A sacred space for Shiva worship is a natural healing place for body and mind. Shiva directs us to meditation in which the mind can naturally heal itself.

Shiva and the Three Doshas

Shiva as Prana and Vayu is associated with the air element and with its corresponding Vata dosha in Ayurveda, which is the most powerful of the three doshas, the main factors behind health and disease. It is Vata dosha as the pranic force that directs and motivates the other two doshas, Pitta as the fire force, and Kapha as the water force. Yet Shiva has his connections with the other two doshas as well. Shiva as Agni relates to the fire element and Pitta dosha at a biological level. As Soma, Shiva possesses affinities with Kapha as the ultimate form of nourishment and as the nectar of immortality.

Shiva relates more specifically to the three vital essences of the three doshas, their subtle master forms as *Prana, Tejas*, and *Ojas*, the healing forms of air, fire, and water. Shiva is the higher Prana that is the supreme force of healing and regeneration. Shiva is the higher Agni or Tejas, the warmth and radiance of vitality. Shiva is the higher Soma or Ojas, the inner grace that grants the supreme strength and stamina.

Shiva as the power of balance or Samatva relates to the balance of the three doshas that is the foundation of health and well-being. As the higher Prana, Shiva energy helps us balance the powers of the five Pranas, and of Agni as the digestive fire on all of its levels. The state of Shiva is the state of health or self-abidance in Ayurveda (svastha), which is abidance in our natural state of peace and healing, our Shiva nature.

Shiva and Healing Touch

Shiva is the deity of healing touch. This reflects his connection to Prana and to the air element, which rules over the heart chakra, the skin and the hands. The hand of Shiva has the supreme healing touch and pranic power. Shaivite Yogis can grant blessings and healing through their hands alone or by raising their palm while greeting a person. This is the grace of Shiva. All practitioners of therapeutic touch should seek the grace and guidance of Shiva and learn to channel his vital force.

Healing Power of Shiva's Bhasma or Sacred Ash

Shaivites use the bhasma or sacred ash of Shiva for various spiritual and healing purposes, as one of the most sacred Shiva symbols. Such bhasmas are an integral part of Shiva pujas, abhishekas and rituals. Some Shaivite gurus initiate their disciples with the bhasma and have them use it as a means of connecting with the teacher, placing it on various parts of the body like the third eye or ingesting small quantities of it.

The bhasma is usually white in color and is an ash containing various herbs, usually including camphor. The bhasma symbolizes the essence of the universe after it has been purified by the fire of Shiva. Many Shaivite ascetics rub their bodies with this bhasma, especially the naked sadhus and Naga Babas. Many temples and ashrams in India prepare their own Shiva bhasmas. A little of the bhasma can increase the healing power of herbs or be a medicine in its own right.

Shiva's Plants

Shiva as Soma holds the healing essence of all the plants, particularly herbs that bring about rejuvenation of the body and heightened awareness to the mind.

Shiva is often associated with intoxicants like alcohol, cannabis and dhatura. The reason for this is that Shiva has the ability to transform all addictions and to take us to the highest bliss in which we no longer need any external comforts and stimulations. Offering our addictive substances like alcohol and cannabis to Shiva is a way in which we can learn to let them go. Shiva has the ability to transform rajas and tamas, the agitation and inertia in the mind, into sattva or peace.

Shiva has several special plants used in his worship, which symbolize aspects of his nature. Yet Shiva as Soma is also the lord of all the plants.

- Rudraksha – The special seed called the eye of Shiva used for making Rudraksha rosaries or malas. It has a blue covering when ripe. A Rudraksha mala helps strengthen physical and psychological immunity. It stimulates the higher Agnis within us, helping to open the third eye or eye of Shiva.

- Bilva or Bael – Its three lobed leaves symbolize the trident or Trishula of Shiva – Its fruit aids in rejuvenation, strengthening absorption in the digestive tract. Bilva leaves are commonly offered to Shiva and often used along with flowers for adorning Shiva statues or Shiva lingas.

- Dhatura – A narcotic plant that his large beautiful, fragrant white flowers sacred to Shiva. The five folds of the flower indicate the five faces of Shiva. The seeds are also offered to Shiva.

- Cannabis – Sometimes smoked by Shaivite Sadhus and offered to Shiva, a good analgesic and antispasmodic in herbal formulas.

- Shilajit – The famous exudation of mountain rocks, particularly in the Himalayas, that holds the rejuvenating power of the mountains. Taken with milk it can rejuvenate the plasma and all other bodily tissues, as well as increase energy and vitality.

- Camphor – The fragrance and resin of camphor is commonly used in the worship of Shiva who is said to be *Karpuragauram* or "white like camphor." Camphor relates specifically to the lunar form of Shiva. Camphor is the primary fragrance of Shiva used in his worship. Burning camphor purifies the air and brings in the power of Shiva, aiding in clarity of perception.

- Calamus (Acorus calamus) – This pungent root called *vacha* in Sanskrit has the ability to open up higher perceptual and mantric powers and can stimulate the third eye or eye of Shiva.

- Deodar (Devadaru) – The tall Himalayan cedar that reflects the steadiness and mountain like strength of Shiva, common in the mid-mountain elevations. The American redwood would be another tree of this type of symbolism.

- Peepal (Ashvattha or Ficus religiosa) – Another important large Asian fig or Ficus, sacred to Agni.

- Nyagrodha or Banyan (Ficus bengalis)- The large Asian fig or Ficus trees that hold the energy of the Earth, Heaven and the supreme Brahman, spreading out with wide branches and aerial roots. It is an ideal tree for the worship of Shiva, particularly connected to his Dakshinamurti or youthful sage form.

- Nagalingam (Couroupita guianensis) – a native Amazon tree that has beautiful flowers like the Shiva linga. Naga Linga means the linga of the serpent. Found at many Shiva temples in South India.

Shiva and Vedic Astrology

The Moon, the Sun, Saturn, Ketu, the planet, the lord of planets, supreme.

Thousand Names of Shiva v. 8

Shiva as the great lord of time (Kala) is called *Mahakala*. Shiva as the lord of Eternal Time is an important deity in Vedic astrology, which is the Vedic science of time and light. Shiva as pure light (Prakasha) is also the light behind all the stars and planets, through whose movement time and karma are measured.

Astrology is said to be the eye of the *Vedas*. That spiritual eye is the third eye of Lord Shiva. Shiva relates to several planetary and constellation influences, starting with the Sun and the Moon.

Shiva and the Sun

As a deity of light, perception, and consciousness, Shiva is naturally associated with the Sun. Shiva is regarded as the supreme deity (pratyadhi Devata) of the Sun in Vedic astrology, with Surya as the solar deity, and Agni, often another manifestation of Shiva, as the overruling deity (adhi Devata) of the Sun. Sometimes the trinity of Hindu deities of Brahma, Vishnu and Shiva relate to the creative, preservative, and transformative aspects of solar energy.

Pashupati, the Lord of the animals form of Shiva, in particular is associated with the Sun. Pashu also means perception and Shiva as the lord of perception is associated with the Sun. The animals of Shiva are also the animal representations of the constellations.

Shiva and the Moon

Shiva is associated with the Moon and is often regarded as a Moon God, which reflects his association with the mind, which is connected to the Moon in Vedic thought, and his calm auspicious energy. Monday is usually the main day of the week for Shiva's worship.

Yet Shiva is more a deity of the dark of the Moon than of the full Moon. The crescent Moon he wears on his head is that of the waning Moon. Shiva is worshipped on the last night of the lunar month that the Moon's disc can be seen before it becomes new. Shiva like the Moon relates to the night, which is the time of mystery.

The Moon relates specifically to the Soma form of Shiva, as the Agni or fire form is that of the Sun. The full Moon is the Soma form of Shiva, while the new Moon, when the Moon is merged into the Sun, is also his Agni form.

The Moon commonly relates to Shakti, specifically to Parvati, Shiva's consort. The Goddesses are associated with different phases and aspects of the Moon's energy. Parvati means "what has parts," which is not simply a mountain, but an allusion to the phases of the Moon. For the Moon, its presiding deity is Chandra or the Moon God. Its overruling deity is the Waters, which also refer to Soma. Its supreme deity is Parvati or Shakti.

Shiva and Saturn

Saturn as the slowest moving of the visible planets relates to the cosmic powers of time, eternity, dissolution, and transformation, much like the powers of Shiva. Saturn relates to the elder or grandfather form of the deities, in the case of Shiva, his Mahakala form, and the grandmother form of Kali (Jyeshta or Dhumavati). Saturn (Shani) is often depicted like Shiva with a trident or Trishula. Shiva can help us overcome the afflictions of Saturn, which cause the most difficulties for us in life, particularly with his Mrityunjaya mantra.

Shiva and Mars

Mars relates to the fire or Agni form of Shiva, which is usually called Rudra. Agni is the child or the youth, *Kumara*. He is the youthful form of Shiva as Dakshinamurti, the giver of knowledge. He is also the son of Shiva as Lord Skanda or Subrahmanya. He is called Karttikeya from his birth in the Pleiades (Krittika Nakshatra). This also relates to Shiva's masculine energy and his ascetic forms.

Shiva and Eclipses: Rahu and Ketu

Rahu and Ketu are the north and south lunar nodes, the Dragon's head and Dragon's tail of western astrology, the cut off head and tail of the serpent in Vedic thought. Each represents half of the body of the serpent. Rahu as the head of the serpent projects a power of illusion or Maya, including unusual desires and creative energies. Ketu as the tail of the serpent indicates death and transformation, including higher knowledge and focused perception.

These two lunar nodes are responsible for eclipses of the Sun and Moon. Though either node can eclipse either Sun or Moon, Ketu is more associated with the eclipse of the Sun and Rahu with the eclipse of the Moon. The two represent subtle astral energies and collective karmas that are hard to overcome and can easily disturb our minds and cause difficulties in our outer lives and communication. They govern over subtle energies of technology as well as poisons and toxins, yet also higher powers of Yoga.

Shiva as the lord of serpents has the power over these two nodes. Of the two, Ketu is closest in energy to Shiva as it rules over liberation and deeper insights. Ketu is sometimes associated with Ganesha as the son of Shiva, as Ganesha has his head cut off before replacing it with that of an elephant. Ketu is also sometimes related the Bhairava form of Shiva, which has a child form as well. Shiva's consort, particularly as Durga, has power over Rahu, as she is the very power of Maya, though Shiva as the lord of serpents can master that force as well.

Eclipses, both of the Sun and the Moon, are important times for the worship of Lord Shiva, who dispels all fear. Eclipses can be used to magnify the power of mantras and take our energy to a higher level of manifestation. They are related to Shiva if they occur on Mondays, the day of the Moon.

Shiva and Venus: The Power of Rejuvenation

Venus is the guru and teacher of the Asuras or anti-Gods of Vedic thought, who represents the outward movement or rajasic quality of Prana. Shiva as the lord of Prana has control over the Asuras as well. Venus governs rajas but also has the power to transform it.

Venus is a morning and evening star that arises from and returns to the Sun. As such it is thought to be a spark or ray from the Sun that is Shiva. It holds the power of rejuvenation and relates to Shiva's Soma form as well, giving longevity and bliss.

Shiva and the Fixed Stars: the Nakshatras

Besides the twelve signs of the zodiac, Vedic astrology uses twenty-seven Nakshatras or lunar constellations. These cover the same ground as the signs but divide up the zodiac differently and have their special meanings. Shiva is associated with a number of lunar constellations or Nakshatras, particularly those in Orion, which can be regarded as Shiva's constellation. It mainly falls in the region of the zodiacal sign of Gemini. It marks the region of the zodiac and Milky Way located opposite to the galactic center in early Sagittarius, through which we can move out from the galaxy into the infinite space beyond the stars.

- Mrigashira (23 20 Taurus–06 40 Gemini) – ruled by Soma or the soft form of Shiva. It is connected to the head of Prajapati or the head of the sacrificed Creator, indicating the crown chakra or lotus of the head, and to the state beyond the mind. The Rudras or sons of Shiva are honored here with Shiva for their drinking of the Soma or the nectar of immortality.

- Ardra (06 40–20 00 Gemini) – ruled by Rudra, the fierce form of Shiva connected to Agni, who is often regarded as a hunter. It relates to the third eye, to focused perception and discrimination. Shiva as Rudra, his fiery or red form, is associated with the red giant star Betelgeuse or Beta Orion.

Shiva as the Lord of Time is mirrored in all the Nakshatras. Yet he has special associations with several other Nakshatras that reflect different aspects of his energy:

- Ashvini (00 00–13 20 Aries) – ruled by the Ashvins, the magical twin horsemen, who reflect Shiva's prana. It is sometimes regarded as a cut off head of a horse, or the sacrificed horse, indicating the sacrifice of the Prana to the deity, which is also the opening up of the higher immortal Prana.

- Bharani (13 20–26 40 Aries) – ruled by Yama, or the God of death, who is a form of Shiva, particularly as the guru or guide that takes us beyond death to immortality, using death and self-sacrifice as the path.

- Krittika or the Pleiades (26 40 Aries–10 00 Taurus) – ruled by the Agni form of Shiva and connected to his son Skanda and his wife as Uma.

- Aslesha (16 40–30 00 Cancer) – relates to the serpents or Nagas, whose Lord is Shiva and to his Nilakantha or poison-drinking form.

- Magha (00 00–13 20 Leo) – relates to the ancestral spirits, particularly the great Rishis and Yogis for whom Shiva is the supreme lord and guide.

- Vishakha (20 00 Libra–03 20 Scorpio) – relates to the electrical form of Shiva and Shakti (Indragni), giving a deep power of intelligence and insight.

- Jyeshta (16 40–30 00 Scorpio) – relates to the transcendent forms of deity as Indra, Shiva and Kali, the independent Supreme Self, and the red star Antares.
- Mula (00 00–13 20 Sagittarius) – relates to the primal or original forms of Shiva and Kali, where the galactic center occurs, the source of all.
- Purva Bhadra (20 00 Aquarius–03 20 Pisces) – relates to Aja Ekapad, which indicates the electrical force of the Sun crossing the sky, the life force that is rooted in the unborn or deathless state.
- Uttara Bhadra (03 20–16 40 Pisces) – relates to Ahir Budhnya, the serpent of the depths, also under Shiva's power, the deeper wisdom at the root of the world.

Shiva along with Vishnu is associated with Shravana (10 00–23 00 Capricorn) as a Nakshatra governing higher knowledge overall. The month of Shravana is sacred to Shiva, marked by the Shravana full Moon. Krishna's birthday is the waning half moon of the Month (Krishna Janmashtami). Shravana usually occurs from late July to late August, with some variability of the lunar calendar. Mondays during this month are particularly sacred to Shiva.

Shiva is associated with the dark of the Moon, particularly the fourteenth tithi or phase, which is the last night that the Moon can still be seen right before sunrise. Shiva Ratri, the night of Shiva, is the most important day of the year for worshipping Shiva. It occurs on the fourteenth tithi or phase of the dark Moon in the month of Magha. On this night the Moon is usually located in Shravana.

Shiva Ratri occurs in late February or March depending on the calendar. Devotes of Shiva stay up all night and perform rituals, mantras and meditations to Shiva, generally in the form of a Shiva linga. Yet on every dark of the Moon and fourteenth tithi, Shiva is honored. These are monthly Shiva Ratris. Staying awake at night or remaining aware during waking, dream and deep sleep is an important part of worshipping Shiva at a higher level. Shiva Ratri is said to be the day of marriage for Shiva and Parvati, also as the Sun and the Moon.

The Thirty-Six Tattvas
The Cosmic Principles of Shiva Yoga

Philosophy that is cosmological in nature is an integral aspect of Shaivite Yoga, just as it is of all Vedic thought. Its purpose is not to simply promote one rational system of ideas over another, but to draw us into the realization of the Absolute beyond all concepts. Vedic philosophies are allied with Yoga and meditation practices in order to help us experience how the universe arises as a manifestation of our inmost awareness. The universal process is the process of our own inner nature, which is reflected in all of nature externally.

This means that all philosophical systems are merely provisional in nature, approached as tools to calm and silence the mind, not to get us caught up in semantic debates. Vedic philosophies lead us to the direct perception of truth that ultimately transcends all philosophies. Yet they can be very helpful for training and purifying the mind, taking it beyond its usual mundane and personal concerns to a contemplation of higher realities.

Different philosophical approaches appeal to different people and their varying temperaments, just as different deities, images or mantras do; so a diversity of teachings and latitude of language and terminology is always helpful. The minds of livings being are different in their karmas and aptitudes, though the inner Self is one. We should always afford the mind freedom in approaching the inner truth. Vedic teachings appreciate this fact and allow many angles of approach to the Divine. Human language also has its limitations and the meanings of words change over time, so that no terminology can ever be final or conclusive.

In philosophical discourses, we must first be very careful about our usage of words and understand their definitions and implications, which are not always fixed. Many Sanskrit terms, which have precise meanings, have been rendered into modern English in a general way, which can cause distortions, as good equivalents for them do not always exist. We may need to learn certain Sanskrit terms and their meanings, rather than accept such approximate translations. Even common English terms like God, soul, or world – the meanings of which we often take for granted – can vary from person to person or philosophy to philosophy. It makes little sense to have a discussion or debate when the definition of the terms we are using may not be clear or even agreed upon.

In order to approach subtle yogic philosophies, we need a certain adaptability of mind, and a reliance on direct perception over verbal semantics. We should grasp what is being suggested and alluded to, rather than interpreting what is said according to outer definitions of words, taking statements literally or rigidly. Shaivite thought has many artistic, poetic, metaphoric, mantra and story based teachings that can point out the higher truth beyond words.

Cosmic Principles or Tattvas

Shaivite philosophies share certain characteristic features. Notably, they recognize the existence of 36 cosmic principles from the subtlest state of consciousness down to gross matter. These principles are not proposed for mere speculative purposes or to constitute a map of the greater universe. They are meant to be experienced inside ourselves as the basis of our inner nature and as constituting our three bodies as causal, subtle, and gross. They constitute a blueprint for Yoga practice. We have alluded to some of these principles in earlier chapters of the book, but will here explain the overall system in greater detail.

The 36 tattvas of Shaivism are not a new invention but are based upon and add to the better known 25 tattvas of Samkhya philosophy. These principles of Samkhya, which Yoga Darshana and many other systems also accept, in turn reflect primary principles of Vedic and Upanishadic thought that can be presented in several formulations. They expand out of the theory of the five great elements of earth, water, fire, air and ether on their various levels of action.

Notably the *Prashna Upanishad* – which likely predates all these philosophical systems – mentions forty-three such cosmic principles. These include all the twenty-five principles of Samkhya. They include the five gross and five subtle elements, the five sense organs and their five sense actions, the five motor organs and five motor actions, the four aspects of the mind and their four functions, light and prana (as higher powers beyond the elements) and their two actions, with the Purusha or consciousness principle beyond.[93]

43 Tattvas or Principles of the Upanishads

1-2. Earth and essence of Earth.

3-4. Water and essence of Water.

5-6. Fire and essence of Fire.

7-8. Air and essence of Air.

9-10. Ether and essence of Ether.

11-12. Eye and what is seen.

13-14. Ear and what is heard.

15-16. Nose and what is smelled.

17-18. Tongue and what is tasted.

19-20. Skin and what is felt.

21-22. Speech and what is spoken.

23-24. Hands and what is grasped.

25-26. Reproductive organ and what is enjoyed.

27-28. Organ of elimination and what is released.

29-30. Feet and movement.

31-32. Mind (manas) and what is thought.

33-34. Intelligence (buddhi) and what is perceived.

35-36. Ego (ahamkara) and ego-thoughts.

37-38. Feeling mind (chitta) and what is felt.

39-40. Light (Tejas) and what is revealed.

41-42. Prana and what is upheld.

43. Atman or Purusha.

All systems of Samkhya, Vedanta and Shaivism agree that the Tattvas, however numbered, are rooted in the pure consciousness principle that is Atman, Purusha, or Shiva. They also reflect a fivefold structure based upon the five elements.

25 Principles or Tattvas of Samkhya Philosophy

The 36 Tattvas of Shaivism begin with and rest upon the 25 Tattvas of Samkhya. The foundation of the 25 Tattvas of Samkhya is the five great elements. The first twenty tattvas reflect the correlations of the five elements with the five sense organs, five motor organs, and five sensory qualities, which yogically relate to the lower five chakras from the root chakra to the throat chakra that are associated with the elements.

Four Groups of Five Element Principles

- 5 elements as Earth, Water, Fire, Air, and Ether Represent the different densities of substance and energy in the universe from the gross to the subtle. Often the term five elements refer specifically to the five gross elements, but the five elements have also subtle and causal forms. [94]

- 5 sensory potentials or subtle elements as sound (ether), touch (air), sight (fire), taste (water), and smell (earth). Allow for the five elements to be experienced by the mind and senses.

- 5 sense organs as hearing (ether), touch (air), seeing (fire), taste (water), and smell (earth). Our instruments of perceiving the subtle elements and their corresponding gross elements.

- 5 motor organs as speech (ether), hands (air), feet (fire), elimination (water) and reproduction (earth). Our means or instruments of working on the five gross and subtle elements.

Three Aspects of Mind, Prakriti and Purusha

To these twenty foundational principles based upon the five elements are added the three aspects of mind as *manas* (outer mind connected to senses and motor organs), *ahamkara* (ego or sense of the self as the doer), and *buddhi* (inner mind or intelligence), along with *Prakriti* and *Purusha*, nature and soul, for twenty-five. Sometimes these tattvas are counted as twenty-four, with the Purusha having an independent status beyond them.

Note that Shaivism looks at the Purusha or Twenty-fifth Tattva of Samkhya only in terms of the individual Purusha or soul in bondage. It adds eleven higher tattvas or principles to these. Other Vedic and Yogic systems have additional principles or slighting different formulations than Samkhya. But we must remember that the infinite and multileveled nature of the universe allows for several angles or views, like the different facets of a magnificent jewel.

Eleven Higher Tattvas of Shaivism

Shaivism's adds to Samkhya eleven higher Tattvas to explain the process of creation at a cosmic level, including the fundamental principles behind the manifest world. Some Shaivite thinkers recognize a higher state of Parashiva, with which its Shakti is merged, beyond the Thirty-six Tattvas as the realm of pure Being, Sat or the Supreme Brahman, though some relate this higher truth to the first, Shiva Tattva.

Yet we should note that the cosmic principles represented by the elements also exist in the higher Tattvas, though not as separate principles. Space, light, and sound, for example, have correlates at the level of Shiva and Shakti Tattvas beyond them. Prana, meanwhile, just as in the Samkhya system, is usually not listed as a separate principle, but is common to all the Tattvas or cosmic principles, and in its higher essence as the immortal Prana is one with Shiva or the supreme Purusha.

Thirty Six Tattvas of Shaivism

The Five Pure Tattvas beyond Ignorance – Divine Foundation of the Universe
The Two Supreme and Transcendent Shiva and Shakti Tattvas

1. Shiva Tattva – Pure consciousness as the Supreme Reality and the basis of all manifestation, the inner essence that is the substratum of all expression. Relates to being (Sat), consciousness, Chit, and to Chit-Shakti or the power of consciousness, Shakti one with Shiva. Those who reach this realm of experience are called Shambhavas for their ability to give blessings to all just as Shiva (Shambhu) himself. Reflects the Shambhava Upaya of Shiva Sadhana.

2. Shakti Tattva – Shakti developing out of the power of consciousness, with the latent seed of creative capacity. Relates to Chit Shakti or the power of consciousness and to Ananda Shakti or Shakti as the basis of all manifestation. Actually Chit-shakti or the power of consciousness is also Ananda. Those who reach this level of experience are called Shaktajas, as they are born of the highest Shakti. Reflects the Shakta Upaya of Shiva Sadhana.

The Three Transcendent States Behind Manifestation – Three Aspects of Shiva as the Cosmic Lord and Lord of Mantra

3. Sadashiva Tattva – state of balance of subject and object prior to any defined manifestation. Relates to Iccha Shakti or the power of the supreme will in its latent state. It is the experience of "I am this," with the "this" indicating all possible manifestation, form or formless, as part of oneself. Those who reach this level of experience are called Mantra Maheshvaras as they reach the supreme level of cosmic sound vibrations.

4. Ishvara Tattva – the universal lord, Shiva as Maheshvara or the Lord of the Universe. Relates to Jnana Shakti or the power of knowledge that rules over all and expresses the Divine Will. It is the experience "This I am," with a sense of rulership over all possibilities. Those who reach this level of experience are called Mantreshvaras as they reach the ruling level of cosmic sound vibrations.

5. Shuddha Vidya Tattva – pure or higher knowledge, the omnipotence of Ishvara relating to the Cosmic Mind. Relates to Kriya Shakti or the power of Divine action through which all energies in the universe operate, including the powers of creation, preservation and dissolution. Those who reach this level of experience are called Mantras as they reach the level of cosmic sound vibration. Six Mixed Tattvas – contain the seeds of ignorance – limiting powers inherent in the process of manifestation Maya as the Illusion of Creation or the Realm of Appearance

6. Maya Tattva – Power of Illusion at a potential level, creation of division, measurement, name and form, often regarded as the creative power of Ishvara in Vedantic thought. Here Maya is the lower power of Ishvara that develops out of the higher knowledge or Shakti Tattva above. Five Manifestations or Functions of Maya These five are not mere philosophical principles but laws and principles of life that we must learn to understand in order to transcend and move beyond Maya.

7. Kalā – division, apportioning, creation of parts according to the measuring power of Maya, apparent division of the indivisible.

8. Raga – Desire and attachment as the basis of manifest existence, generally identified with desire or Kama.

9. Vidya – limited knowledge relative to time and desire, name, form and action in the outer world, the basis of ignorance or Avidya.

10. Kāla – The seed of time as the basis of all manifestation. On this level Brahma, Vishnu and Shiva or the creative, preservative, and transformative powers arise.

11. Niyati – law, destiny and karma, the basis of bondage but also the regulatory laws of nature. Twenty-Five Impure Tattvas Tainted by Ignorance The Principles of Samkhya Philosophy

12. Purusha Tattva – Here indicating only the individual Purushas or bound souls, not the Supreme Purusha that is ever free. Such individual souls are operating in the field of Maya, which obscures the higher Tattvas beyond Maya.

13. Prakriti Tattva – Process of becoming and evolution through the world of nature, power to create the seen or realm of material forms. From Prakriti downward is the objective side of creation, with its inertia and unconsciousness.

14. Buddhi Tattva – Intelligence at a manifest level in the individual soul, the higher mind.

15. Ahamkara Tattva – Ego identity or sense of I am this or that, main principle of division, the basis of life and action for the separate individual soul.

16. Manas – Outer sensory mind that can coordinate sensory and motor organs. Five Sense Organs: Not just the organs but the inner capacity

17. Ears and hearing capacity on gross and subtle levels. Not just the outer organs but the inner capacity.

18. Skin and capacity for touch on gross and subtle levels.

19. Eyes and seeing capacity on gross and subtle levels.

20. Tongue and capacity for taste on gross and subtle levels.

21. Nose and capacity for smell on gross and subtle levels. Five Motor Organs: Not just the organs but the inner capacity

22. Voice and capacity for speech on gross and subtle levels. Not just the outer organs but also the inner capacity.

23. Hands and capacity for grasping on gross and subtle levels.

24. Feet and capacity for movement on gross and subtle levels.

25. Organs of elimination on gross and subtle levels.

26. Organs of reproduction on gross and subtle levels. Five Tanmatras or Subtle Elements

27. Shabda, sound as the subtle element of ether. The realm of manifest sound but connected to the space of Shiva consciousness beyond.

28. Sparsha, touch as the subtle element of air.

29. Rupa, sight as subtle element of fire.

30. Rasa, taste as subtle element of water.

31. Gandha, fragrance as subtle element of earth. Five Gross Elements

32. Ether as a gross element, space as the etheric state of matter on all levels of its manifestation.

33. Air as a gross element, gaseous state of matter.

34. Fire as a gross element, condition of light and heat.

35. Water as a gross element, liquid state of matter.

36. Earth as a gross element, solid state of matter.

37. Vedic Cosmological Connections.

As such cosmic principles are beyond ordinary speech and mind, a number of formulations are possible when we put these into human language. Ganapati Muni, in his study of Shiva and Shakti, relates these principles to the higher lokas or realms of Vedic and Puranic thought.[95]

- **Satya Loka** or the principle of Sat (pure being) to Shiva, and to the principle of Pure Light or Prakasha. He further relates this to the cosmic mind of the Purusha or Shiva principle.

- **Tapo Loka** or the principle of Chit or consciousness to Shakti and the Principle of Reflection or Vimarsha. Tapas is often a synonym for Shakti. He further relates this to the cosmic prana of the Purusha or Shiva principle.

- **Jana Loka** or the principle of Ananda or bliss, to the seed of manifestation arising from Shakti. Jana refers to generation or creation. He further relates this to the cosmic body of the Purusha or Shiva principle.

- **Mahar Loka** or the principle of Vijnana or intelligence to the foundation of creation through the cosmic mind or cosmic intelligence. Mahat is the principle of vast knowledge.

Philosophy of Shaivism and Other Schools

We can surmise much about early Shaivite thought through the *Vedas*, *Agamas*, and *Puranas* in which it is indicated. Yet we do not possess many independent works from the earlier periods not only for Shiva but also for Vishnu. The *Shvetashvatara Upanishad* is the most central of the older Shaivite texts and integrates the worship of Vedic Rudra-Shiva with Vedantic and Samkhya views and the practice of Yoga. This *Upanishad* is perhaps the key text of ancient Shaivite philosophy. It precedes scholastic philosophy and its differing opinions, taking a more integral approach.

Note that I take a different view of Shaivite philosophy than some thinkers and academics. I do not regard Shaivism as significantly different from other Vedic philosophies, but as representing their essence. What Vedic and yogic schools have in common far outweighs their differences, which can usually resolved by a slight shift of terminology.

There is a tendency today to focus on the system of Kashmir Shaivism as unique, and not give much attention to other Shaivite schools. Kashmir Shaivism is the most popular, best translated, and most well known system of Shaivism – and in many ways perhaps the best. It is one of the most brilliant philosophies in the world, and contains a great summation of Indian thought and spirituality.

Yet Kashmir Shaivism is not unique in Shaivite thought and has much in common with other Shaivite schools, especially with the Nath and Siddha Yoga traditions that have a wide following throughout India.[96] Kashmir Shaivism is similar to Shaivism throughout India, including schools in the east (Bengal)[97], south (Tamil Nadu and Kerala, Shaiva Siddhanta) and west of the country (Maharashtra),[98] extending into traditions in what is now Pakistan and Bangladesh. Shankara, the great teacher of Advaita Vedanta, reflects Shaivite teachings in his *Saundarya Lahiri* and his other Shakti works. We must remember that Shankara predates Kashmir Shaivism by some centuries.

Shaivism and Vedanta

Some thinkers like to emphasize the differences between the philosophies of Kashmiri Shaivism, Advaita Vedanta, and Samkhya. I would rather emphasize their similarities and note their common background. From whatever angle one is able to reach the ultimate state of consciousness does not matter when that is reached.

Shaivite philosophy is an important development of Vedantic thought through the *Vedas, Upanishads, Agamas*, and *Puranas*. It follows the language and terminology of Vedanta, such as Purusha and Prakriti, karma, rebirth and liberation. Like all Vedic systems it emphasizes that the supreme truth is beyond words and one must realize it through Yoga and meditation.

Shaivite philosophies are of several types and comprise both dualistic and non-dualistic schools. Dualistic schools are usually devotional in nature and emphasize communion with Shiva as the highest reality, in which the individual soul does not entirely disappear, such as occurs in the higher realm of Shiva Loka. Non-dualistic schools are knowledge oriented and emphasize mergence of the individual soul into the Supreme Reality of Shiva and the realization "I am Shiva." In this regard, Shaivism resembles Vedanta with its dualistic and non-dualistic schools.

Dualistic and non-dualistic views can be complementary. In the manifest world the dualistic view prevails, as at an individual level one is a servant of Lord Shiva working out his will in the world. In the unmanifest realm, the non-dualistic view prevails in which Shiva is the sole reality. When asked by people about the validity of dualism and non-dualism, which they find to be contradictory, I state that "the closest thing to one is two."

Shaivism and Advaita Vedanta

Vedanta in the broader sense refers to all philosophies that accept the authority of the *Vedas* and *Upanishads*. This extends to all schools of Vedic thought, and to Tantra that shares a Vedantic terminology. More specifically, Vedanta is identified with the *Uttara Mimamsa School* among the six Vedic schools, but even that school has dualistic and non-dualistic lines, the schools of Dvaita and Advaita Vedanta.

Advaita Vedanta refers primarily to the non-dualistic school promulgated by the great teacher Shankara, which holds that the world is Maya or illusion and that the supreme Reality is beyond all manifestation, though other Vedantic formulations of non-dualism can also be found.[99]

Kashmir Shaivism and other Shaivite schools may criticize some Vedantic schools but we must remember that they still accept the authority of the *Upanishads* and *Bhagavad Gita*. The noted Kashmiri Shaivite philosopher Abhinavagupta wrote a commentary on the *Bhagavad Gita*. *Shaivite schools can all be called Vedantic in the sense that they accept the authority of the Vedas and Upanishads.* "Shaivism" versus "Vedanta" meaning versus the Advaita Vedanta of Shankara is not Shaivism versus all Vedantic schools or opposed to Vedic thought, but only a critique of certain aspects of Shankara's philosophy. In addition, many Shakti *Tantras* and Shaivite *Tantras* do follow the non-dualistic philosophy of Shankara, including texts like the *Shiva Gita* and *Devi Bhagavata Purana*.

Non-dualistic Shaivism and Shankara Advaita Vedanta accept a non-dual Absolute of Being-Consciousness-Bliss. The debates revolved around whether the manifest world is real, in what manner and to what degree. Shaivite philosophy holds that the world is real as a manifestation of Shiva but not apart from him. Advaita Vedanta holds that the world is real as its substratum in Brahman, but not in its own accord. These views do not differ by much. We could say that the Shaivite and Tantric view has a more aesthetic approach, appreciating the world as symbolic of the higher truth. The usual Advaita Vedanta view is more ascetic and rational, holding to the pure Absolute beyond the world.

Shaivite schools are not realistic in the sense of accepting the physical world as real in the materialist view. Shaivism recognizes the power of Maya and its ability to confuse, delude, and bind the individual soul, but it derives the world manifestation ultimately from the power of consciousness or Chit-Shakti beyond Maya. Maya is the sixth Tattva of Shaivite thought prior to the ignorant soul but there are five Shiva and Shakti Tattvas beyond it.

Shaivite schools regard the world as an appearance like images reflected in a mirror (pratibimba vada), while the Advaita Vedanta school of Shankara, though also using the mirror metaphor, adds to this the idea of superimposition – that the world is false and unreal like rope mistaken as a snake. Shaivite non-duality would not usually compare the universe as a manifestation of Shiva with a rope confused for a snake, though it would accept such a metaphor for the misperception of reality by the individual soul. However, some Advaita Vedantins have this view as well, regarding superimposition as a psychological rather than a cosmological metaphor.[100]

Some thinkers hold that Shaivite non-dualism adds a finishing touch of clarity to that of Shankara Advaita and helps us understand the process of cosmogenesis in greater detail. Others may argue that Shankara Advaita is more simple and clear in its approach, linking the individual directly with the Supreme.

Earth Existence and Shiva Sadhana

Shaivism holds that the world is real as a manifestation of Shiva and Shakti. As such, each creature and each world has its sacred place in the cosmic order of Shiva and Shakti, and need not be negated as irrelevant, unreal, or unimportant, however limited it may be. Shiva and Shakti manifest on all levels of existence down to the Earth and are reflected in all dualities of nature, with distinctive forms and patterns found on every level. Each world and level of existence has an eternal and integral place in the reality and play of Shiva and Shakti.

The Earth serves an important place in the cosmic order and life here should be honored as part of the sacred order of the universe. The Earth plane affords certain opportunities to the soul in terms of energy and expression that are not present in other worlds. The Earth as the root world holds all the higher worlds as well. No doubt the Earth life is daunting but that also affords greater gains for those who are able to progress on their spiritual path in this world where the dualities and powers of ignorance are strongest.

We need not look or go elsewhere to find truth or curse our karma for being born in this lowly physical world. We should strive to understand how the two forces of Shiva and Shakti unfold within our life-experience, seeking to align ourselves with their inner reality. If we can discover Shiva and Shakti here we can bring a great power of knowledge and transformation to the whole of life. We can discover the supreme Shiva in the ground on which we stand. This is perhaps the most significant thing that we can achieve as human beings.

That being said, we should not forget that our sojourn on Earth or in any world is transient and only a small part of our greater journey through the boundless reality of Shiva and Shakti. To take this material world as real in itself, or to regard the achievement of worldly goals as the real purpose of our lives is truly ignorance and will not aid in the development of our souls, or help humanity in any lasting manner. The physical is the grossest and densest of the worlds, a challenging place to live or be aware, and not without its karmic dangers. It has challenges, but also beauties and rewards. What we gain here we can gain for all the worlds and for all time, but we need the awareness of Shiva and the power of Shakti in order to handle this obscure world, whose power of illusion should not be underestimated.

Similarly, all worlds and all creatures of the cosmos, gross, subtle and causal, bound and liberated, individual or cosmic have their place in the greater Reality. There is an integral Reality that includes both the Supreme Shiva above and the manifest realms of Shiva and Shakti below without any necessary contradiction. Yet behind all these Shiva and his inherent Shakti remain the supreme Reality.

Shakti, Maya, Prakriti, Avidya

In Advaita Vedanta there is a simple equation of the main terms for the power of creation – Shakti, Maya (Illusion), Prakriti and Avidya (Ignorance) – regarded as synonyms. Ignorance as an individual principle and Maya as a cosmic principle are sometimes identified. Other texts identify Maya with Ishvara as the cosmic creative power and Avidya only with the Jiva as a power of ignorance, making a clear distinction between them. Sometimes these terms are regarded as referring to different levels of teaching, with the world as a creation of God (Ishvara) being the outer view, and the world and God as illusory divisions in the same transcendent Reality comprising the inner view.

In Shaivism these four terms (Shakti, Maya, Prakriti, Avidya) are related but slightly different in meaning.

- **Shakti** is of many types starting with Para Shakti, the supreme Shakti, which is the power of the Absolute or Supreme Shiva beyond all mani-festation and all the tattvas. In the pure tattvas of Shaivism, Chit-Shakti and Shakti Tattva are beyond ignorance, Prakriti and Maya.

- **Maya** is the power of Shakti to create name and form, the realm of the measurable, which occurs as the basis of the realm of multiplicity. Maya is a power of illusion but not necessarily one of ignorance, though it makes ignorance possible. Maya is like the power of the ocean to produce waves. Ignorance is to take the illusion as real, to confuse the waves with the sea.

- **Prakriti** is the process of manifestation of the forces of nature, nature's organic unfoldment through the gunas and elements, which occurs for the sake of the individual soul or Purusha. Prakriti implies the produc-tion of unconscious or mechanical forces and the creation of various bodies and worlds.

- **Ignorance** at a cosmic level is the power to create that which appears to be unconscious as material and physical reality, and also limited awareness or minds in embodied creatures. The creaturely mind has an inherent ignorance or limitation as it is bound to a living organism and its perpetuation. This ignorance is natural to embodied existence but can be removed by investigation, inquiry and meditation.

- **Ignorance** at an individual level consists of misperception of reality, which sets in motion the process of karma and rebirth. This ignorance consists of confusing the Self for the body and the world of appearances for the ultimate reality. It is on this level of individual avidya that the superimposition process of Advaita Vedanta has its relevance. We confuse the Self for the body like mistaking a rope for a snake in dim light. Yet ignorance is never total. Ignorance is a limited or partial knowledge that is taken as a complete knowledge. It is not a complete absence of knowledge.

Ignorance, Unconsciousness, and Evil

The manifest universe consists of a veil of unconsciousness upon the unmanifest pure consciousness of Shiva. To create form out of the formless, division must occur, in which the original unbounded nature of conscious must become apparently diminished. Matter is nothing but a form of apparent unconsciousness. We say "apparent" because matter is nothing but consciousness in its hidden or devolved state, crystallized as it were into form. As matter further evolves into life and mind, it unfolds by degrees the consciousness existing behind in it all along.[101]

This power to create unconscious or material conditions is part of the cosmic creative force. It reveals potentials like stars and planets, rocks, plants and animals hidden in Brahman and has its own beauty and purpose. Creatures under the influence of this ignorance will not know their true nature, unless they learn to question and move beyond it.

Living creatures combine both conscious and unconscious aspects of reality together as mind and body. We human beings have a limited consciousness in a partially unconscious body. We confuse the conscious with the unconscious, Self with body, the Divine reality with the appearance of the world. This is the basic ignorance that we must overcome. It requires sadhana, extending over many lives as the ignorance is so deep seated.

Evil occurs when the ignorant individual or group deliberately resists the light of consciousness and truth and willfully opposes it to the extent of violence. Evil is an extreme manifestation of ignorance, but not all ignorance or unconsciousness is evil. We cannot say that a rock, a plant or an animal is evil, though they are under unconscious forces. Evil is a perversion of ignorance that can also be removed by knowledge.

Karma

All schools of Vedic and Shaivite thought, dualistic or non-dualistic, world-negating or not, accept the law of karma. One can transcend the law of karma only through Self-realization, but at an outer level of body and mind one should always respect the law of karma and avoid creating negative karmas. One cannot simply dismiss karma as illusion or ignorance. One can only transcend karma by transcending illusion and ignorance. Similarly, all Vedic and Tantric schools recognize a principle of consciousness as our true nature and higher reality beyond karma and beyond all names and forms as Shiva, , or Purusha.

Shaivism and Samkhya

Samkhya philosophy emphasizes twenty-five principles, as occurs in the *Bhagavad Gita*[102] of a combination of the eightfold Prakriti (Prakriti, Buddhi, Ahamkara and the five elements), the sixteenfold Purusha (Purusha, mind, five sense organs, five motor organs, five tanmatras or sensory potentials), with the liberated Purusha beyond as the twenty-fifth.

For Shaivism, Purusha Tattva stands for the individual Purusha only, while in the Samkhya system Purusha stands for the Shiva principle of pure consciousness. The higher principles of Shaivism can be included under Mahat Tattva in Samkhya, which in Samkhya governs such principles as time, space and causation. Mahat Tattva in Samkhya is more than the individual intelligence or buddhi, which is but its limited manifestation in the individual soul.

Samkhya is also not atheistic, as sometimes thought, rejecting any God or Cosmic Lord. Rather it is "trans-theistic," including theism as a lesser manifestation of the Supreme Purusha. Samkhya recognizes Ishvara or God in his three manifestations and Brahma, Vishnu, and Shiva, the cosmic powers of creation, preservation, and dissolution as the three functions of Mahat Tattva or Cosmic Mind.[103] Samkhya Mahat Tattva includes Maya and its functions under Prakriti, not as a separate principle as in Shaivism.

There is little difference between the systems of Samkhya and Shaivism, except relative to the highest principles that Shaivism explains in more detail. Samkhya emphasizes the reality of the Purusha or Shiva principle, the seer or consciousness factor, much like the Shaivite schools. Yet it affords a lesser place to the Shakti principle, which is largely reduced to Prakriti or its unconscious side. We could perhaps call Samkhya a kind of "Shiva without Shakti philosophy," emphasizing the withdrawal of the individual soul from the world manifestation back into the Shiva principle as the Supreme Purusha, *Para Purusha*.

Samkhya teaches more a path of detachment, withdrawing from Prakriti, while Tantra has more a path of sublimation, moving from Prakriti to Shakti. Samkhya does not list Chit-Shakti as an independent principle but only Prakriti as a power of unconsciousness, objectivity, or materiality. Shaivism shows how Shiva and Shakti are both reflected in the world of nature. Yet we could include Shakti in Samkhya as the inherent power of the Purusha.

Samkhya does admit from the highest truth that bondage and liberation are but a play of Prakriti alone, and that the Purusha in its true nature is ever free, just like the nature of Shiva. Seven forms of Prakriti bring bondage and one grants liberation, which is her knowledge form.

> *There is no bondage or liberation, there is no one who is born or dies, in the realm of Samsara. It is only Prakriti in its various forms that is born and dies, is bound and liberated.*
>
> *With seven forms, Prakriti binds herself by herself. She again with one form for the sake of the Purusha liberates herself.*[104]

Prakriti's knowledge form that brings about liberation can be connected to Shakti as a power of knowledge. Yet it remains short of Shaivism's Chit-Shakti or power of consciousness, which is the power of the Purusha itself. We do not find the concept of Purusha-Shakti given prominence in Samkhya, however.

Samkhya's diminished role for Ishvara (God as the cosmic lord) as a function of Mahat Tattva under Prakriti is not much different from the Advaitic view that Ishvara exists only relative to Maya. The Shaivite view that elevates Ishvara above Maya is a further enhancement of the Vedantic idea not emphasized in Samkhya. As an historical note, the *Shvetashvatara Upanishad* that emphasizes Rudra-Shiva also honors Kapila, the founder of the Samkhya system.[105]

Yoga Darshana/*Yoga Sutras*

The *Yoga Sutras* of Patanjali is the primary text of the Yoga Darshana School among the six schools of Vedic philosophy. Yoga Darshana is coupled with Samkhya by way of its philosophical views as Samkhya-Yoga. Yet Yoga Sutra thought can be integrated into Shaivism with a few added explanations.

Yoga Sutras like Samkhya aims at the realization of Atman or Purusha of Vedic thought, which can be equated with Shiva. *Yoga Sutras* gives a special emphasis to Ishvara, which suggests Shiva, particularly as OM and Pranava or primal sound.[106] The *Yoga Sutras* equate Ishvara with the state of the liberated Purusha, making him a special Purusha beyond Prakriti, which is a higher status than Ishvara as the functioning of Mahat Tattva within Prakriti that we find in Samkhya. It can perhaps be identified with the principle of Sat or Pure Shiva. In the *Yoga Sutras*, according to Vyasa's commentary, Ishvara assumes a created mind (Nirmana chitta) to guide living beings, which can be connected to Shiva as the first guru.[107]

The *Yoga Sutras* does not seem to emphasize Shakti but curiously does end with the word Shakti, not as mere Prakriti but as the power of consciousness or the Purusha.

> *Kaivalya (liberation) is the return of the gunas to their origin or when the power of consciousness (chiti shakti) dwells in its own nature.*[108]

Shaivism also regards the universe as a play of the power of consciousness, which in its own nature is one with Shiva. *Yoga Sutras* regards bondage as the confusion of the seer with its power of seeing, with the state of liberation defined as the power of seeing resting in its own nature, which is the nature of the seer. Shaivite Yoga, as in the *Hatha Yoga Pradipika*, identifies the highest Nirvikalpa Samadhi of the *Yoga Sutras* with Advaita or non-duality and the unitary state of Shiva.[109] Clearly there are subtle correlations of what sometimes appear as different terms, with Patanjali Yoga and Shaivite Yoga.

Brief History of Shaivite Yoga

Shiva, as the indicator of Eternal Consciousness, stands outside of time and human history and reflects higher realities than the known universe. But that same power of Shiva as the power of time is behind many important changes in human history and in human evolution.

Shaivite Yoga has a long history, several different layers, and relevance to all humanity. It is one of the most important spiritual traditions not only of India but of the entire world. The purpose of the following chapter is not to reduce the reality of Shiva to historical ideas, movements, or cultural trends. The intent here is to introduce the reader to the enduring nature of Shiva Dharma along with its key representatives and teachings, particularly its connections with Vedic teachings overall.

There are many Shaivite Yoga texts and Shaivite gurus known throughout history. Shaivite texts afford a great prominence to Yoga, including Hatha and Raja approaches in all aspects. Yet many of its greatest teachers are unknown and the greatest texts were either not recorded or were lost over time. Such lost teachings can still be accessed through higher levels awareness and in realms like Shiva Loka. Nevertheless, there remains a richness of teachers and teachings that have been remembered and recorded, many of which are not yet available in the English language. These teachings are not only in Sanskrit but extend to all the languages of India.

Vedic Shaivite Yoga

The history of Shaivism cannot be separated from Hinduism, Vedic or *Sanatana Dharma*, "the eternal tradition." The image of Lord Shiva dominates the history of Yoga going back to the *Vedas* and ancient Harappan seals. Yet even the existent *Vedas* are but the last of an ancient series of compilations that take Yoga back to different world-ages long before what we know of as history began. Vyasa Krishna Dvaipayana, who compiled the existent Vedic texts right after the time of Lord Krishna, is regarded as the twenty-eighth Vyasa, not the first.[110] In every yuga or world-age, Shiva prevails as the lord of time and eternity, assuming different names, forms and representations. As the lord of immortality he is the lord of Yoga as well.

Traditional Yoga in India goes back to the Vedic Yoga, which is rooted in the *Rigveda* as the oldest recorded Vedic text. The *Rigveda* forms the oldest core text of the compilation of the *Vedas* that we have. The other three *Vedas* (*Sama*, *Yajur* and *Atharva*) are developed around it. The *Rigveda* is rooted in the mantras of the Rishis, which reflects their insights and realizations of the supreme truth and Divine Word.

Classical Yoga, as explained in the *Yoga Sutras,* is rooted in Mantra Yoga as OM and primordial sound (pranava),[111] which is the Divine Word of Ishvara, God as the original guru, *whose traditional manifestation is the Vedas*. Shiva is the deity of OM and primordial sound and its manifestation through the *Vedas*, and can be identified with Ishvara.[112]

Vedic Yoga is primarily a Mantra Yoga, consisting of chants and invocations to the Divine through Vedic truth principles, predominantly Agni (Fire), Soma (Moon/Nectar), Indra/Vayu (Air/Lighting) and Surya (Sun). Shiva is an all Vedic deity representing the synthesis of these four primary Vedic deities of light, which are Shiva's four light forms, his three eyes (Sun, Moon and Fire) and their background lightning force.[113]

Vedic Yoga is first of all a twofold Yoga of Agni and Soma, which are the two primary forms of Shiva as fiery and watery, harsh and soft, purifying and regenerating. Shiva and Shakti Yogas consist of the internalization of the Vedic Agni and Soma ritual (yajna), with Agni as the Kundalini fire in the root chakra below, and Soma as the nectar of the thousand petal lotus of the head above, which relates to the Moon. The unification of Fire and Moon results in the Sun of awareness or the Atman in the spiritual heart. The background force is Prana, Vayu or Vidyut, the air and lightning force that sets all energies in motion and is ultimately the power of the Spirit.

Rudra, the Vedic name for Shiva, is sometimes portrayed as the great father of all the Vedic deities and all the worlds, with Vedic deities called "Rudras" or his sons. Rudras are often called "Maruts," the Vedic atmospheric deities reflecting Rudra's power as Prana and Vayu.

Shaivite Yoga is reflected in Vedic deities like Rudra, Indra, and the Maruts or Rudras, which rule over Prana at a subtle level and its corresponding atmospheric realm. The Maruts or Rudras are usually eleven in number, the number of the different types of lightning or pranic forces. The Rudras or Maruts are also portrayed as sages with "tongues of Fire and eyes of the Sun."[114] Krishna in the *Bhagavad Gita* states that he is Shankara (Shiva) among the Rudras.[115]

Shiva is similar to Vedic Indra, the foremost of the Vedic deities. While Shiva represents more the sound power or thunder of the Vedic mantras, Indra represents more the light power or lightning perception.[116] These two must always go together. While Rudra is the father of the Rudras or Maruts, Indra is their leader (Marutvan) and Vishnu is the foremost among them (Evayamarut[117]).

Vedic Shaivite Yoga also relates to the Ashvins in the *Vedas*, the twin horsemen or powers of Prana, who are called "Rudras" and can represent Agni (Rudra) and Soma as complementary forces. The Ashvins are lauded among the early teachers of Ayurvedic medicine, Vedic astrology and the *Upanishads*.[118] They hold all miraculous powers and deeper knowledge, especially that of Soma, bliss and immortality.

Shiva and the Vedic Rishis
Shiva is closely associated with several important Vedic Rishis and their families. He can be easily regarded as the supreme Guru behind all of them.

- Vamadeva is the seer of the fourth book of the *Rigveda* and the seer of the Hamsa mantra that is connected to Shiva.[119] Vamadeva later became an important name for Shiva, while in the *Rigveda*, Vamadeva refers to Indra and Surya (Sun). Vamadeva's family, the Gotamas, were an important Vedic family of the Angirasa line. They became the main priests or Purohits of the kingdom of Videha from which Sita came and many enlightened kings of the Janaka lineage that extended into the Upanishadic era.

- Vasishta is the seer of the famous Mrityunjaya or Tryambakam mantra to Shiva as the one who takes us across death.[120] Vasishtha is the seer of the seventh book of the *Rigveda* and has the greatest number of hymns in the *Rigveda* attributed to him of any seer. The Vasishtas became the main priests or Purohits of the kingdom of Kosala, from which Rama came and were renowned for their purity.

- Agastya is the elder brother of Vasishta in the *Rigveda*,[121] prominent in South Indian Shaivism, who is the seer of about twenty-five hymns in the first book of the *Rigveda*, mainly to Indra and the Maruts. To Agastya is attributed the founding of the Tamil language and Tamil culture as well as the spread of Hindu culture throughout Southeast Asia. He also connects Vedic and Shaivite traditions to the South of India, particularly through his mentorship of Vasishta.

- The Angirasas, the largest family of Vedic rishis, are connected to Agni and Skanda (Shiva's son and the deity of the planet Mars) and through them to Shiva himself. Skanda as Sanat Kumar or the eternal child is the first of the Angirasa Gurus. Yet the Angirasas also relate to Brihaspati or Jupiter, which has associations with Ganesha.

- The Bhrigus, the other main Vedic seer family, is connected to Shiva through his Soma form and the planet Venus. They are associated more with the southwest of India, particularly Gujarat, yet are mentioned in Persian Zoroastrian lore as well, with some affinities with Venus based cultures of the Middle East, Egypt and Mexico.

Relative to the famous Vedic Gayatri mantra to the deity *Savita* as the solar deity of enlightenment, there is a special Shiva connection. The mantra is to the "most adorable radiance (Bharga)" of the solar Godhead. That term for radiance, Bharga, is identified with Agni and with Rudra, the most powerful and purifying flame of tapas. This connects Shiva with the Rishi Vishvamitra, the seer of the Gayatri mantra, and guru of the Vedic martial arts and Kshatriya traditions.

Rudra's Supremacy in the later Vedas

Shiva as Rudra becomes the dominant deity in the *Yajurveda*, notably in the Rudram section. Shiva is worshipped in the *Atharvaveda* as Rudra, Bhava, Sharva, Manyu, Bhima and Ugra. Rudra is the main deity personifying the Vedic fire altar in the *Shatapatha Brahmana*[122] and represents the Vedic ritual overall.[123]

The main Shiva text in the *Upanishads* is the *Shvetashvatara*, the name of the teacher, a famous Shaivite guru. The *Katha Upanishad*, taught by Yama, another name for Shiva, is also associated with him. The *Isha Upanishad*, whose name "Ish" reflects Ishvara or Shiva forms another possible connection to Shiva. *Kena Upanishad* mentions Shiva's wife as Uma. The *Kaivalya Upanishad* is another important Shaivite work and there is an entire set of Shaivite *Upanishads* that refer to special Yoga practices. Most *Yoga Upanishads*, another later set of the literature, prominently mention Shiva, including a special set of Shiva Upanishads.

Puranic Shaivite Yoga

The *Puranas*, the great Hindu encyclopedic teachings, begin at the time of the *Mahabharata* in the ancient period and extend to the time of the *Tantras* in the medieval period. There are many Shaiva *Puranas* among the twenty main *Puranas* including the Agni *Purana, Vayu Purana, Skanda Purana, Linga Purana,* and *Shiva Purana*. Shiva is discussed in detail in all the *Puranas*. All aspects of Shaivite philosophy, Yoga and worship are covered in various places in the *Puranas*, including sacred sites, rituals and mantras. These rich and powerful texts deserve much more study and hold the key to many higher teachings. The Mahabharata, often called the fifth Veda, is famous for its *Thousand Names of Shiva* as well as its many stories of Shiva, like the Puranas.

Pashupata Yoga, Lakulish Tradition

Shaivite Yoga under the name of Pashupata Yoga is examined in the *Mahabharata*, often regarded as the fifth Veda, where it is mentioned in a number of places. Relative to the story of the Mahabharata War, Arjuna received Shiva's Pashupata bow as his weapon in the Himalayas.[124] The *Mahabharata* not only contains the *Bhagavad Gita* and the *Thousand Names of Vishnu*, it also has the *Thousand Names of Shiva*, given by the Rishis Tandi and Upamanyu, which has been widely used.

Lakulish is the most famous Shaivite guru of the Pashupata line and a great Yogi. He is regarded as the twenty-eighth incarnation of Lord Shiva in the Pashupata line, which begins with Dakshinamurti, and is dated at two thousand years ago or more. His main center is Kayavarohan in Gujarat, but his representations are commonly found in the Himalayas, particularly at the Jageshwar temple in the Kumaon region. Lakulish is usually presented as holding a staff, and regarded as an ascetic and yogi. Earlier Hatha and Raja Yoga traditions can be traced to Lakulish before the Nath Yogis like Gorakhnath and through him back to older Vedic traditions.

Shankara and Advaita Vedanta Shaivite Yoga

Shankara, the great teacher who revived the tradition of Advaita Vedanta, taught the worship of all the main Hindu deities but emphasized Shiva and Shakti. He is regarded as a manifestation of Lord Shiva himself. Shankara has left many important works on Shiva, which later Advaitic teachers have expanded.[125] Shiva has probably been the most popular deity in Advaita Vedanta. Shankara helped renovate many sacred sites in India, including such important Shiva temples as Kedarnath, as noted earlier in the book. Many Advaitic Swamis honor Lord Shiva through Shankara and forms like Dakshinamurti.

Shiva and Buddhism

Both Shiva and Buddha reflect the India image of the teacher or deity seated in meditation. The sitting forms of Shiva and Buddha are the most common in the iconography of Asia. Joint Shiva-Buddha movements existed in medieval times in India, Central Asia and Southeast Asia. Tibetan Buddhism honors Shiva as the deity of Mount Kailas and as Mahakala. Shiva relates to Nirvana as the ultimate state of samadhi, nirodha and release. One could call Shiva the personification of Nirvana. Shiva resembles the impersonal Buddha and the Buddhist clear light of awareness. The famous ancient Buddhist university of Nalanda in east India also had a depiction of Shiva. We do not know if Buddha came from a Shaivite family, but Shiva was a common deity among the princes of North India at his time.

Buddhist Tantra, particularly the Vajrayana School, resembles much of Hindu and Shaivite Tantra, particularly in terms of practices, with differences more in philosophy. Vajrayana practices include deity worship, pujas, homas, abhishekas, Sanskrit mantras, yantra and mandalas, Kundalini (Chandali), chakras and nadis, with special teachings from Ayurveda and Vedic astrology, much like the Hindu Tantras. The Buddhist One Mind of pure light (Prabhasvara Chitta) resembles the Shiva principle of pure awareness,[126] though formulated in a different way.

Tantric, Nath and Siddha Shaivite Yogas

Tantric texts honor Lord Shiva as their primary deity and include his mantras, rituals and teachings. Tantric Yoga is a development of Shiva Yoga. There are numerous Tantric texts throughout India, much like the *Puranas* reflecting all aspects of life, religion and spirituality.

Hatha Yoga, which is largely a Tantric tradition, goes back to the older Pashupata and Lakulish traditions and ultimately to the *Vedas* and the tradition of *Dhanur Veda*, the martial arts taught by the seer Vishvamitra. Hatha Yoga is mentioned by Shankara,[127] who preceded Gorakhnath by some centuries.[128] In the works of the later Natha Yogis like Gorakhnath and Matsyendranath, Hatha Yoga and its related Raja Yoga become prominent again. Most existing Hatha Yoga texts like the *Hatha Yoga Pradipika* derive from them.

Nath Raja Yoga is also called Siddha Yoga. The Siddhas are largely great Shaivite Yogis and are attributed with great longevity and special occult powers. The Siddhas are prominent in South India also, particularly in Tamil Nadu, with many ancient Tamil Siddha Yogis like Tirumular and his famous text *Tirumandiram*, one of the national literature classics of the area. All these Yoga approaches begin with Shiva as the original guru.

Kashmiri Shaivism

Kashmiri Shaivism is one of the most important branches of Shaivism and also Tantric in nature. Its prime guru Abhinavagupta is teacher of monumental stature like Buddha, Krishna, and Shankara. Abhinavagupta's corpus of works covers all aspects of Yoga, philosophy, art and culture, with depth, profundity and refinement. Kashmir has long been a land of Shiva. The main lake in Kashmir, now called the "Dal Lake," was earlier called the "Lesser Manasa Lake" or lake of the mind, as associated with the "Greater Manasa Lake" of *Manasarovar* by Mount Kailas in Tibet. The same lake is also called *Satisarovar* as sacred to Shiva's wife as Sati. Shankaracharya also has a famous temple on a hill by Srinagar in Kashmir. Kashmir Shaivites were strongly connected to the Nath and Siddha traditions as well.

Shakti Shaivites

Most followers of Shakti, Devi, the Goddess or the Divine Mother naturally worship Shiva. They regard Devi as Shiva's consort and counterpart (Uma, Parvati, Durga, Kali, Sundari, Lalita). Shiva Yoga is related to and affords an important place to the worship of Shakti. The worship of Durga and Durga puja, the Dasha Mahavidya (Ten Wisdom Forms of the Goddess), and Sri Yantra that highlight the Goddess are common in Shaivite teachings.

Avadhutas

Avadhutas are wandering realized sages beyond all social boundaries. They wear minimal clothes and have no money, possessions, or homes, not even ashrams. They seldom write, speak or formally teach anyone. They live at the fringe of the human world and more in the world of nature. Most avadhutas relate to Shiva energy. The great Avadhuta *Dattatreya* is often related to the Dakshinamurti form of Shiva.[129] One of the most important modern Avadhutas was Swami Nityananda, the guru of Swami Muktananda.

Shaivite Yoga and the Future of Our Species

Shaivism is one of humanity's oldest and most important spiritual traditions. Shaivism is continuing to grow worldwide as one of the main movements in modern Yoga, and one of the core components of Hinduism or Sanatana Dharma, which is also spreading worldwide. I have discussed earlier my own encounter with Shiva that reflects many of the great Shiva gurus and traditions in the world today, but there are many more.

Lord Shiva is emerging as an important deity not only through the Yoga tradition but also through the world revival of native and pagan traditions, with which he is closely connected and has many counterparts. As the spirit in nature once more asserts itself against the depredations of modern humanity, the Shiva energy is likely to manifest more strongly. As we begin to understand the cosmic nature of sound, language, universal speech and communication, the mantric power of Shiva will become more relevant.

Many new movements in meditation, healing and ecology can draw that Shiva power back into humanity for the greater well being of our species and of our planet. Shiva Dharma and Shiva Yoga will continue to guide humanity for centuries to come, and new great teachers of Shaivism will likely arise all over the world.

Shiva holds the supreme power of transformation. There can be no real change in humanity unless we once more discover that inner Shiva power of stillness, peace and mastery and let go of our outer desires, wants, obsessions, and compulsions. No force of mere science and technology can compare to Shiva's force or lift us beyond the deep-seated limitations of our ego nature. The display of Shiva's energy puts all the glamour of the media into the dust. Shiva is the power of eternity that dwarfs all our transient ventures and ambitions, extending to our highest individual and collective achievements, which are but the shadow of his universal dance.

Shiva holds the key to all evolutionary changes in humanity and to a new inner birth that takes us beyond the karmic and genetic limitations of our species to a truly conscious and universal awareness as our natural state. Shiva grants us the Shakti or inner power that can hold the entire universe within our own hearts in the equanimity of meditation as if it were but a fragile flower.

Shiva is the power of the true Self that is the master of the universe. From the sound vibration of Shiva originates all higher teachings. Shiva is the inner guru that we must discover in order to reach our true destiny as souls. We must let go of our arrogance to know and embrace his presence as the great unknown. If even a few of us today can do this, it can create a wave of transformation beyond time and number that can reverberate through the entire world around us.

May that Shiva consciousness come forth in every person and radiate through every place on Earth!

May you connect with the presence of Shiva and his representative powers in this and all the worlds!

OM Namah Shivaya!

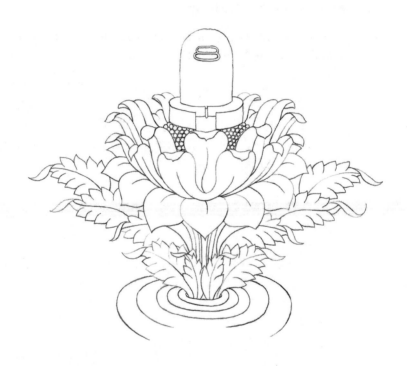

10. Shiva Linga 2

Part VI

Appendices

Appendix 1
Names and Terms for Shiva

1. Achala – unchanging, a mountain
2. Adiguru – the primal guru
3. Adinatha – the primal lord
4. Adi Purusha – the primal Person or Purusha
5. Aghora – not fierce
6. Agni – cosmic principle of fire and light
7. Ahipati – lord of serpents
8. Akshara – letter or imperishable point
9. Amrita – immortal nectar
10. Ardhanareshvara – combined Shiva and Shakti
11. Ashutosha – quick to give blessings
12. Ayus – longevity and duration
13. Bhagavan – blissful lord
14. Bhairava – fierce, often relates to Vayu or air
15. Bhasmadhara – anointed with the sacred ash or bhasma
16. Bhava – power of existence
17. Bhima – fierce
18. Bhuta-pati – Lord of the spirits
19. Bindu – the primal point or singularity
20. Chidambaram – who wears the space of consciousness
21. Chandrashekhara – who wears the crescent moon on his head
22. Dakshinamurti - youthful knowledge form of Shiva
23. Damarudhara – who carries the drum
24. Gangadhara – who carries the river Ganga on his head
25. Gauranga – who has white limbs
26. Ghora – fierce or terrible
27. Girijapati – husband of the daughter of the mountain
28. Girisha – dweller in the mountains
29. Hara – the one who captivates or takes things away

30. Haumkara – pranic seed mantra Haum

31. Humkara – fire seed mantra Hum

32. Indra – Supreme lord in the Vedas

33. Indupati – Lord of the Moon

34. Ishana – ruling force from the northeastern direction

35. Ishuhasta – who holds an arrow in his hand

36. Jatadhara – who has matted locks of hair

37. Jyotir Linga – the linga or emblem of light

38. Kailasapati – Lord of Mount Kailas, the cosmic mountain of Shiva

39. Kala – time and the lord of Time, Mahakala

40. Kalagnirudra – Rudra who is the fire of time

41. Kala Bhairava – fierce power of time

42. Kameshvara – Lord of desire or love

43. Kapali – who carries a skull

44. Kapardin – with matted hair

45. Kashi – illuminating perception or city of Varanasi (Benares)

46. Kedarnatha – main Himalayan Shiva temple

47. Linga – emblem of Shiva or the Cosmic Masculine force

48. Mahadeva – great god or divinity

49. Mahayogi – great Yogi

50. Maheshvara – great Lord

51. Manasarovara – the mind lake of Shiva by Mount Kailas in Tibet

52. Manyu – wrath and the power of protection

53. Marut – power of the air and atmosphere

54. Mayavin – Lord of Maya

55. Moksha – state of liberation or release from Samsara, the cycle of birth and death

56. Mriga-dhara – who carries a deer as his ornament

57. Mrityunjaya – conqueror of death

58. Mukteshvara – great lord of liberation

59. Nageshvara – Lord of serpents

60. Nandi-vahana – whose vehicle is the bull called Nandi

61. Nataraj – Lord of the dance, specifically the cosmic dance of fire and light

62. Nilakantha or Nilagriva – who has a blue throat

63. Nirodha – state of cessation

64. Nirvana – state of dissolution

65. Ojas – vital essence

66. Omkara – the primal sound or seed mantra OM

67. Panchavaktra – who has five faces for the five directions of space

68. Parabrahman – the Supreme Brahman

69. Paramatman – the Supreme Self

70. Parameshvara – Supreme Lord

71. Parashiva – Supreme Shiva

72. Parvati-Pati – Lord of Parvati

73. Pashupati – Lord of the animals

74. Pinaki – who holds the bow

75. Prakasha – pure light

76. Prana – vital energy, spirit

77. Pranava – primordial sound vibration

78. Purusha – Cosmic Person

79. Pashupati – Lord of the animals or lord of perception

80. Rudra – fierce or the maker of sound

81. Sadashiva – always auspicious

82. Sadyojata – immediately manifest

83. Samba – who is with the cosmic Mother or amba

84. Satisarovara – lake of Sati or Shakti in Kashmir

85. Shaktiman – wielder or lord of Shakti

86. Shambhu – dispenser of blessings

87. Shankara – giver of blessings

88. Shanta – state of peace

89. Sharva – wielder of the arrow

90. Shitikantha – who has a white throat or neck

91. Shulapani – who has a spear in his hand

92. Shiva – the auspicious one

93. Soma – immortal nectar

94. Sphatika Linga – the crystal linga

95. Sthambha – the pillar

96. Sthira – state of steadiness

97. Sthanu – a post or pillar

98. Sundareshvara – Lord of beauty

99. Surya – the Sun

100. Suvarna Linga – the golden linga

101. Swami – who is master of himself

102. Tandava – Shiva's thundering dance of transformation

103. Tapas – fire of yogic transformation

104. Tat Purusha – that Purusha or cosmic being

105. Tejas – fire and vigor

106. Taraka – the one who takes us across the darkness of ignorance

107. Trimurti – having three forms as Brahma, Vishnu and Shiva

108. Trinayana or Trinetra – who has three eyes as Sun, Moon and Fire

109. Tripurahara – destroyer of the three cities

110. Trishula-dhara – who carries the Trishula or trident

111. Tryambakam – who has three eyes or three mothers

112. Ugra – fierce

113. Vaidyanatha – lord of the doctors

114. Vamadeva – the blissful deity

115. Vishvanatha – Lord of all

116. Vayu – cosmic air principle

117. Vratya – the outcaste

118. Vrishabha – the bull

119. Yama – deity of death

120. Yogeshvara – Lord of Yoga

Appendix 2
General Terms

Advaita – non-duality

Akasha – space

Agamas – Shaivite and Tantric texts

Agni – cosmic fire principle

Amrita – nectar

Ananda – bliss

Atman – higher or true Self

Avidya – ignorance, unconsciousness as a power

Ayurveda – Vedic system of medicine

Bhakti – devotion as a yogic principle

Bhasma – sacred ash

Bija – seed or seem mantra

Bindu – point

Brahman – Absolute or formless Godhead

Chakras – energy centers of subtle body

Chit – consciousness

Devi – Goddess

Dharana – concentration

Dharma – cosmic and natural law

Dhyana – meditation

Dosha – biological humors of Ayurveda

Ganesha/ Ganapati – elephant headed son of Shiva

Hamsa – swan, bird, prana, Atma

Jnana – knowledge as yogic principle

Jyoti – light as a cosmic principle

Jyotish – Vedic astrology

Ishvara – God as cosmic lord

Kala – cosmic design

Kala – time

Kali – Goddess of eternal time

Karma – action, ritual

Kriya – power of action

Kundalini – inner serpent power of Yoga

Lalita – Goddess as power of delight

Laya – the state of mergence

Linga – Shiva's symbolic form

Maya – power of illusion

Mudra – gesture, action

Nada – cosmic sound vibration

Parvati – Shiva's wife as daughter of the mountain

Puranas – Hindu texts

Prakriti – nature and its process

Prana – breath, spirit

Pranava – primordial sound

Purusha – cosmic person

Rudraksha – malas or rosaries of Rudraksha seeds

Sakshi – witness or observer

Sadhana – Yoga practice

Samadhi – state of absorption

Samatva – state of balance

Sat – being, truth, existence

Satya – truth or reality

Shabda – sound vibration

Shakti – Goddess as Supreme cosmic power

Skanda – Shiva and Parvati's second son as the deity of Fire and knowledge

Soma – Power of bliss, immortal nectar

Stotra – devotional hymn

Svara – sound vibration, resonance

Tantras – medieval Yoga and Hindu texts

Tattva – truth principle

Uma – Shiva's wife as the giver of knowledge

Upaya – method of practice

Vayu – cosmic air element

Vedas – mantras of the ancient Rishis

Vishnu – Divine power of sustaining the cosmic order

Yajna – sacrifice, ritual, worship

Yantra – geometrical meditation design

Yoni – origin, source

Appendix 3
Transliterated Sanskrit letters found in the text

Note that we have only used these in the case of a few mantras, not for all Sanskrit terms. We have included mainly those letters that are pronounced rather differently than their normal English equivalents

a as in *a* book

ā as in f*a*ther

i as in *i*t

ī as in st*ea*m

u as in p*u*t

ū as in shoot

ṛ as in

e as in c*a*ke

ai as in f*i*re

o as in h*o*me

au as in h*ou*nd

c as in *ch*urch

ch as in i*tch*

ś as in s*h*ip

ṣ as s*h*ut

ḥ soft h sound

Appendix 4
Bibliography

Abhinavagupta. PARATRISIKA VIVARANA (Jaidev Singh translation). Delhi, India: Motilal Banarsidass, 1988.

Abhinavagupta. TANTRASARA (Sanskrit only). Delhi, India: Bani Prakashan, 1983.

AKASHA BHAIRAVA TANTRA (Sanskrit and Hindi). Nanak Chand Sharma, editor. Delhi, India: Motilal Banarsidass, 1980.

ATHARVA VEDA SAMHITA
BRIHAT STOTRA RATNAKARA
Chopra, Shambhavi. YOGINI: UNFOLDING THE GODDESS WITHIN. Delhi, India: Wisdom Tree Books, 2006.

Chopra, Shambhavi. YOGIC SECRETS OF THE DARK GODDESS. Delhi, India: Wisdom Tree Books, 2007.

COLLECTED WORKS OF VASISHTHA KAVYAKANTHA GANAPATI MUNI (Sanskrit only), in eleven volumes, edited by K. Natesan. Tiruvannamalai, India: Sri Ramanasramam 2003–2007.

HATHA YOGA PRADIPIKA of Svatmarama. Adyar, India: Adyar Library and Research Centre, The Theosophical Society, 1972.

MAHABHARATA, INCLUDING BHAGAVAD GITA
Swami Muktananda, INTRODUCTION TO KASHMIR SHAIVISM. Ganeshpuri, India: Sri Gurudev Ashram, 1977.

Murty, Dr. Sivananda, KATHA-YOGA. New Delhi, India, Aditya Prakashan, 2009.

M., THE GOSPEL OF RAMAKRISHNA. Chennai, India: Sri Ramakrishna Math, 2000.

PASUPATA SUTRAS WITH PRANCHARTHABHASHYA OF KAUNDINYA, Edited by R. Ananthakrishna Sastri, Trivandrum, India: Oriental Manuscripts Library of the University of Travancore, 1940.

Patañjali, YOGA SUTRAS. Varanasi, India: Bharatiya Vidya Prakashana, with commentaries of Vachaspati Mishra and Vijnana Bhikshu, 1983.

Bhagavan Ramana Maharshi, SADDARSHANA BHASHYA, Tiruvannamalai, India: Sri Ramanasramam, 1968.

RIGVEDA SAMHITA
Satguru Sivaya Subramuniyaswami. DANCING WITH SHIVA. India and USA: Himalayan Academy, 2004.

Satguru Sivaya Subramuniyaswami. LIVING WITH SHIVA. India and USA: Himalayan Academy, 2001.

Satguru Sivaya Subramuniyaswami. LOVING GANESHA. India and USA: Himalayan Academy, 1993.

Satguru Sivaya Subramuniyaswami. MERGING WITH SHIVA. India and USA: Himalayan Academy, 2004.

Shankaracharya. SAUNDARYA LAHARI (V.K. Subramanian trans.). Delhi, India: Motilal Banarsidass, 1986.

SHIVA SAMHITA. Delhi, India: Chaukhambha Sanskrit Pratishthan, 2004.

SIDDHASIDDHANTA PADDHATI of Goraknath. Poona, India: Poona Oriental Book House, 1964.

SIVA GITA. Chennai, India: Centenarian Trust, 1997.

UPANISHADS, ONE HUNDRED AND EIGHTY EIGHT (Sanskrit only). Delhi, India: Motilal Banarsidass, 1980.

VIJNANA BHAIRAVA (Commentary by Swami Lakshman Joo). Varanasi India: Indica Books, 2002.

YAJURVEDA SAMHITA

Yogananda, Paramahansa. AUTOBIOGRAPHY OF A YOGI. Los Angeles, CA: Self-realization Fellowship, 2007.

By the Author

Frawley, David. GODS, SAGES AND KINGS: VEDIC SECRETS OF ANCIENT CIVILIZATION, Twin Lakes, WI: Lotus Press, 1991, 2012.

Frawley, David. INNER TANTRIC YOGA. Twin Lakes, WI: Lotus Press, 2008.

Frawley, David. MANTRA YOGA AND PRIMAL SOUND. Twin Lakes, Wi.: Lotus Press, 2010.

Frawley, David. SOMA IN YOGA AND AYURVEDA. Twin Lakes, Wi.: Lotus Press, 2012.

Frawley, David. TANTRIC YOGA AND THE WISDOM GODDESSES. Twin Lakes, WI: Lotus Press, 1994.

Frawley, David. VEDIC YOGA: THE PATH OF THE RISHI. Twin Lakes, WI: Lotus Press, 2014.

Frawley, David. WISDOM OF THE ANCIENT SEERS: SELECTED MANTRAS FOR THE RIG VEDA Twin Lakes, WI: Lotus Press, 1993.

Frawley, David. YOGA AND AYURVEDA: SELF-HEALING AND SELF-REALIZATION. Twin Lakes, WI: Lotus Press, 1999.

Frawley, David. YOGA AND THE SACRED FIRE. Twin Lakes, WI: Lotus Press, 2004.

Appendix 5
Resources

Vedacharya Dr. David Frawley (Pandit Vamadeva Shastri)

Dr. David Frawley (b. 1950) is the author of more than thirty five published books and several distance learning courses over the past thirty years. His books are available in twenty different languages and include important publications in the fields of Ayurvedic medicine, Vedic astrology, Raja Yoga, Veda, Vedanta, and Tantra. His works are noted for their depth and specificity and often serve as textbooks in their respective fields.

Vamadeva is one of the most respected *Vedacharyas* or teachers of the ancient Vedic wisdom in recent decades, East and West. He has a D.Litt and in Yoga from S-VYASA (Swami Vivekananda Yoga Anusandhana Samsthana) and a special *Padma Bhushan* award from the government of India for "distinguished service of a high order." He is honored in traditional circles in India, where his writings are well known and frequently quoted. He is regarded as a teacher or acharya of Yoga, Ayurveda and Vedic astrology as well, reflecting his rare ability to link different Vedic disciplines together and teach them in an integral manner.

American Institute of Vedic Studies, *www.vedanet.com*

The American Institute of Vedic Studies is an internationally recognized center of Vedic learning, with affiliated organizations worldwide. Directed by Dr. David Frawley (Pandit Vamadeva Shastri) and Yogini Shambhavi Devi, the Vedic institute serves as a vehicle for their work, books, CDs, programs, and activities. The institute, which is primarily web-based, offers in depth training, including distance-learning programs in Ayurveda, Raja Yoga, and Vedic astrology. Its courses are available in a number of different languages and through several affiliated organizations worldwide.

The institute participates in regular retreats in different countries in order to bring students for a deeper level of instruction with Vamadeva and Shambhavi. It also participates in various international programs, events and conferences. The institute website features extensive on-line articles, on-line books, and a full range of Vedic resources for the serious student, including a regular newsletter. His Facebook account is Dr. David Frawley.

Yogini Shambhavi Devi

Yogini Shambhavi Chopra is one of the foremost traditional women teachers coming out of India today. She is the author of several important books on the Goddess (*Yogini: Unfolding the Goddess Within* and *Yogic Secrets of the Dark Goddess*), noted for their experiential approach to higher consciousness. Her *Yogini Bhava* and *Jyotish Bhava* CDs provide powerful guides for traditional chanting and mantra sadhana, invoking the Divine presence and power of Shakti in our lives.

Shambhavi offers consultations in Vedic astrology and spiritual guidance, reflecting her understanding of the Divine powers of the planets and their karmic connections. She also offers special initiations into Shakti Sadhana and Shakti Dharma for select students from all over the world who seek her guidance. She has a proficiency in both Vedic and Tantric mantras that she shares with her students. She is a great inspiration for all who come into contact with her. Her Facebook account is Yogini Shambhavi.

Pieter Weltevrede

In 1977 Pieter Weltevrede met his guru Sri Harish Johari, a multitalented artist, yogi and spiritual teacher who created the Harish Johari wash-technique. Since 1980 Pieter has devoted his time to master this technique and study Sanatana Dharma. In 1988 he met the teacher of his teacher: Sri Chandra Bal. which culminated in the book "the Birth of Ganga." After that Pieter created together with Harish Johari and his brother Suresh Johari the book "Little Krishna."

Pieter published three more children's books: "How Ganesha got his Elephant Head," "How Parvati Won the Hearth of Shiva," and "Ram the Demon Slayer." He contributed to many books of his guru like "Chakras," "Numerology,"' 'Leela," "Ayurvedic Massage" and "the Monkey and the Mango Tree."

Pieter has been teaching yantra, mandala and deity painting in Holland and the USA. He conducts workshops in the Johari House in Haridwar together with Mavis Gewant. Pieter and his wife Geva travel to India every year. His paintings can be viewed at sanatansociety.org or at pieter.weltevrede.com.

Appendix 7
Quotes

Vamadeva Shastri has been a spiritual guide and mentor of mine for several decades. For anyone who is serious about their journey to higher divine consciousness this book is yet another jewel from him. I'm immensely grateful that he is in our lives.

Dr. Deepak Chopra

For someone like me, who is a devout Shiva worshipper, this book is a treasure. But even for those who may not be Lord Shiva devotees this book is a path to wisdom. Dr. Frawley has conveyed the intricate philosophies of Lord Shiva through language that is simple and beautiful, through a means that makes complex ideas easily understandable.

A few lines that remained with me (among many others!) is when Dr. Frawley wrote wonderfully in the book: "Shiva is the resonance of the cosmic silence." Or this other beautiful line: "The light of Shiva is the inner light behind all outer light forms in the universe." Or this: "To find Shiva we must create a space for Shiva to manifest... Yoga is about developing higher forms of space inside ourselves, through which the cosmic forces can manifest".

"Shiva: The Lord of Yoga" is wonderful book of wisdom. I strongly recommend that you read it.

Amish Tripathi, best-selling author of the Shiva Trilogy

Sri Vamadeva Shastri (Dr. David Frawley) is no mere academic or intellectual researcher. His present book on Lord Shiva that has flowed from his pen is an in-depth work of both erudition and insight, reflecting many years of both study and meditative experience.

Sri Sadguru Sivananda Murty

Vamadeva reflects the living reality of Shiva that pervades all of nature and fills all life with mystery, wonder and awe. He brings us all into the presence of Shiva.

Yogini Shambhavi Devi, author Yogic Secrets of the Dark Goddess

This mind-shattering book ushers us into a far vaster universe than we in the West are accustomed to. We meet a wild and exultant divinity who strips us of everything we are, to show us we actually are everything. Fantastic book—a superb evocation of one of the world's great spiritual traditions.

This book is a head-on collision with reality. The primordially ancient tradition of Shiva confronts us with a Supreme Deity who is unfathomably transcendent yet radically present. Shiva is not a doting celestial father figure but reality itself, in all its magnificence and terror, bracingly alive, the very essence of ecstasy, and closer to us than our own thoughts. This book is blazingly spiritually vibrant, a mind-blasting encounter with the deepest part of our own being.

Linda Johnsen, author, The Living Goddess:
Reclaiming the Tradition of the Mother of the Universe

"Shiva: The Lord of Yoga", by Vamadeva Shastri/David Frawley, is without a doubt the most authentic, masterful, comprehensive and profound presentation of the essential nature and lore of Shiva/Yogeshvara that has been presented in the English language. I highly recommend that all yoga practitioners and those interested in Vedic wisdom make this book one of their "Gurus" for perfecting the yogic journey they have begun.

Kavindra Rishi/Jeffrey Armstrong

Appendix 8
Footnotes
(Endnotes)

1.   Līyate gamyate caracarām idam sarvam yatra lingam iti abhidhīyate.

2.   Kushanas and Hunas, as well as Indo-Scythians. Kushanas strongly promoted Buddhism through Central Asia to China but earlier and later Kushana kings were Hindus. Hunas overall were Hindus. Indo-Scythians had Shiva and Skanda in their coinage.

3.   Note Amish Tripathi's Shiva Trilogy that has been the best selling novel in modern India.

4.   Hatha Yoga Pradipika I.1.

5.   Dionysius was originally a Thracian God. The Thracians were likely an Indo-Iranian people with possible connections to India. The Orphic mysteries around Orpheus, another Thracian deity, contained a belief in karma and rebirth, as did many other European pagan traditions.

6.   Note Gundestrup Cauldron, which has a depiction of a deity resembling Shiva as the Lord of the animals, dating from Denmark around two thousand years ago.

7.   This includes the Turkish-Mongol deity Tengri, the God of the Sky of the Shamans, who has connections to Shiva.

8.   Note teachings of Bhagavad Gita, II.12,16,20.

9.   Chandogya Upanishad, Chapter VI. Sadvidya.

10.   Bhagavan Ramana Maharshi, Saddarshana. I.1.

11.   Yoga Sutras IV.34.

12.   Brihadaranyaka Upanishad II.5.18.

13.   This is the direct or Anupaya approach of Shaivism that we will discuss later.

14. Brihadaranyaka Upanishad, I.III. 28.

15. Omkara Stotra. Brihatstotra Ratnakara.

16. The anahata shabda, the non-material or non-element related sound.

17. Mahanarayana Upanishad 12, Dahara Vidya, Yo vedādau svaraḥ prokto vedānte ca pratiṣṭitaḥ☐ tasya prakṛtilīnasya yaḥ parasya maheśvaraḥ.

18. This mantra is prominent at Jageshwar in the Himalayas and connects to Lakulish and his tradition of older Pashupata Yoga Shaivism. Jageshwar is a Lakulish site.

19. Rigveda VII.59.10, Tryambakam yajāmahe sugandhim puṣtivardhanam; urvārukam iva bandhanāt, mṛtyor mukṣīya māmṛtāt.

20. By Shankara, Shivananda Lahiri, Lingashtakam, Kala Bhairavashtakam, Nirvanashtakam, among many others. For other hymns to Shiva, Shiva Mahimna Stotra by Pushpadanta, Upamanyu Shiva Stotra, Shiva Tandava Stotra of Ravana, and the Thousand Names of Shiva (Shiva Sahasra Nama) from the Mahabharata.

21. OM Namah Shivaya itself is a common kirtan, or longer chants like Hara Hara Mahadeva Shambho, Kashi Vishvanatha Gange!

22. Isha Upanishad 6.

23. Katha Upanishad I.2.20.

24. Yama in the Katha Upanishad.

25. Saundarya Lahiri

26. Notably, Tantric Yoga and the Wisdom Goddesses.

27. Such as the teachings of Ramana Maharshi.

28. Such as in the Integral Yoga of Sri Aurobindo.

29. Hinduism Today crystal Shiva linga

30. There are special five element forms of Shiva lingas in Tamil Nadu in South India. They consist of various stone forms, though Chidambaram consists of the linga of space.

31. Like Shatchakra Nirupana.

32. Note the famous Sanskrit drama, Kumara Sambhavam of Kalidas.

33. Such are the ideas of the demiurge that we find in Gnostic thought, which has an evil being create this world, and the higher Divine force as the liberator from it.

34. Kavyakantha Ganapati Muni, Prachanda Chandi Trishati, Collected Works, Volume 2.

35. Kavyakantha Ganapati Muni, Rigveda Mantra Bhashyam, Gritsamada's Sukta, Collected Works, Volume 7.

36. Kavyakantha Ganapati Muni, Rudra Kutumba Sutram 22-39, Collected Works, Volume 5.

37. Krishna Yajur Veda Taittiriya Samhita Chaturtha Vaishvadevam Kandham Prathama Prapathaka.

38. Rudram 8, Namas tārāya ca namaś śambhave ca mayobhave ca namaḥ śankarāya ca mayaskarāya ca namaḥ ṣivāya ca śivatarāya ca.

39. Rudram 1.

40. Rudram 12.

41. Rudram 12.

42. Shiva Mahimna Stotra of Pushpadanta, 28.

43. Satapatha Brahmana, Agni Chayana.

44. Mahanarayana Upanishad 16-25, Shivopasana Mantras.

45. Note author's book Tantric Yoga and the Wisdom Goddesses.

46. Shiva Mahimna Stotra of Pushpadanta 7.

47. Shaivite or Pashupata Yoga is also there in the Mahabharata and Shvetashvatara Upanishad that commonly call Rudra as Pashupati.

48. Yoga Sutras I.3.

49. Yoga Sutras, I.2. Note Vyasa's commentary for more information on Yoga as Samadhi and the pursuit of Samadhi as the nature of the mind.

50. Yoga Sutras I.2.

51. Yoga Sutras I.26. Sa eṣa pūrveṣām api guruḥ. Ishvara as the guru suggests Brahma, Vishnu and Shiva as the three forms of Ishvara relative to creation, preservation and dissolution, though the term Ishvara more commonly refers to Shiva.

52. Hatha Yoga Pradipika 1. Shiva as Adi Natha.

53. Siddhasiddhanta Paddhati of Gorakshanath, Ādinātham namaskṛtya śaktiuyuktam jagadgurum.

54. Yoga Sutras I.22-23.

55. Yoga Sutras I.27, Tasya vācakaḥ praṇava.

56. Brihat Yogi Yajnavalkya Smriti XII.5.

57. Shvetashvatara Upanishad III.5.

58. Brihat Yogi Yajnavalkya Smriti XII.5. Eka eva hi vijñeya praṇava yoga sādhanam.

59. Bhagavad Gita II.48.

60. Such as Hatha Yoga Pradipika, Shiva Samhita, Gheranda Samhita, though in no Hatha Yoga text does asana constitute the main portion of the teaching.

61. Hatha Yoga Pradipika I.1. Śri Ādi nāthāya namo´stu tasmai yenopadiṣṭha hathayogavidyā.

62. Katha Upanishad I.2.20.

63. With nada as Sadashiva Tattva and Bindu as the next Tattva, Ishvara Tattva.

64. Nada and Bindu on this higher level or Shakti and Shiva tattvas.

65. Yoga Sutras IV.29, Dharma Megha Samadhi.

66.   Nada as Sadashiva Tattva.

67.   These three bindus reflect the three higher tattvas of Sadashiva, Ishvara and Shuddha Vidya. These three Bindus can be generally correlated to mind as Bindu, speech as Nada and Prana as Bija in other correlations.

68.   Often identified with Lord Skanda as the son of Shiva and Shakti.

69.   Ahamkara also means the maker (kara) of a and ha as the first and last letters of the alphabet.

70.   Note author's book Mantra Yoga and Primal sound, page 128.

71.   Note author's book Mantra Yoga and Primal Sound page 129. Also Yogini Shambhavi's rendition of this mantra in her Yogini Bhava chanting CD.

72.   Rigveda IV.55.10.

73.   Tantrasara III. Shambhava Upaya. Tadā svātantrya śaktim eva adhikām paśyan nirvikalpam eva bhairavasamaveśam anubhavati.

74.   Tantrasara III. Shambhava Upaya. Sarvam idem bhāvajātam bodhagagane pratibimbamātram.

75.   Tantrasara III. Shambhava Upaya.

76.   We follow that practice from Sadguru Sivananda Murti.

77.   I will write about these experiences later as they become more complete.

78.   Aruna Prashna, Taittiriya Aranyaka, 94-96.

79.   Ayush Sukta 1.

80.   Rigveda I.114.5. Haste bibhrad bheṣajā vāryāṇi.

81.   Rigveda II.33.4 unno vīrām arpaya bheṣajebhir bhiṣaktamam tvā bhiṣajām śṛṇomi.

82.   Rudram 1, prathamo daivyo bhiṣak.

83. Rudram 10. Yā te Rudra śivā tanūḥ śivā viśvāha bheṣajī, śivā rudrasya bheṣajī tayā no mṛḍa jīvase.

84. Rigveda VI.74.3, somārudrā yuvam etanyasme viśvā tanūṣu bheṣajāni dhattam.

85. Rigveda X.97.19, yā oṣadhīḥ somarājnīr viṣtitāḥ pṛthivīm anu.

86. Rigveda V.57.1.

87. Rigveda VII.59.10.

88. Rigveda VII.59.7.

89. Rigveda VIII. 22.1, Yam aśvinā suhavā rudravartanī.

90. Brihadaranayaka Upanishad II.5.16-18.

91. Rigveda V.78.

92. Pandit Nanak Chand Sharma of Delhi in recent times spoke of a special Shiva Ayurveda tradition from the Himalayas, connected to Tantra, and of a special Shiva Samhita or Shiva text of Ayurveda that he followed. Note his Akasha Bhairava Tantra.

93. Prashna Upanishad IV.

94. The subtle forms of the elements are the five sensory qualities. The five causal elements are inherent in Mahat and Prakriti along with the three gunas. The five causal elements refer also to the ideas beyond the elements like harness, solidity, and density in Earth.

95. Uma Sahasram I. of Kavyakantha Ganapati Muni.

96. The influence of the Nath Yogis has extended to Vaishnava schools as well with Goraknath as Shiva and Matsyendranath Nath as Vishnu.

97. Note the many good books on Tantra by Sir John Woodroofe (Arthur Avalon).

98. The Jnaneshvar tradition is also a Nath Yoga tradition.

99. Like that of Sri Aurobindo, who has a school of Purna Advaita.

100. Kavyakantha Ganapati Muni was of this view in his commentary on Shankara's Brahma Sutras.

101. Note Sri Aurobindo's philosophy, notably the Life Divine, for an explanation of both cosmic and human evolution according to a yogic perspective.

102. Bhagavad Gita XIII.5.

103. Samkhya Karika 22. Mathara commentary.

104. Samkhya Karika 62-63.

105. Shvetashvatara Upanishad V.2.

106. Yoga Sutras I.23-29.

107. Yoga Sutras, I.25. Vyasa commentary.

108. Yoga Sutras IV.34. Puruṣārtha śūnyānām guṇānām pratiprasavaḥ kaivalyam svarūpapratiṣṭhā vā citi śaktir iti.

109. Hatha Yoga Pradipika IV.1.

110. Vishnu Purana III.3. 9-20 for the 28 Vyasas.

111. Yoga Sutras I.27.

112. Vedic Yoga the Path of the Rishi

113. Vedic Yoga: the Path of the Rishi

114. Rigveda I.90.7.

115. Bhagavad Gita X.23.

116. Author's Vedic Yoga: the Path of the Rishi, note chapter on Vedic Shaivism.

117. Rigveda V.87.

118. Brihadaranayaka Upanishad II.5.16-18.

119. Rigveda IV.40.10.

120. Rigveda V VII.59.10.

121. Rigveda VII.33.10.

122. Shatapatha Brahmana, Agni Chayana, Fire altar as Rudra

123. Laghu Nyasa of the Rudram honors Rudra as all main Vedic sacrifices extending to Rudra as Sarvakratvatman, the Self or soul of all rituals.

124. Mahabharata, Arjuna's bow is received from Rudra-Shiva.

125. Notably the great poem Sivananda Lahiri of Shankara.

126. As frequently mentioned in the Vajrayana Guhya Samaj Tantra.

127. Aspects of Hatha Yoga occur in Shankara's Brahma Sutra Bhashya and Hatha Yoga is mentioned in his Aparokshanubhuti.

128. Modern scholarship places Shankara around 800 AD and Gorakhnath around 1100 AD, though traditional scholarship makes Shankara earlier.

129. Note Avadhuta Gita of Dattatreya for his profound teachings of Advaita Vedanta.

Index